Keaton Campbell

Keaton Campbell

Quintessential
Dzogchen

RANGJUNG YESHE BOOKS • WWW.RANGJUNG.COM

PADMASAMBHAVA • *Dakini Teachings*
Advice from the Lotus-Born • *Treasures From Juniper Ridge*

PADMASAMBHAVA AND JAMGÖN KONGTRÜL
The Light of Wisdom, Vol. 1 • *The Light of Wisdom, Vol. 2* •
The Light of Wisdom, the Conclusion

PADMASAMBHAVA, CHOKGYUR LINGPA, JAMGÖN KONGTRÜL, TULKU URGYEN,
AND ORGYEN TOPGYAL RINPOCHE
Great Accomplishment

YESHE TSOGYAL • *The Lotus-Born*

GAMPOPA • *The Precious Garland of the Sublime Path*

DAKPO TASHI NAMGYAL • *Clarifying the Natural State*

TSELE NATSOK RANGDRÖL • *Mirror of Mindfulness* • *Empowerment* •
Heart Lamp

CHOKGYUR LINGPA • *Ocean of Amrita* • *The Great Gate*

JAMGÖN MIPHAM RINPOCHE • *Gateway to Knowledge, Vol. 1*
Gateway to Knowledge, Vol. 2 • *Gateway to Knowledge, Vol. 3* •
Gateway to Knowledge, Vol. 4

TULKU URGYEN RINPOCHE • *Blazing Splendor*
Rainbow Painting • *As It Is, Vol. 1* • *As It Is, Vol. 2* • *Vajra Speech*
Repeating the Words of the Buddha

ADEU RINPOCHE & TULKU URGYEN RINPOCHE • *Skillful Grace*

KHENCHEN THRANGU RINPOCHE • *Crystal Clear*
Songs of Naropa • *King of Samadhi* • *Buddha Nature*

CHÖKYI NYIMA RINPOCHE • *Present Fresh Wakefulness*
Indisputable Truth • *Union of Mahamudra & Dzogchen*
Bardo Guidebook • *Song of Karmapa*

TSIKEY CHOKLING RINPOCHE • *Lotus Ocean*

TULKU THONDUP • *Enlightened Living*

ORGYEN TOBGYAL RINPOCHE • *Life & Teachings of Chokgyur Lingpa*

TSOKNYI RINPOCHE • *Fearless Simplicity* • *Carefree Dignity*

DZOGCHEN TRILOGY COMPILED BY MARCIA BINDER SCHMIDT
Dzogchen Primer • *Dzogchen Essentials* • *Quintessential Dzogchen*

ERIK PEMA KUNSANG • *Wellsprings of the Great Perfection*
A Tibetan Buddhist Companion • *The Rangjung Yeshe Tibetan-English
Dictionary of Buddhist Culture* • *Perfect Clarity*

MARCIA DECHEN WANGMO • *Confessions of a Gypsy Yogini*

ADEU RINPOCHE • *Freedom in Bondage*

TRAKTUNG DUDJOM LINGPA • *Clear Mirror*

Quintessential Dzogchen

Confusion Dawns as Wisdom

Introductory Teachings by

Tulku Urgyen Rinpoche

Translated & compiled by

Erik Pema Kunsang & Marcia Binder Schmidt

RANGJUNG YESHE PUBLICATIONS
Boudhanath, Hong Kong & Esby
2006

Rangjung Yeshe Publications
Flat 5a, Greenview Garden,
125 Robinson Road, Hong Kong

Address letters to:
Rangjung Yeshe Publications
p.o. box 1200
Kathmandu, Nepal
WWW.RANGJUNG.COM

3 5 7 9 8 6 4

First edition 2006
Printed in the United States of America
on recycled acid-free paper

Publication Data:
Schmidt, Marcia Binder, Erik Pema Kunsang,
Quintessential Dzogchen: Confusion Dawns as Wisdom.
Introductory Teachings by Tulku Urgyen Rinpoche.
Includes bibliographical references.
ISBN 962-7341-58-4 (alk. paper)
1. Eastern philosophy—Buddhism. 3. Vajrayana—Dzogchen
(Nyingma).
I. Title.

Cover art detail: oil painting by Dzigar Kongtrul Rinpoche
Design: Rafael Ortet

Contents

The door of the Great Perfection has been opened by noble beings and the fortune of enjoying its wealth is within reach of ordinary disciples. It is, by all means, of vital importance to attain complete liberation through practice to make having met this profound path meaningful.

Kyabje Dilgo Khyentse Rinpoche[1]

Preface

How amazing to be able to connect with the rich, awe-inspiring
   tradition of Dzogchen!
How propitious to live in a time when we can meet these instructions and
   the lineage masters who propagate them!
How unbelievably fortunate to be able to actually practice and realize the
   teachings!
We rejoice in being able to have the opportunity to share some of this
   precious wisdom
And aspire that such an undertaking will bring immeasurable benefit!

The teachings in *Quintessential Dzogchen* fall under the fourth Dharma of
Longchenpa and Gampopa, "confusion dawns as wisdom," which involves
acknowledging and training in our intrinsic buddha nature. "When our
confusion is purified, the wisdom that is our basic wakefulness becomes
apparent."[2] Once we have been introduced to this basic wakefulness and
have managed—through the combined power of our devotion and prior
training—to recognize it directly and definitively, then, through training in basic wakefulness (*rigpa*), we enter the ranks of *true* practitioners of
the Great Perfection. Looking back, we then realize that all the previous
spiritual practices we were engaged in—though earnestly undertaken and
immensely beneficial as stepping-stones—were based on only a theoretical
understanding.

To enter the Vajrayana path, we need to mature our being through empowerments. The essentials for practice are the ripening empowerments,
the liberating instructions, and the supportive reading transmissions. If we
start practice without ripening our body, speech, and mind through receiving empowerments, the blessings will not enter our stream-of-being. The
four empowerments are the vase empowerment, the secret empowerment,
the knowledge empowerment, and the word empowerment. *Quintessential
Dzogchen* covers the section of the Dzogchen path that is connected with the
fourth empowerment: the precious word empowerment.

On the Dzogchen path, we practice in close association with and under the guidance of a genuine lineage holder of this tradition. Such a teacher must possess the ripening empowerments, reading transmissions, and liberating instructions, as well as accomplishment in these practices. For the blessings of realization to arise within our own experience, our master needs to be authentic and qualified. *Quintessential Dzogchen* is offered as a handbook of teachings to request from such masters, as well as an encouragement in carrying them out by providing source materials for practitioners to use when seeking pith instructions.

As was done with the previous books in this series (*The Dzogchen Primer* and *Dzogchen Essentials*), the teachings in *Quintessential Dzogchen* are arranged in the sequence used in Padmasambhava's and Jamgön Kongtrül's *Light of Wisdom*: an explanation of the ground and how sentient beings become deluded, ways to practice the path, and how the final fruition is accomplished. This structure is designed to assist practitioners in carrying out these practices in a traditional order.

To help engender confidence in your practice, we begin with three introductory teachings to give an overview of the entire path. We continue with the historical background as well as sources of the Dzogchen teachings. It is crucial to take the support of genuine texts when doing these practices. As Tulku Thondup says, "It is extremely important to rely on authentic scriptures such as the tantras and the writings of Longchen Rabjam as the basis and to have the teacher's instructions as the keys. But some people rely on the oral instructions from a teacher and do not know anything about scriptures, the source of the teachings. In addition to conveying the blessings of the lineal Buddhas, Vidyadharas and masters, these scriptures contain various levels and means of practice in both detailed and condensed forms."[3]

The importance of this is underscored in the biography of Khenpo Ngakchung, one of the greatest Dzogchen khenpos of recent times, when his teacher, Nyoshul Lungtok, told him, "From now on refine your own mind with the meaning of the *Seven Treasuries* of Longchenpa as well as *The Mother and Son Heart Essences*. There are people who just listen to the words of an old lama and put the *Seven Treasuries* and *Four Volumes* aside and say, 'These books are textual expositions. The unexcelled oral tradition is given to me by so and so Lama,' and they give new meanings to dwelling, moving and aware, to the tranquility with or without characteristics. These (tendencies) deceive trainees (of Dzogchen) of both higher and lesser (intellect) and are teachings influenced by demonic forces."[4] Nyoshul Lungtok's words summarize the tendency of half-baked "Dzogchen practitioners" to pridefully believe their understanding of rigpa's awakened state. Tulku Urgyen Rinpoche often stated that when one "settles the case" prematurely while still limited by inadequate learning and training experience, one's rigpa is often no more than a state of formless shamatha that *feels like* nondual awareness. To slay this demon, we need honesty and humility, while combining a study of the original scriptures with oral instructions and practical experience.

Following the background material presented in part 1, in part 2 we return to where we started in *The Dzogchen Primer:* teachings on the ground. *The Light of Wisdom* introduces us to the whole perspective from the very beginning because there is a need for it from the start. The ground is our basic nature and is an underlying principle of not only the Great Perfection but also the entire Buddhist path. However, we have somehow lost direct contact with our intrinsic nature. To quote Tulku Urgyen Rinpoche again:

> A seeming confusion obscures the recognition of the ground. Fortunately, this seeming delusion is temporary. This failure to recognize the ground is similar to dreaming. Dreaming is not primordial; it is temporary, it can be purified. Purification happens through training on the path. We have strayed from the ground and become sentient beings. To free the ground from what obscures it, we have to train. Right now, we are on the path and have not yet attained fruition. When we are freed from obscuration, then the fruition—*dharmakaya*—appears. The liberated ground, path and fruition are all perfected in the realm of the single essence, the continuity of rigpa.
>
> In fact, there is no difference whatsoever between ground and fruition. In the state of the ground the enlightened qualities are not acknowledged, but they are manifest at the time of fruition. These are not new qualities that suddenly appear, but are like the qualities of a flower that are inherent in the seed. Within the seed are the characteristics of the flower itself. The seed holds the potential for the flower's color, smell, bud and leaves. However, can we say that the seed is the fruition of a flower? No, we cannot, because the flower has not fully bloomed. Like this analogy, the qualities of the fruition are contained

in the state of the ground; yet, they are not evident or manifest. That
is the difference between ground and fruition. At the time of the path,
if we do not apply effort, the fruition will not appear.[5]

Part 3, which makes up the bulk of this book, covers the path aspect.
It begins with Padmasambhava's explanation of the pointing-out instruction, continues with the Trekchö view of primordial purity, and ends with
a brief description of the Tögal meditation of spontaneous presence. Under
the rubric of the path are the topics of view, meditation, and conduct. It is
said that at the time of the ground, the practitioner needs to distinguish
between the all-ground and the basic state of dharmakaya; at the time of
the path, to distinguish between *sem* and rigpa; and at the time of the fruition, to distinguish between consciousness and wakefulness. The book concludes with part 4, on the fruition, followed by Longchen Rabjam's "Bardo
Aspiration."

As in the previous volumes in this series, *The Dzogchen Primer* and
Dzogchen Essentials, the teachings here are presented for the *kusulu*, the
simple meditator. "For this type of person, the main point of the Buddha's
teaching involves nothing more than understanding the difference between
recognizing and not recognizing mind-essence. Not recognizing is samsara,
while recognizing is nirvana or liberation. It's from this perspective that we
say that all of the Buddha's teachings are simply about the mind."[6]

Study helps us clear away the doubts that often plague our practice. We
need to know exactly how to go about these trainings. Without reflecting
upon the teachings and understanding all their aspects, we might find ourselves even more confused. There are many pitfalls to avoid on this path.
One of the common sidetracks in Trekchö is to develop a mind-made version of emptiness and to regard the meditation as the task of continually
recreating it. With regard to Tögal, the major sidetrack is to be caught up
in hoping for special experiences and fearing their absence. It is always necessary to compare our understanding and experiences with the instruction
manuals and, most important, to consult with our teacher.

In the end, the one to be the most honest with is yourself. Candidly investigate: "Is my practice in accordance with what I have been taught and what
I have read? Am I progressing? What do I need to do?" Really examine
yourself to see if you are integrating these four Dharmas into your stream-
of-being: "Have I turned my mind toward the Dharma? Has my Dharma

practice become the true path? Does the path that I am practicing clarify confusion? And is confusion truly dawning as wisdom?" To help with this crucial exercise, selections in part 4 give guidelines for such self-examination. In order to make these evaluations, we need to rely on our own integrity and intelligence as well as our teacher's supervision. Sometimes, would-be Dzogchen aspirants find that even after spending years at the feet of great Dzogchen masters and practicing diligently, progress seems elusive. Such practitioners do not lack the necessary intelligence or perseverance, yet they still seem unable to resolve the natural state and progress in these practices. It is taught that we must have the karmic propensities for Dzogchen. If we do not have that readiness now, we can endeavor to create it by generating merit, purifying obscurations, and making aspirations to be able to practice Dzogchen at a later time. In fact, the training that facilitates this readiness is integrated into all the Dzogchen scriptures in the form of the preliminary practices.

An important consideration in compiling this book was the limitations placed on us with regard to the material that we could include. Many of the texts that we wished to use are restricted and could not be made available to a general readership. Kyabje Dilgo Khyentse Rinpoche and Tulku Urgyen Rinpoche clearly defined what could be openly shared and what needed to be kept more secret. Though different lamas and translators hold varying points of view on this subject, we follow what we have been told personally. However, these restricted works are meant for the many sincere practitioners out there, and they can be obtained through Dharma centers under the guidance of a qualified teacher. If a text we wanted to include was restricted, whenever possible we tried to substitute similar material. In light of the sensitivity of the subject matter and the necessity of the practitioner's being in close association with a lama, we did not include any facilitator guidelines in this volume. Nothing can substitute for a direct link with the living word of a qualified master, and we encourage Dzogchen yogis to be in close contact with their teachers. Finally, we ask the reader to find glossary terms as well as a recommended reading list on our website (www. rangjung.com).

Heartfelt appreciation goes to all the teachers, translators, and editors who contributed material to all three volumes, in particular Kerry Moran, Ward Brisick, Mim Coulstock, and Michael Tweed. Sincere thanks go once more to Tulku Thondup, who supports this project with his compassionately brilliant insights; to my husband, coauthor, and translator, Erik Pema Kunsang, without whom this work would be impossible; to Steven Goodman, who lent his wonderful translation; and once more especially to Michael Tweed, who edited so many of these pieces and softened up the language with his poetic style. In particular, thanks are offered to the gifted typesetter and designer, Rafael Ortet, to the constant and kind Zachary Beer for proofreading, and to the talented editor Tracy Davis, who improved every aspect of the book.

May confusion truly fall away and allow the dawn of wisdom for all of us struggling yogis on the path.

Marcia Binder Schmidt, Nagi Gompa Hermitage
February 5, 2006

INTRODUCTORY TEACHINGS

A Mirror to Reflect the Most Essential

The final instruction on the ultimate meaning

Longchen Rabjam

Single embodiment of compassionate power and activities
Of infinite mandalas of all-encompassing conquerors,
Glorious guru, supreme lord of a hundred families,
Forever I pay homage at your feet.

Ema! Listen here, you fortunate yogis.

At present we have achieved the perfect human body of freedoms and riches. We have met the precious teachings of the greater vehicle. We now have the independence to genuinely apply the sacred Dharma, so do not squander your life on pointless things. Instead, pursue the lasting goal.

The categories of teachings are endless. The entrance doors to the vehicles are innumerable. The words to be explained are extensive. Even if you succeed in memorizing millions of volumes of Dharma scriptures, unless you are able to practice the essential meaning, you can never be sure that they will help you at the moment of death. And even if your education in studies and reflections is boundless, unless you succeed in being in harmony with the Dharma, you will not tame your enemy, negative emotions. Even if you succeed in being the owner of a trillion worlds, unless you can curtail your plans from within with the feeling that nothing more is needed, you will never know contentment. Unless you prepare yourself with the attitude that your death could happen at any time, you cannot achieve the great aim that is surely needed at the time of death.

You must tame your own shortcomings and cultivate impartial pure perception, for a biased attitude will not let you shoulder the Mahayana teach-

From Longchen Rabjam's collected writings (Boudhanath: Rangjung Yeshe Publications, 2005).

ings. Since all the sentient being among the six classes in the three realms have without exception been your own parents, unless you make pure aspirations with ceaseless compassion and bodhichitta, you cannot open the jewel mine of altruistic actions. Unless you generate a devotion toward your kind guru exceeding even that of meeting the Buddha in person, you will not feel the warmth of blessings. Unless you genuinely receive the blessings, the seedlings of experience and realization will not sprout. Unless realization dawns from within, dry explanations and theories will not help you achieve the fruit of enlightenment.

In short, unless you mingle your mind with the Dharma, it is pointless to merely sport a spiritual veneer. Keep to the bare necessities for sustaining your life and warding off the bitter cold; reflect on the fact that nothing else is really needed. Practice guru yoga and supplicate one-pointedly. Direct every spiritual practice you do to the welfare of all sentient beings, your own parents. Whatever good or evil, joy or sorrow befalls you, train in seeing it as your guru's kindness.

Within the vastness of spontaneous self-knowing, let be freely, uncontrived and free of fabrication. Whatever thoughts arise, be sure to recognize your nature so that they all dissolve as the play of dharmata. Even though you practice in such a way that there is not even as much as a hair tip of a concrete reference point to cultivate by meditating, do not stray into ordinary deluded diffusion, even for a single moment. Instead, make sure that every aspect of your daily activities is embraced by an undistracted presence of mind. Whatever occurs and whatever you experience, strengthen your conviction that they are all insubstantial and magical illusions, so that you can experience this in the bardo as well.

In short, at all times and in every situation, make sure that whatever you do turns into the sacred Dharma and dedicate every virtuous action toward enlightenment. By doing so, you will fulfill your guru's wishes and be of service to the Buddhadharma; you will repay your parents' kindness and spontaneously accomplish the benefit of yourself and others. Please keep this in your heart.

Even if you were to have met me in person, I would have had no superior advice to give you, so bring it into your practice in every moment and in every situation.

Longchen Rabjam Zangpo wrote this on the slope of White Skull Snow Mountain (Gangri Tökar).

Dzogchen Key Points

Tulku Urgyen Rinpoche

Our basic nature is essentially identical with the ground, has two basic aspects: primordial purity *(kadag)* and spontaneous presence *(lhundrub)*. Our mind's empty essence is related to primordial purity, while its cognizant nature is linked to spontaneous presence.

Spontaneous presence literally means "that which appears and is present by itself" and—besides our cognizant nature—includes the deities that are experienced in the bardo, as well as all the Tögal displays. In the same way, the pure wisdom realms that unfold out of the expanse of the three *kaya*s, which is the state of rigpa devoid of clinging, are also experienced as a natural presence. To rephrase this, all the self-appearing and naturally present Tögal displays, the kayas and wisdoms, that unfold out of the state of dharmakaya, free of grasping, manifest from the primordially pure essence and spontaneously present nature, kadag and lhundrub.

This lhundrub quality also pertains to samsaric experience. Spontaneous presence includes everything that "appears automatically" due to ignorance of our true nature: the worlds, beings, the three realms, the six classes, and all the rest of samsara. These all appear automatically; we don't need to imagine any of them. In other words, the samsaric states that unfold out of the ignorant dualistic mind are all experienced vividly and clearly. Mind and its objects—the perceived objects in the three realms of samsara and the perceiving dualistic mind with its three poisons—all unfold within the arena of dualistic mind, *sem*. We don't need to visualize our world. The sem experiences include the different experiences of the six classes of beings,

From an oral teaching at Nagi Gompa, November 24, 1995.

which are visible yet intangible. Currently our "impure" samsaric experience is clearly present and quite tangible. We can touch the things around us, right? In "pure" awareness, known as the kayas and wisdoms, experience takes place in a way that is visible yet insubstantial. This immaterial or nonphysical quality means that the experience is something that you can see but not grasp—like a rainbow.

The *sambhogakaya* buddhas and realms unfold, visible yet intangible; they are insubstantial like a rainbow in the unconfined sky of dharmakaya. After you first recognize your basic state of primordial purity, then perfect its strength and attain stability, your body returns to rainbow light. In other words, within this very body, your realization is equal to that of sambhogakaya. All the inconceivable adornments and sceneries belonging to sambhogakaya are then as visible as rainbows in the sky. Unlike sentient beings in samsara's three realms, who experience things in a material way, the kayas and wisdom displays are immaterial and unconditioned. Have you ever heard of a sambhogakaya buddha needing to visit the toilet? That's because they are insubstantial, not material. The six types of beings, on the other hand, must defecate and urinate after they eat. That's direct proof of their corporeality. Deities are in an incorporeal state, celestial and rainbow-like. You can't eat rainbows and then shit them out! With a rainbow body there is no thought of food, but ordinary sentient beings, who have material bodies, can't go without food; if they do, they die of starvation.

The materiality I am speaking of here has three aspects: the material body of flesh and blood, the material disposition that needs food as fuel, and the material mind that is born and dies, arises and ceases. The deities' immaterial purity lies beyond those three, beyond every kind of materiality, and this is why we say their bodies are made of rainbow light. In short, samsara is material substance and nirvana is insubstantial.[7]

We hear the deities described as having bodies of light and living in an insubstantial mansion in an immaculate realm—but that is only how it appears from our point of view. The notion of being beyond corporeality is an adaptation to the habitual tendencies of samsaric beings, because we live in material places, in material houses, and have material bodies. From the deities' point of view, there is no such concept whatsoever.

The complete aspects of the Dzogchen empowerments authorize the yogi to embark on Tögal practice. But *without cutting through with Trekchö, one doesn't directly cross with Tögal*. Trekchö means that you have the basic state of primordial purity pointed out to you, at which point you must recognize it and then train in stabilizing that recognition.

The way to approach Dzogchen practice is this: Begin with the *ngöndro*, the preliminaries; follow that with *yidam* practice, for instance, the recitation of the peaceful and wrathful deities; then continue with the actual training in Trekchö. Later, as an enhancement of Trekchö, there is Tögal practice. All these Dharma practices should be applied. When training in Trekchö, leave your mind free of clinging. When practicing Tögal, though there is no clinging, one still applies four key points.

For all Dharma practice, you need preliminary steps, just like laying the foundation when you construct a house. We begin the Dzogchen path with the ngöndro and the reason is this: Throughout innumerable past lives we have created immeasurable negative karma and obscurations. The ngöndro purifies every misdeed and obscuration created through our physical, verbal, and mental actions.

Having gone through a complete ngöndro, next comes the main part, which is like building a palace upon the solid foundation. It may have many stories, but no matter how many there are, they will now all remain stable. The main part is composed of two stages: development and completion. Development stage, in this case, is the visualization of and recitation for one's personal yidam deity. Yidam practice is then followed by the completion stage, which is Trekchö.

Trekchö means recognizing that our essence is primordially pure. The basis for Tögal is recognizing, at the same time, that our natural display is spontaneously present. Then, recognizing that the natural display, the spontaneous presence, is insubstantial and devoid of any self-nature is the ultimate path—the unity of primordial purity and spontaneous presence, which we call the unity of Trekchö and Tögal.

There is a correspondence between Trekchö and Tögal and the two aspects known as the path of liberation and the path of means. By combining Trekchö and Tögal in the Dzogchen system, you experience the natural displays of the peaceful and wrathful deities within this lifetime, without having to wait for the bardo. Since the entire path has been traversed during your life, there is nothing more to train in or to purify during the bardo state.

To reiterate, having thoroughly done the ngöndro, you then proceed with the development stage of the yidam deity. The tantras mention that you have to quadruple all practices during our age. Whereas in the past it was sufficient to chant 100,000 mantras for each syllable, these days one must chant 400,000 per syllable. Spend however many months it takes to do the recitation in retreat. There are set numbers for the ngöndro practices and recitations, but there is no set number for Trekchö, not even a time limit. One doesn't "finish" Trekchö after a couple of months or years—as long as there is life, there is Trekchö training. You never hear anybody say, "Now I've finished Trekchö!" Throughout one's entire life, the nature of mind must be recognized. On the other hand, you can *master* or *accomplish* Trekchö. This is when there is absolutely no delusion anymore, neither day or night; at that point you can truly say you have gone beyond Trekchö. However, I do believe that for the rest of this life there will be sufficient reason to practice. Read the guidance manuals thoroughly, many times. When you really understand them, you will understand the meaning of Dzogchen.

Neither Trekchö nor Tögal is a formal meditation practice. Trekchö means simply acknowledging that your basic essence is empty, and Tögal is the natural displays that are spontaneously present. The essence and its displays are not our creation; we do not create them by practicing. In both Trekchö and Tögal you do not create anything with your imagination but merely rest in the natural state.

To express it slightly differently, Trekchö is recognizing that our natural state or basic essence is primordially pure. Tögal is recognizing that the natural displays of this primordial purity are spontaneously present. And recognizing that this natural display is insubstantial—that the natural manifestations of the five wisdoms as five-colored light are not something you can take hold of—is the unity of primordial purity and spontaneous presence. These two aspects, primordial purity and spontaneous presence, are not separate and distinct like your two arms. They are an *indivisible unity* because the empty quality of mind-essence is primordial purity, while the cognizant quality is spontaneous presence. Hence, they are totally indivisible, and therefore Trekchö and Tögal are fundamentally indivisible.

You wouldn't describe Tögal as a meditation practice, but you could say that it is a training, because there are key points to apply. I would like to stress again that Tögal is not a matter of imagining or meditating upon anything; the displays that appear are the expressions of natural purity. If you train properly and apply the key points, all the Tögal displays evolve naturally.

The reason many Dzogchen teachings are connected to a sadhana involving the peaceful and wrathful deities is that the displays include these deities. The practice lets whatever is already present within you become visible; nothing else manifests. Since the peaceful and wrathful deities are already present within your body, they become visible during Tögal practice. The deities in Tögal are the same ones that will appear in the bardo. So, if the complete mandala has manifested during your life, no second mandala needs to appear in the bardo state—it doesn't manifest twice. This is why many Dzogchen teachings emphasize the mandala of the peaceful and wrathful deities.

There are many levels of practice for the peaceful and wrathful deities, such as in Mahayoga, Anu Yoga, and Ati Yoga. Chokgyur Lingpa, for instance, revealed sadhanas for all three vehicles. For Ati Yoga he revealed the *Kunzang Tuktig,* as well as one belonging to the *Dzogchen Desum*. You can also base your Dzogchen practice on the guru principle, since the enlightened master embodies everything. For example, the mind treasure of Jigmey Lingpa called *Tigle Gyachen* is based on the single figure of Longchenpa. In this way there are various approaches, and it is really good to do such practices.

Whether you are sitting down or moving about, whatever situation you are in, always remember Trekchö—recognizing the nature of mind. It is the very core, the very heart of Dzogchen practice.

The first experiences we will have at the moment of death are the sounds, colors, and lights, but these will not be vague, feeble, or limited, as they are now, but intense and overwhelming. The colors then are iridescent hues, while the lights are sharp like needle points, similar to looking directly into the sun. The colors are indications of enlightened body, the sounds indications of enlightened speech, and the lights indications of enlightened mind. That is why *The Tibetan Book of the Dead* reminds the dying person, "Do not be afraid of these lights. Do not fear the sounds. Do not be terrified by the colors."

In the bardo, yogis who grew somewhat familiar with Tögal practice during their lives can remain unafraid, free of terror or dread, because they know that the colors, sounds, and lights are their own manifestations—the natural displays of their buddha nature's body, speech, and mind. These initial manifestations are a prelude for the rest of the bardo. Ordinary people, however, become totally overwhelmed by the immensity of the displays. The sounds in the bardo are not small noises—they roar like 100,000 simultaneous thunder claps—and the lights and colors shine with the brilliance of 100,000 suns. Later, when the deities begin to appear, the largest are the size of Mount Sumeru, while the smallest are no bigger than a mustard seed. The deities are vibrantly alive and dance about. Faced with this spectacle, you have two options: either you panic with fright or you recognize them as your natural displays. This is why it is of incredible benefit to practice in this life so that you grow familiar with your natural displays. Otherwise, facing them in the bardo will result in deep confusion and bewilderment.

Even if you are an accomplished Buddhist scholar who knows a lot of Dharma, can debate, and all the rest, without this familiarity you will still become terrified and panic at the awesome display in the bardo. You can't debate with these deities; you can't explain them away. But if you follow the Vajrayana path and grow familiar with the unified path of development and completion, you can ensure that you will recognize all this to be your own manifestation—which will be of real benefit.

That is why *The Tibetan Book of the Dead* emphasizes, "Do not be afraid of your own displays." There is no reason to be afraid of yourself, no need to be overwhelmed by your own sounds, colors, and lights. You can also cross the bardo successfully if you have become fully trained in Mahamudra and the Six Doctrines, but success is guaranteed if you have attained stability in Trekchö and Tögal. Trekchö is recognizing that the *dharmata* of mind and the colors and lights are all dharmata's natural displays and that the sounds are the self-resounding of dharmata. We must recognize that these manifestations, visible yet insubstantial, come from nowhere else. Understand this, truly, and the Lord of Death will have no hold upon you.

It is incredibly important to grow familiar with these displays during this lifetime by practicing the unity of Trekchö and Tögal, because sooner or later everybody ends up in the bardo and these manifestations definitely will appear. These intense bardo experiences are not exclusive to just a few people or to Buddhists, nor does it help to say, "I don't have to worry about those bardo experiences because I don't believe in anything after death." The bardo experiences don't care what you think. They appear to everyone.

Avoid the sorry fate of most people, who get completely overwhelmed believing the displays of their own buddha nature to be devils coming to torture them and carry them off to hell. What a pity that would be!

THE VITAL ESSENCE

Bringing together the crucial points from the stages of the path according to the luminous heart essence of the Great Perfection

Shakya Shri Jñana

Homage to glorious Samantabhadra.

Here I shall present the pith instructions of the Great Perfection—the liberating advice of the *Luminous Heart Essence* that is the summit of the nine gradual vehicles, the Great Perfection of Ati—under five headings.

1. The qualified disciple to whom instructions are given

A qualified disciple is someone who has gathered a vast accumulation of merit for numerous eons, who has no other aim or thought besides the guru and the oral instructions, and who is stable-minded and of a gentle character. On the outer level, for the sake of the guru and the instructions, he can sacrifice body and wealth, reputation and position. On the inner level, he perfectly trusts and is dedicated to the general teachings and teachers of the nine gradual vehicles. On the innermost level, such a disciple trusts completely, and always regards as a buddha in person, the vajra master who teaches the ripening and liberating instructions of the Great Perfection. In this way it is a matter of utmost importance to be a suitable vessel for the Great Perfection.

2. The qualified vajra master who imparts the instructions

In general, a vajra master should be skilled in both the words and meaning regarding teaching and practicing the nine gradual vehicles. In particular,

From Shakya Shri Jñana's collected writings (Boudhanath: Rangjung Yeshe Publications, 2004).

he should be fully capable of teaching the gradual stages of the path of the Great Perfection, in both its theoretical and practical aspects. This includes, at the beginning, being able to distinguish, in both words and meaning, between nirvana's ground of liberation and samsara's ground of confusion, between ground-space and ground-displays, and between all-ground and *dharmadhatu*. In the middle, in regard to practicing the path, he should be able to distinguish between Trekchö and Tögal, the thinking mind (*sem*) and awareness (*rigpa*), consciousness (*namshe*) and wakefulness (*yeshe*), and so forth. Concerning the ultimate fruition, he should not be ignorant of, but able to thoroughly and intelligently explain, the words and meaning in their entirety, detailing how all the manifestations of outward brilliance composed of the kayas and wisdoms dissolve into the expanse of the Youthful Vase Body, the inner brilliance; about how awareness captures the unchanging royal stronghold of dharmakaya; and then how the two form bodies overturn samsara from its depths. Especially, it is of utmost importance that the qualified vajra master, ideally, has perfected the great strength of experience in both the mental states and displays of Trekchö and Tögal and has reached exhaustion in dharmata or, the next best, has brought awareness to culmination.

3. The instruction to be given

Among the nine gradual vehicles, the *Luminous Heart Essence of the Great Perfection* is especially exalted in being the great liberation through encounter or through hearing. Here I shall explain it in the proper order.

4. How the instructions are given

The instructions should be given when the auspicious connection is arranged between a master who possesses the potent elixir and a disciple who is like a receptive vessel. First comes the essential guidance in the seven points of training the dualistic mind. Give the outline first, the detailed explanation next, and conclude with summarizing all the words and meaning. In this way the instructions should be explained and then experientially applied.

In particular, the disciple should be required to achieve a high degree of stability in thought-free shamatha. Following that, he should be given the empowerments of awareness-display that mature him for the luminous Great Perfection, and also the explanatory lineage that instills comprehension by employing the words of the *Self-Arising Tantra* or the like. Especially, he should thoroughly receive the profound instructions of Trekchö and Tögal by being taught all the words and meaning in a manner that is direct and reveals what is hidden.

Having received all of the above, here is what you should do: Visualize your guru vajra master above the crown of your head or in the center of your heart, call upon him intensely, and invoke the passion of sincere devotion. Mingle your minds into one and then, while not moving away from the state of shamatha, thoroughly examine your body, speech, and mind. Determine carefully who, in both spiritual and mundane contexts, is the most important, who feels the joy and sorrow, and who is the doer of good and evil.

When, at the end of this, you have concluded that mind is most important, carefully examine this mind, which seems to vividly arise and then utterly vanish, and in which there doesn't seem to be any difference between it as the basis for arising and the multitude of conscious thoughts. At first, concerning material things, carefully investigate where this conscious mind comes from. Does it come from somewhere in the external world of the inanimate universe? Does it come from sentient beings, the animate inhabitants, or from your own aggregates, elements, and sense bases? Does it come from any place from the hairs on your head down to the toenails on your feet?

When you have settled that this conscious mind does not come from any material thing, then investigate, as before, if it comes from immaterial space—from above or below or from one of the cardinal or intermediate directions.

If it happens that you feel persuaded that there is something that originates in either a material or immaterial location, and a process by which this origination happens, then return to the presence of a sublime master, thoroughly clarify this point in both words and meaning, and then repeat this training.

Next, investigate thoroughly, as before, both the conscious mind's dwelling place and finally its point of departure.

Once you have firmly resolved that the conscious mind cannot be found to have a location of origin, a dwelling place, or a departure point, continue investigating the subject—that which experiences pleasure and pain, good and evil, and is the seed of all of samsara and nirvana.

Does this mind, the creator of every single activity, both spiritual and mundane, possess even the slightest trace of form, color, shape, or dimension in terms of being something concrete? Or is it inconcrete—a complete void like the open and empty midair?

It is essential and of utmost importance that you investigate this thoroughly until you are certain that this mind—which falls into no category such as being concrete or inconcrete, eternal or nonexistent—is both groundless and rootless.

The Main Part

Once you have thoroughly settled upon this, the second section is the main part, the practice of Trekchö.

At the beginning, if your body, speech, and mind are too relaxed, you may stray into the ordinary state. Therefore, place your body in the seven-fold posture of Vairochana. In particular, straighten your spine and remain freely like a great, majestic mountain.

With open eyes, direct your gaze toward the vast sky and remain freely like an ocean that is undisturbed by waves.

The mind's basis for confusion is the fourfold all-ground, while the circumstances for confusion are the three types of ignorance. These are the factors of dependency between wind (*lung*) and mental states that during delusion give rise to every type of thought, be they coarse or subtle. In every instance there is an aware quality that is both empty and cognizant and neither altered nor corrupted by any thoughts. Simply keep this natural state and remain without straying from it. That is the sublime and vital point here.

While you are in this state, there are sense impressions—the objects of the six consciousnesses—that appear vividly and unobstructedly in various ways, both coarse and subtle. Even so, do not stray from the nature of self-existing awareness.

While you sustain this continuity, the expression of this empty and cognizant awareness may appear in the form of all different kinds of coarse and subtle thoughts, but you should not reject them as in the lower vehicles, nor transform them as in the bodhisattva teachings.

The teachings in the Mind and Space Sections, as well as in the Mahamudra system, tell us that the very core of the practice is to allow coarse and subtle thoughts to naturally vanish by looking into their essence and letting them be in naturalness. Though this may be so, it conflicts directly with the view of the Great Perfection. Therefore it is extremely important that while having recognized the natural state you allow all coarse and subtle thoughts—whatever arises as the expression of this empty and cognizant awareness—to be groundless and rootless and to be liberated simultaneously with arising, just like a wave naturally subsiding back into the water. This is the sublime and vital point.

Then, as you attain greater stability in this awareness, here are the three means of placement that are specific to the approach of the Great Perfection itself:

Like a bundle of straw when a string has been cut, leave your body in whatever way you are comfortable and at ease.

Like the strings of a sitar that have been severed, leave your voice in its natural state—uninvolved in mundane conversation, mantra recitation, and the deliberate focusing upon the channels and energies.

Like a water mill where the water has been diverted, leave your mind in its natural state—without straying from the natural state in which the empty and cognizant awareness is unimpaired. Do not try to do anything at all even though thoughts of the three times of past, present, and future may stir. In this way, transcend into the state in which they exhaust themselves within the nature of dharmata.

Moreover, in the context of establishing this view of the *Luminous Heart Essence of the Great Perfection*, the primordial purity of Trekchö, it is an extremely vital point not to intermingle this view with the "views of assumption" that belong to the nine gradual vehicles. This is because the emptiness or the views of the teachings and the practitioners of the other vehicles—from that of the shravakas up to that of Secret Mantra—are all exclusively established by means of analytical meditation.

The Great Perfection does not require analysis nor cultivation. Rather, it is merely a matter of recognizing, as your own nature, this very wakefulness of natural knowing that is self-existing and spontaneously present throughout samsara and nirvana.

This recognizing is unlike the rigid clinging of intellectual or conceptual meditation training—as in the lower vehicles, which involve hope and fear, permissions and prohibitions concerning what to accept and reject—that is like a deer being caught in a hunter's trap. It is also unlike the lower sections of tantra in which the practitioners of Secret Mantra, in all the gradual stages of the path, engage in mental effort and conceptual involvement, as in the practices of the development stage, completion stage, and so on, which all require mental discrimination.

These perspectives may each have their individual view, meditation, and fruition, but they are entirely different from the Great Perfection's fresh essence of primordially pure awareness, which is unchanging throughout the three times.

So, unless you perfect the great strength of such awareness, you will not attain the kayas and wisdoms of ultimate fruition—the result of having captured the natural state of awareness within the basic space of primordial purity, which is the place of liberation of the entirety of samsara and nirvana. This difference, as vast as heaven, is therefore of utmost importance.

According to this king of views, our Dzogchen tradition—whether expressions of thought movement occur, remain, or dissolve, the essence does not change but remains a fresh, basic state of naturalness.

No matter the variety of samsaric or nirvanic displays that may arise, there is nothing else to be attained apart from or superior to this unchanging essence suffused with awareness, which transcends being liberated, even though the labels "buddha" or "fruition" may be given to it.

Since this essence has never been tainted by confusion, it is free from the seeds for taking rebirth within the worlds comprised of the three realms, the six classes of beings, and the four modes of rebirth.

Consequently, both samsara and nirvana are merely words and mind-made labels that do not possess a shred of real existence, not even as much as an atom—just like the space in a container is not really separate [from that outside of it]. Through personal experience you must realize this in actuality.

Primordial purity (kadag) means that the basic nature of awareness belongs to neither samsara nor nirvana, and therefore its identity is primordially pure. No type of virtuous karmic cause and effect improves this primordial purity, nor does any type of unvirtuous karmic cause and effect worsen it.

In short, this wakefulness of self-existing knowing is not improved upon—not even one speck—by any amount of relative or conceptual virtue belonging to the view, meditation, and conduct of the nine gradual vehicles. Also, it is not harmed in the slightest, even though one accumulates a tremendous amount of relative or superficial negative misdeeds, including the ten unvirtuous actions and the five actions with immediate consequences.

This primordially pure identity of awareness can be neither improved nor harmed by anything whatsoever. All types of cause and effect from wholesome and unwholesome actions appear as its expressions—just like the apparitions conjured by a magician. Realize that they are all unreal and empty, a magical display, and you will transcend the practices of cause and effect, which demand effort.

Nakedness (*jenpa*) means that the fresh, basic nature—empty, cognizant, and unchanging like the sky—is completely untainted, even as much as a hair tip, by feeling drowsy, foggy, or dull; by the meditation experiences of bliss, clarity, and nonthought; or by the conceptual speculations of a view, meditation, and conduct.

Openness (*zangtal*) means that the wide-open, natural state of aware-ness is neither composed of nor produced by conceptual thoughts. It is a complete openness that is not obscured by the world and beings, the ani-mate and inanimate, nor even the aggregates, elements, or sense bases. It is a complete lucidity that is not divided into the categories of outer, inner, and in-between. It is an unchanging openness of awareness that continues throughout the day and night.

In short, when the confused manner of experiencing along with its vari-ous aspects are all exhausted within the basic space of dharmata, all exter-nally perceived objects appear while being devoid of even as much as a hair tip of true existence, just like the reflection of the moon in water.

There's not even the slightest intellect that speculates, "Is it or isn't it?" concerning all the various types of sounds that are presented to your ears. Sounds and words to communicate do not cease, however, but are heard like an echo.

All the various types of thoughts belonging to cognitive acts and men-tal states become self-arising and self-dissolving within the basic nature of awareness.[8]

Then, as you reach an increased level of experience in this wakefulness of self-existing knowing, thoughts vanish by themselves, like a design drawn on water.

When you reach even greater stability, at the stage of the culmination of awareness, thoughts arise and dissolve simultaneously, like tiny particles of moisture in midair.

After this, as you reach the stage of exhaustion in dharmata, all expres-sions, however they may manifest, transcend in the identity of awareness the categories of arising or dissolving, like a design drawn in midair.

At this stage—having perfected the great strength of awareness in the ex-haustion of dharmata—even the subtlest type of consciousness (*namshe*) has dissolved into the empty and cognizant nature of awareness. This is like a vessel that formerly held camphor or any of the other five major types of scent but is now free of even the subtlest hint of an odor. In the same way, all the aspects of confusion—the confused way of perceiving due to the ground of confusion—are completely exhausted, and in a single lifetime you have captured the royal stronghold within the basic space of Samantabhadra's mind.

How wonderful! How utterly amazing!

Additionally, for applying the numerous key points for Tögal of spontaneous presence—the preliminaries, the three body postures, the three eye gazes, the key points for breath and awareness, and for using the supports of the sun, the moon, flame, and so on, and the supportless expanse of midair or the empty sky—you should first receive the pointing-out instruction from a sublime guru.

Next, train with strong perseverance until you have reached manifest dharmata in actuality, increased experience and displays, the culmination of awareness, and the exhaustion in dharmata.

For the final fruition, the foremost is to be liberated into the basic space of primordial purity, without any physical remainder. The next best is that liberation into the basic space of the ground is simultaneous with the interruption of the outer and inner breath. The least best is to recognize all the manifestations belonging to the bardo of dharmata, or the bardo of spontaneous presence, to be your own displays. By "making the distinction in a single instant," you are reborn in a realm beyond return, just like an arrow flying from a strongly shot bow. In the very least is that all your confused experiences belonging to the bardo of becoming dissolve into themselves so that, beyond return from the *nirmanakaya* realms in which the five kayas are spontaneously present, you become endowed with a status that is equal to all the bodhisattvas of the ten bhumis.

The gradual stages of the path of Tögal are described elsewhere.

For a person who has completed the Trekchö training in this way and perfected the great strength of awareness, conditioned attributes become exhausted within the basic space of unconditioned dharmata and awareness becomes unchanging. For such a person, the material body dissolves into immaterial particles—an occurrence the conquerors state to be "like a sky-soarer" or "like space."

Next best is to capture, simultaneously with expiring, the natural seat within the basic space of primordial purity that is the site of liberation of all buddhas and accomplished yogis, so as to be unchanging from the essence itself. From this great basic space of empty essence, an activity by means of the two types of form kaya will appear unceasingly for the benefit of beings for as long as samsara lasts.

Those of even lesser capacity will mingle the mother and child luminosities of the ground and path during the bardo of dharmata and then awaken to true and complete enlightenment within the "upper directness."

Those of slightly lesser capacity will recognize the sounds, colors, and lights during the bardo of spontaneous presence to be their own displays, remain in equanimity within this recognition, and within that equanimity reach the state beyond return, just like an arrow released by a great archer.

A person of the lowest capacity who has received the ripening and liberating instructions of the Great Perfection—although his stream-of-being fails to be liberated by practice—yet who has not damaged his samaya with the guru or the teachings does not possess a degree of progress sufficient for him to be liberated during the former bardos. Therefore, when the experience of the bardo of becoming dawns upon him, all his deluded perceptions will dissolve into themselves. Like a dream or a magical illusion, he will then miraculously take rebirth from within a lotus flower in one of the five buddha realms: the Truly Joyful to the east, the Glorious Realm to the south, the Lotus Realm to the west, Fulfilled Action to the north, the Densely Arrayed realm of Akanishtha in the center, and the like.

Here he will behold the countenance and hear the voice of the buddha residing there. After the coarse and subtle emotional obscurations are purified, he will become equal in status to all the bodhisattvas that dwell on the eighth to the tenth bhumis. After five hundred years he will take rebirth in the realm known as Blazing Fire Mountain charnel ground that is situated above all other pure realms. Here he will behold the countenance of the Youthful Warrior of Great Strength, purify the cognitive obscurations, and awaken to true enlightenment within the basic space of primordial purity.

5. The benefits of the instructions

These precious teachings of the luminous Great Perfection, the summit of all vehicles, are the quintessential essence of the precious teachings of all the perfect buddhas who teach and reside in the realm of the three kayas.

All sublime masters, who uphold the Dharma and remain for so long in the realms of the Saha worlds, began by entering these essential teachings, the summit of vehicles. Next, they retained these teachings, and finally they never forsook them. These knowledge holders and sublime beings realized for themselves the state of the luminous Great Perfection exactly as it is. Having done so, they benefit others by means of the knowledge that perceives all possibly existing things, overturning every state of samsara to the very depths. Thus they carry out the profound and perfect activities for both self and others—like suns rising in the sky.

These gradual stages of the Great Perfection, the condensed quintessence of the entire practice of the Luminous Heart Essence—*so difficult to encounter throughout the three times—were written down by someone who many times has received the ripening and liberating instructions of the* Luminous Heart Essence *from Jamyang Khyentse Rinpoche and numerous other masters who uphold the teachings of the Great Perfection in both scripture and realization. In particular, they were written, in a single session, by Shakya Shri Jñana—a yogi of the Great Perfection who repeatedly has been blessed by the three secrets of the Precious Master of Uddiyana and the omniscient Longchen Rabjam—in the glorious forest of Chikchar at Tsari. My son Tsering Rinchen devotedly took the dictation. This is of extreme profundity and belongs to the innermost section.* ITHI. *May it be virtuous!*[9]

PART ONE

BACKGROUND

1

THE WRITTEN NARRATION:
IN INDIA

The ka section: The written narration from the secret heart essence
of the Great Perfection, the most profound quintessence

Vimalamitra

Homage to Glorious Vajrasattva.

Primordial state, spontaneously perfected twofold well-being,
Nature in which the kayas and wisdoms are indivisible,
This you have realized, deathless vajra body,
Pandita of the five fields known as Jemala.
May you look upon me, Nyangben, with compassion.
Grant your blessings that we may be inseparable.

Ema,
This land of Tibet, in the northern part of the ax-shaped Jambu continent,
May be a barbarian borderland untouched by the Buddha's feet,
But the noble Avalokiteshvara
Has blessed it and brought it within his sphere of influence.

The incarnated Dharma king Toto Nyanshel
Founded the sacred Dharma and merely uttered its name.
The Dharma king Songtsen Gampo
Built temples and made the law of the ten virtues.
Through Avalokiteshvara, he cared for beings.

At present the sovereign lord King Trisong
Has built Glorious Samye and other temples.
He has invited the assemblies of learned panditas,

From *Dzogchen Sangwa Nyingtig: Dzogchen Sangwa Nyingtig Yangzab Düpey Nyingpo*,
Rinchen Terdzö, Vol. LI (Boudhanath: Rangjung Yeshe Publications, 2006).

And with numerous lotsawas, they have thoroughly translated
All of the sacred Dharma of Sutra and Mantra
And established the sanghas of monks and ngakpas.

In particular, the great pandita, a second buddha,
Samantabhadra in person, known as Jemamudra,
Has compassionately looked upon me, through the Dharma king's
    kindness,
And bestowed upon me the Secret Hearing Lineage of the Great Perfection.
Afraid that it may be forgotten, I write these words of reminders.
May they be retained by a few fortunate people with the karmic connection!

The following is the history of this quintessence of all the tantras of the
Great Perfection, the pinnacle of the entire 84,000 sections of the Dharma.

In the palace of five-colored lights in the dharmakaya realm, the chief of
all buddhas, the glorious Samantabhadra's body, speech, mind, and activity,
emanated as the buddhas of the five families to enact the boundless activities of influencing whoever is in need in any way that is necessary.

Next, in the abode of Tushita, the realm of the immaculate Abundant
Delight, on a lotus flower with one thousand petals, the great Vajradhara
of the Sixth Family taught the tantras of the *Secret Heart Essence*, including
the *Dra Talgyur Root Tantra*, to the one thousand buddhas of the Fortunate
Aeon, Glorious Vajrasattva, Vajrapani the Lord of Secrets, and others.

Then, the bhagavan Vajrapani the Lord of Secrets, in the palace of the
great Blazing Fire Mountain charnel ground, turned, throughout day and
night, the wheel of Dharma to the human and deva *vidyadhara*s as well as
the four classes of *dakini*s.

It was at this time that in the land of Uddiyana in the western direction, King Uparaja and Queen Radiant gave birth to a daughter, a nun by
the name of Dharma Sun. While she practiced meditation in the district
of the world ocean known as Jungle of Trials, she dreamed that a boy of
white crystal placed a nectar-filled vase made from five types of precious
substances upon the crown of her head.

Nine months and ten days later, she gave birth to a beautiful boy, without
any physical discomfort, but in shame she hid it in a heap of ashes. When
she saw that the wisdom dakinis, along with the young *deva*s and *devi*s,
paid homage and made offerings to it, she asked for forgiveness and took

the child up from the ashes. He was then given the name Resurrected Ash-Colored One. As he grew up, at the age of seven he understood much of the meaning of the Buddha's words.

When on the eighth day of the last autumn month he went to a forest to refresh himself, he beheld the countenance of Buddha Vajrasattva within a sphere of swirling five-colored rainbow lights in the expanse of the sky. Vajrasattva gave him this direction:

> "Kye, son of a noble family,
> Within the expansive sky of emptiness, rainbows of empty
>   cognizance radiate.
> Self-occurring sounds resonate the *Ali-Kali*—ringing, clanging.
> There is perfect fragrance, taste, and texture; exquisite but devoid of
>   attachment.
> To be vividly awake within this expanse of nonarising is called self-
>   existing wakefulness, but it transcends both symbol and meaning.
> Emaho!"

Having said this, he accepted the boy as a disciple.

About this time, his mother asked, "Where have you been?"

"I went to hear the Dharma from Glorious Vajrasattva. As I know all the teachings realized by Vajrasattva, I will go to debate with the panditas serving at the court of Uddiyana's king, so, Mother, please ask permission from His Majesty, your father."

His mother asked her father, who replied, "It will not do for a young child to debate. However, I shall inquire of the court panditas."

He went to the assembly of panditas at the noon meal and said, "The nun Dharma Sun has an intelligent eight-year-old child who says he wants to debate with all the panditas at the court."

The panditas replied, "Great king, let the young child come and debate. If he wins, we will become his followers. If we win, he should be punished by the king."

The child and the panditas then began the debate, and Resurrected Ash-Colored One won. The king was delighted and named him Garab Dorje, Delightful Vajra.

Later on, when he remained composed in samadhi at Mount Radiance, Vajrasattva again appeared in the sky before him and said, "Kye, child of a noble family, go to the great Blazing Fire Mountain charnel ground!"

Garab Dorje went to the Blazing Fire Mountain charnel ground, where he met Glorious Vajrapani. He received all the 6,400,000 tantras of the Great Perfection in their entirety and then went to the summit of Mount Malaya. There he wrote down all the tantras, statements, and pith instructions of the Great Perfection. After entrusting them to the care of the wisdom dakinis, he remained in meditation in the great Cool Grove charnel ground.

At this time, in the western part of India, in the city named Twofold Stages, the brahmin Fortunate and his wife Effulgent Lamp had a son by the name of Manjushrimitra, a pandita learned in the five fields of knowledge.[10] He received this prophecy from Manjushri: "Kye, son of a noble family. If you wish to attain enlightenment within this same body and life, go to the great Cool Grove charnel ground!"

In accordance with this prediction, he went to the great Cool Grove charnel ground, where he met the master Garab Dorje. After bestowing all the teachings of the Great Perfection, the master Garab Dorje departed into the expanse of space within a mass of light. Manjushrimitra fell to the ground in a faint. Then he uttered deep-felt cries of despair, whereupon a small casket of five precious substances containing the testament entitled *Three Words Striking the Vital Point* fell down into his hands.

The master Manjushrimitra then committed to writing all the tantras, statements, and pith instructions of the *Secret Essence Hearing Lineage*, after which he concealed them as a terma treasure in the Vajra-Cross Boulder to the northeast of the Vajra Throne in India. He then remained composed in samadhi in the great Sosaling charnel ground.

Meanwhile, in the Chinese city called Black Shokhyam, the householder Virtuous Attitude and his wife Wise Light had a son known as the great pandita Shri Singha. While he was traveling along the road to the city of Serling, in the middle of the vast plain, the mighty Avalokiteshvara appeared in the sky before him and said, "Listen, son of a noble family. If you wish to attain enlightenment within this same body and life, go to the great Sosaling charnel ground to the west of the Vajra Throne in India!"

In accordance with this prediction, Shri Singha went in a swift manner, with his feet one cubit above the ground, and reached the great Sosaling charnel ground in the course of nine days. There he met with the master Manjushrimitra. He presented innumerable mandala offerings and made numerous prostrations and circumambulations. After begging to be accepted, he was taught all the instructions in their entirety. Then he was told,

"Take out the scriptures that are concealed as a terma treasure in the Vajra-Cross Boulder to the northeast of the Vajra Throne in India!"

Having given this direction, Manjushrimitra departed into the expanse of space within a mass of light. Shri Singha uttered deep-felt cries of despair, and from amid the mass of light descended a small casket one inch in size and made out of eight precious substances, within which was the testament entitled the *Sixfold Meditation Experience.*

The learned Shri Singha then went to the Vajra Throne in India, where he took out the terma treasure scriptures that were concealed in the Vajra-Cross Boulder. Then he went to the Bodhi Revealing Tree in China, where he arranged all the scriptures. He concealed them in the side of a pillar in the Auspicious Ten-Thousand-Gate Temple and remained in the Cooling charnel ground.

During this time, in the city called Kamala in the eastern part of India, the low-caste Shanti and his wife Virtuous Heart had a son known as the sublime Jñanasutra. And, in Kashmir in the western area of India, in Elephant Ridge, the householder Blissful Wheel and his wife Bright Mind had a son known as the great pandita Jemalamudra.[11] While they were staying at the Vajra Throne, they went to refresh themselves at Reed Grove. In the middle of the expanse of the sky appeared Glorious Vajrasattva, who gave them this prophecy:

> "Kye, you two sons of noble families. For five hundred lives without interruption, you have taken birth as panditas, but you have not yet attained the essential fruition. So, if you wish to attain enlightenment within this same body and life, go to the Cooling charnel ground!"

Jemalamudra went there and met the learned Shri Singha, who gave him the entire cycle of the Great Perfection. When he returned to India, he met Jñanasutra again. Jñanasutra remembered the previous prophecy and asked, "Jemalamudra, did you meet Shri Singha?"

"I met him," Jemalamudra replied. After telling the whole story, he remained in samadhi at the Little charnel ground.

Following this, the sublime Jñanasutra also went to the Cooling charnel ground and met the learned Shri Singha. After making prostrations and circumambulations, he pleaded, "Please accept me!" Consequently, Shri Singha bestowed upon him the cycles of the Hearing Lineage and all the instructions belonging to the cycle of the *Secret Heart Essence of the Innermost*

Quintessence. Shri Singha then gave him this direction: "The scriptures for this are concealed as terma treasures in a pillar in the Auspicious Ten-Thousand-Gate Temple. Go take them out and apply them."

Having given this direction and prediction, Shri Singha departed into the expanse of space by letting his material body disappear within a mass of light. At that moment, the sublime Jñanasutra fell to the ground in a faint. He then uttered deep-felt cries of despair, whereupon a small casket of precious white crystal containing the testament entitled the *Seven Spikes* fell down [into his hands].

As he was told, he removed the scriptures from the cavity in the pillar of the Auspicious Ten-Thousand-Gate Temple, after which he remained composed in samadhi in Bhasing charnel ground.

Meanwhile, the dakini Resplendent Wisdom appeared in actuality to Jemalamudra and said, "Kye, son of a noble family. If you wish to receive even more profound instructions than before, go to Bhasing charnel ground!"

According to this prophecy, Jemalamudra went to Bhasing charnel ground, where he met with the sublime Jñanasutra. After making innumerable prostrations and circumambulations, he presented a boundless amount of ganachakras and mandala offerings. Then he made this request: "Kye, most compassionate protector. Please accept me!"

As Jemalamudra beseeched in this way with deep devotion, Jñanasutra bestowed upon him all the instructions in their entirety, without a single exception. Having entrusted him with all the scriptures, he departed into the expanse of space within a mass of light. At that moment, Jemalamudra fell to the ground. As he uttered deep-felt cries of despair, the testament entitled the *Fourfold Means of Settling*, within a small casket of precious *sona* studded with five types of precious stones, fell down [into his hands].

Following this, Jemalamudra was invited by King Singhabhadra[12] to Kamala in the eastern part of India, where he resided as the foremost officiating priest at the court. Here he turned the wheel of the Dharma during the daytime for the king, queens, children, ministers, retinue, and all the subjects. At night he remained in the Spontaneously Present Treasure charnel ground teaching the Dharma to the dakinis.

These details complete a brief history of the Buddha's mind transmission and the vidyadhara's symbolic transmission.[13]

2

THE STORY OF
VIMALAMITRA AND VAIROTSANA

Yeshe Tsogyal

King Trisong Deutsen then reflected deeply and formed this intention: "Here in Tibet I will make the sacred Dharma shine like the rising sun. Therefore, I must invite the great master Vimalamitra, who is reputed to be the most learned among the five hundred panditas in India."

The master Vimalamitra was an emanation of the Great Compassionate One. The Indian king Dharma Ashoka had a daughter named Dharmabodhi, a ravishing beauty who resembled a divine maiden. Once, while sleeping in a flower garden, she dreamed that an extremely handsome white man came and anointed her with a full vase of nectar. As the liquid passed down through the crown of her head, her whole body was filled with bliss.

After twenty-one days, without any physical discomfort, she gave birth to a baby boy. Thinking that it was dreadfully shameful to have given birth to a child without a father, she took the baby and abandoned him in the desert. Later, when she went looking for the child, he was sitting with his eyes wide open and wakeful. Feeling pity for the baby, she took him home and nurtured him.

Over the months and years, the boy grew up much faster than other children. When five years had passed, he went to the monastery of Nalanda. With the panditas there, he studied the five sciences and the Tripitaka. In particular, he became learned in all the tantras.

He took ordination from the master Shri Singha and was given the name Vimalamitra, Immaculate Renown. Living up to his name, he became the most eminent among the learned ones. He acted as the officiating

From *The Lotus-Born* (Boudhanath: Rangjung Yeshe Publications, 2004).

priest for the Dharma king Dharmachakra and resided in the monastery of Vikramashila with five hundred panditas.

King Trisong Deutsen gave the translators Kawa Paltsek, Chok-Ro Lui Gyaltsen, and Rinchen Chok of Ma each one *drey*[14] of gold dust and sent them off with this order: "Offer some gold to the Dharma king Dharmachakra at the Indian temple of Vikramashila. Beseech the king to send me the gift of a pandita who is learned in all the outer and inner teachings. You three translators shall then invite the pandita and return!"

The three translators presented the gold to the king of Vikramashila and said, "Since you are a monarch who sustains the Dharma, King Trisong Deutsen, the Dharma king of Tibet, requests you to give him the gift of a pandita who is expert in all the outer and inner teachings." King Dharmachakra replied, "Well, we must ask my court assembly of five hundred panditas, who will congregate tomorrow at noon."

The next day at noon the king called upon the five hundred panditas, presented each of them with a mandala offering of gold, and said, "The Dharma king of Tibet has presented me with a gift of gold and has requested me to send a pandita who is learned in all the outer and inner teachings. He has furnished these three translators as escorts, so I beseech the most learned of you to go."

Master Vimalamitra, the most learned among the five hundred panditas, was seated in the middle row. All five hundred panditas—the 250 to his right and the 250 to his left, looked toward Vimalamitra, and the king said, "This means that you must go."

Vimalamitra reflected, "The king of Tibet may have great faith in the Dharma, but his ministers are antagonistic toward the teachings of the Buddha. It is well known that they had the translator Vairotsana expelled. It is not sure whether I can tame them. I should not, however, turn my back on the Tibetan king's faith. In order not to transgress the command of the king of India, I must go!" Having reflected in this way, he stood up and exclaimed "Bodhisattva dathim!" three times.

The three translators interpreted this in different ways. Kawa Paltsek understood it to mean that he agreed to go, saying,

> When the arrow supported by the bow
> Is sent off by the strength of the man's finger,
> The arrow can reach the target.

Rinchen Chok of Ma understood it to mean that he agreed to go, saying,

> When the boat supported by the ocean
> Is rowed by the strength of the man with oars,
> The boat can cross the waters.

According to the understanding of Chok-Ro Lui Gyaltsen, it meant:

> In a place that is not his own country,
> The person endowed with qualities
> Will pour the river of his mind
> From the full vase of his body.

And so, having obtained permission from the king and all the panditas, the translators invited Master Vimalamitra.

Vimalamitra went to Samye holding a *kapali* four fingers in height on which were written eight Indian characters. King Trisong Deutsen and all the subjects formed a welcome party. When Vimalamitra arrived at Samye, they escorted him to Khorsa Chenmo. The master neither bowed to the king nor paid homage before the divinities; because of this the ministers said, "In the past we have invited many panditas here to our temple. We also will invite them in the future. Why is it that you, a pandita, neither bow to the king nor pay homage in the shrine hall?" Vimalamitra replied, "Do you, king and ministers, know the meaning of homage?"

"I don't know the meaning of homage," the king answered. Vimalamitra responded, "I pay homage by being indivisible from the deity. Because of this, the symbolic deities cannot bear my gesture of respect. Therefore, I do not bow down to the statue of a deity. Also, I do not bow down to a king."

King Trisong Deutsen then thought, "I wonder if he is really a Buddhist or a heretic." Vimalamitra knew his thought and said, "Are you displeased, King?"

Vimalamitra then put on his Dharma robes and made a gesture of homage to the statue of Buddha Vairochana, the image of the personal practice of the king, saying:

> To Vairochana, the form body of the supreme deity,
> Vimalamitra, the wisdom deity, bows down
> Within the relative state of illusion.

As a result of his making this gesture of homage, the image of Vairochana split apart from the top of its head down to the base of its pedestal. King Trisong Deutsen thought, "He really is a heretic!" and showed an utterly depressed face. Again Vimalamitra inquired, "Your Majesty, are you displeased?"

"I am not pleased," the king responded. Making another gesture of homage, Vimalamitra uttered:

> To Vairochana, the supreme wisdom deity,
> The form aggregate of Vimalamitra
> Confers the true empowerment endowed with the five wisdoms.

As he placed his hands at the top of the head of the Vairochana image, it became even more splendid than before. Countless rays of light issued forth, filling the three-story central temple with light. Vimalamitra then performed a consecration by permeating all the divine images at Samye with rays of light.

At this King Trisong Deutsen exclaimed, "I bow down to you!" He prostrated and said, "Outwardly, you wear the dress of a monk, but within you are a yogi who has attained accomplishment of Secret Mantra. Henceforth I beg you not to pay homage to me!" Vimalamitra replied, "Since you are a king who upholds the Dharma in Tibet, I surely must show you respect." He made the gesture of joining his palms, and the lights rays from his hands scorched the king's garment. The king then again prostrated.

King Trisong Deutsen requested the great master Vimalamitra to sit upon a lion throne with nine layers of cushions, offered him a huge brocade cape, various kinds of food, and a silver vase filled with three drey of gold dust. The master looked extremely displeased and did not say a thing, so the king thought, "This covetous man from south of Nepal is still not satisfied!" The master perceived this and said, "King, hold up your sleeve!" The king did so and Vimalamitra filled three drey of sand into his sleeve, saying, "Keep this for a moment!" King Trisong Deutsen couldn't hold it and let it slip out. The sand had turned into gold and Vimalamitra said, "Great king, for me all appearances are gold. But to fulfill Your Majesty's aspirations, just for now, I shall accept your gift."

On the meadow in front of the central temple a Dharma throne was erected and Vimalamitra was requested to teach the Dharma. The master reflected, "Formerly Vairotsana taught the resultant vehicle, but it did not tame the Tibetans and he was expelled. Therefore I must now teach gradually, beginning with the causal vehicles." While he was expounding the causal vehicles of philosophy to King Trisong Deutsen and the ministers, the king sent for tea from the area of Shangpo. On their way the traders reached Gyalmo Rongkhar, where Vairotsana asked them, "Where do you come from?" The traders answered, "We come from Central Tibet. We are sent by our king to fetch tea." Vairotsana asked, "Well, is the king's health good? Is the yoke of the royal law steadfast? Is the silk knot of the Dharma law tight? Who is the court priest? What are the titles of the teachings being translated?"

In reply, they said, "The king is in good health. The royal law is strict. The Dharma law is also tight. The court priest is Vimalamitra, who has been invited from India. They are translating the teachings known as the causal vehicles." The master Vairotsana then said, "I was expelled when translating the resultant vehicle such as the sacred Great Perfection, but now they are listening to the causal vehicles. Yudra Nyingpo, go there and do something to satisfy these Tibetan ministers who hate the Dharma."

Yudra Nyingpo put on a coat of woven cloth and a canvas sorcerer's crown and took a wooden sword in his hand. He made the Early and Later Translation of the Great Perfection into two scrolls on which he wrote the *Six Vajra Lines* and tucked them behind his left and right ears. Then he departed for Tibet.

Yudra Nyingpo arrived at Samye, where Vimalamitra was teaching the causal vehicles to King Trisong Deutsen and the ministers. Stripping naked, he mounted his wooden sword as if it were a horse and rode in using a whip on his rear end, shouting, "Kakapari, kakapari!" Due to the ministers' hostility toward the Dharma, Vimalamitra, afraid of being punished under the law, had never been seen to smile even once since having arrived in Tibet. But when he saw this yogi, he smiled and said, "Dathim, dathim!"

Vimalamitra was later invited to the palace. After food was offered, King Trisong Deutsen asked, "Since you have arrived in Tibet, master, you haven't been seen to smile even once, but today you smiled. Why was that?" Vimalamitra replied, "I never smiled in the past because it depresses me that the Tibetan ministers revile the Dharma. I smiled today because I was delighted that such a yogi lives in Tibet."

"Well," the king said, "What did it mean when the yogi said, 'Kakapari, ka-kapari'?" Vimalamitra replied, "He was talking about the teachings, saying:

> Buddhahood is not attained through the immature teachings of the
>   shravakas.
> A jumping crow cannot travel a great distance.
> Without teaching the resultant vajra vehicle,
> What is the use of teaching the causal vehicle?

"Well," King Trisong Deutsen asked, "why did you say, 'Dathim, da-thim,' master?" Vimalamitra replied, "It meant that all the teachings are the realization of the victorious ones and are without duality. Just like the nature of molasses or salt, all the Buddhadharma is devoid of duality."

The king sent someone to find the yogi, saying, "Find out who that yogi is!" The yogi was found sitting and drinking while flirting with a barmaid. When asked, "What is your name? Who is your teacher? What is the name of your teaching?" he answered, "I am Yudra Nyingpo. My teacher is Vairotsana. My teaching is the sacred Great Perfection."

This was reported to King Trisong Deutsen, who declared, "Invite him here! I must ask him for teachings!" Yudra Nyingpo was then placed on a throne of precious substances and offered a mandala of gold. The king and the close disciples received teachings from Master Vimalamitra in the morning and from Yudra Nyingpo in the afternoon. Thus they received the *Five Early and Thirteen Later Translations of the Great Perfection*. As the teachings of the two masters turned out to be identical, the Tibetan ministers felt regret for having expelled Vairotsana. Three emissaries were sent off with a gold ingot as a gift and invited Vairotsana back from Tsawarong. King Trisong Deutsen and the ministers placed his feet above their heads and venerated him as a supreme object of respect.

This was the sixteenth chapter in the Immaculate Life Story of the Lotus-Born Master, on how master Vimalamitra was invited and Vairotsana's expulsion regretted.

3

THE HISTORY OF THE
HEART ESSENCE OF THE DAKINIS

Padmasambhava

Homage to all the sublime masters.

In order to create trust and authenticate the source, here I shall briefly mention the succession of lineage masters. To quote the *Union of Sun and Moon Tantra*:

Unless the meaning of the history is explained,
The flaw of distrust will develop
Toward these teachings of the Definitive Great Secret.

As for the history of how this transmission occurred, this same tantra continues:

Through blessings the teacher Samantabhadra with consort
Entrusted the sovereigns,
Who are the Sattva recipients not inferior to himself,
So that all dharmas were liberated by knowing one,
Beyond the confines of bondage and liberation.

Through the blessings of Vajrasattva
They arose in the mind of the self-appeared Garab Dorje,
Who entrusted the tantras to Shri Singha.
The *Tantras That Liberate by Wearing* of the utterly perfect fruition
He entrusted to Padma of Uddiyana.

From Khandro Nyingtik, *The Heart Essence of the Dakinis* (Boudhanath: Rangjung Yeshe Publications, 2006).

Reveal them to the fivefold disciples.
Thus it was said.

To explain, in the dharmadhatu palace of Akanishtha of the utterly pure space, the glorious Bhagavan Samantabhadra with consort, the dharmakaya beyond defilement, is not made out of any entity whatsoever but is manifest in a form with face and arms. From within this unconstructed state of dharmakaya, in the realm of Akanishtha, he taught glorious Vajrasattva by means of natural blessings.

Glorious Vajrasattva, the sambhogakaya adorned with the major and minor marks, in the celestial palace of the Blazing Fire Mountain charnel ground, taught, with few words, the emanation Garab Dorje, the one who though remaining in the world of men is equal to the buddhas in realization. Garab Dorje taught the master Shri Singha in the charnel ground of Wild Jungle by establishing the actuality in Shri Singha himself. Shri Singha then taught the great vidyadhara known as Padma Tötreng Tsal, the one whose vajralike body is beyond birth and death, passing and transmigration, in the great charnel ground of Sosaling, by revealing the natural state free of assumptions.

Padma Tötreng Tsal then taught Tsogyal, the Lady of Kharchen, the one who received the prophecy from all the dakinis, in the Tidro Cave at Upper Zho, by divesting her of deluded meditation, assumptions, and mental darkness and revealing the fivefold wisdom essence by establishing it as a self-luminous actuality. I, the Lady of Kharchen, then acted as the compiler and gave my blessings that these teachings may be transmitted to the minds of those in the future who are endowed with a karmic link. Thus I entrusted them to the dakinis and concealed them as a precious earth treasure. May they meet with the destined one in the future!

Samaya. Seal, seal, seal.

4

HISTORICAL BACKGROUND

Tulku Urgyen Rinpoche

The main teaching of the original teacher Buddha Samantabhadra is Dzogchen, the Great Perfection. The teachings of Dzogchen are the pinnacle of all nine vehicles. Before the Dzogchen teachings arrived in our human world, they were propagated through the mind transmission of the conquerors in the three divine realms: first in Akanishtha, then in Tushita, and lastly in the Abode of the Thirty-three Gods, the world of Indra and his thirty-two vassal kings located on the summit of Mount Sumeru.

Akanishtha is of two types: The ultimate Akanishtha, often called the palace of Dharmadhatu, refers to the state of enlightenment of all buddhas. There is also the symbolic Akanishtha, which is the fifth of the Five Pure Abodes and is still within the realms of form, located in the sky above Mount Sumeru. The symbolic Akanishtha is the highest among the seventeen worlds in the realms of form, situated just below the formless realms. The whole of samsara consists of three realms—the desire realms, the form realms, and the formless realms. Above the desire realms, seventeen worlds make up the form realms. Above them are the four formless realms, also known as the four spheres of infinite perception. The statement "All buddhas awaken to complete and true enlightenment within the realm of Akanishtha" refers to dharmadhatu, not the symbolic realm of Akanishtha.

To reiterate, after Akanishtha, the teachings were disseminated in the realm of Tushita, another of the form realms, where Buddha Maitreya now abides. Then, in the desire realms below, the teachings were spread in the realm called the Abode of the Thirty-three Gods. Samantabhadra,

Adapted from Tulku Urgyen Rinpoche, *Rainbow Painting* (Boudhanath: Rangjung Yeshe Publications, 1995), "Background."

as Vajradhara, taught in Indra's palace, called the Mansion of Complete Victory, on the summit of Mount Sumeru. This was about the three divine realms.

Generally, it is said that the 6,400,000 Dzogchen teachings entered this world via Garab Dorje, the first human vidyadhara, who directly received the transmission from the Buddha in the form of Vajrasattva. These teachings first arrived in Uddiyana and later were propagated in India and Tibet. Before the era of Buddha Shakyamuni, the Dzogchen teachings were propagated in our part of the universe by other buddhas known as the Twelve Dzogchen Teachers. Buddha Shakyamuni is usually counted as the fourth guide in this Excellent Aeon in which one thousand fully enlightened buddhas are to appear in our world. Although in this context he is known as the fourth guide, Shakyamuni is the twelfth in the line of Dzogchen teachers.

No Dzogchen teachings have occurred apart from the appearance of a buddha in this world, so we must count Buddha Shakyamuni as one of the chief teachers through whom the teachings were transmitted. He did, indeed, convey Dzogchen teachings, though not in the conventional manner. His conventional teachings were primarily received by those who had a karmic connection with the teachings appropriate to *shravakas*, *pratyekabuddhas*, and *bodhisattvas*. It was not that they were not allowed to receive the Dzogchen teachings; their karmic fortune was such that they received the teachings to which they were suited. The Buddha gave Dzogchen teachings, as well as other Vajrayana instructions, by first manifesting the mandala of a deity and then imparting the tantric teachings to a retinue seated within that setting. This, however, does not lie within the scope of what was perceived by ordinary people.

The Dzogchen teachings are sealed with three types of secrecy: *primordial secrecy* means that they are self-secret; *hidden secrecy* means that the teachings are not evident to everyone; and *concealed secrecy* means that they are deliberately kept secret. All other buddhas also teach Dzogchen, but never in as open a way as during the reign of Buddha Shakyamuni. During this period, even the word *Dzogchen* is world-renowned and can be heard as far as the wind pervades. Despite their widespread nature, the teachings themselves, the pith instructions, are sealed with the stamp of secrecy.

Through his immaculate wisdom, Buddha Shakyamuni always taught after taking into account the abilities of the recipients. In other words, he would not teach at a level above a person's head. He adapted his teachings to what was suitable and appropriate to the listener. Therefore, we can say that those who heard his teachings only assimilated what was comprehensible to someone of their aptitude. Later, when they repeated what Buddha Shakyamuni had taught, their account was according to what they had perceived in their personal experience. But his teachings were not only limited to the personal experience of the recipients, who according to some historical texts were shravakas, pratyekabuddhas, or bodhisattvas. The teachings they experienced are contained in the different versions of the Tripitaka, the three collections of Sutra, Vinaya, and Abhidharma. The reason that the Buddha did not give the shravakas, pratyekabuddhas, and bodhisattvas deeper teachings is that these would not fit into their scope of comprehension. What they received is called the general Sutra system. In addition to delivering these general Sutra teachings, Buddha Shakyamuni also taught in various locations throughout the universe. Manifesting in the form of a deity as the central figure of innumerable mandalas, he taught the tantras. In this way, we should understand that Buddha Shakyamuni himself, appearing in other forms, was the crucial figure in the transmission of Vajrayana teachings. This is not in the conventional sense but in the extraordinary sense. So, when we hear that the Dzogchen aspect of Vajrayana was transmitted through Garab Dorje, we should know that it actually came from Buddha Shakyamuni in the form of Vajrasattva. From there it was continued through other masters—first through Garab Dorje, then through various Indian masters, and eventually through Padmasambhava and Vimalamitra.

Our main teacher, Buddha Shakyamuni, appointed Padmasambhava as his chief representative to teach Vajrayana. He said that Padmasambhava was the body emanation of Buddha Amitabha, the speech emanation of Avalokiteshvara, and the mind emanation of Buddha Shakyamuni himself.

Padmasambhava arrived in this world without a father or mother, appearing in the center of a lotus blossom. He lived in India for more than a thousand years and remained in Tibet for fifty-five years before departing from this world at a pass called Gungtang, the Sky Plain, on the Nepal-Tibet border. Four dakinis appeared to support his horse and carried him to a pure land known as the Copper-Colored Mountain.

Since the time he left Tibet, he has sent a ceaseless stream of emissaries representing him. They are called *tertöns*, or treasure revealers, and are the reincarnations of his twenty-five main disciples. Today, we refer to these masters in their various incarnations as the 108 Great Tertöns. Through the centuries they have appeared to reveal the terma treasures that Padmasambhava concealed throughout Tibet for the sake of future generations. These termas are discovered in the form of scriptures, instructions, sacred substances, precious gemstones, holy objects, and so forth.

Many of these tertöns uncovered in such an impressive fashion what Padmasambhava had hidden that even people who harbored great doubt were forced to admit the validity of termas. Sometimes a tertön would open up a solid rock before a crowd of four hundred or five hundred people and reveal what had been concealed inside. By openly performing such feats and permitting people to witness the revelations with their own eyes, they completely dispelled all skepticism. Through the ceaseless activity of Padmasambhava, this type of tertön has continued to appear right up to the present day. So, the terma teachings come from Padmasambhava himself and are revealed in an undeniably direct way. This is not some mere legend from long ago. Even until recent times, these great tertöns could perform miraculous feats like passing through solid matter and flying through the sky.

The Vajrayana teachings, in particular the Dzogchen teachings that consist of seventeen chief tantras, were brought to Tibet and spread by Padmasambhava and Vimalamitra. While these teachings had been propagated in India by many other masters, their transmission in Tibet is chiefly due to the kindness of Padmasambhava and Vimalamitra. Many centuries later, when Atisha arrived in Tibet, he visited the extensive library at Samye and was amazed. He said, "These treasures must have been taken from the dakini realms! I have never heard that tantras existed in such numbers anywhere in India." Atisha acknowledged that Vajrayana teachings flourished to a much greater extent in Tibet than they did in India.

Since the time of the introduction of Buddhism into Tibet right up until the present day, a continual revelation has occurred in the form of new terma transmissions. Some of the most renowned are: Longchenpa's *Nyingtig Yabzhi,* the *Four Branches of Heart Essence*; Dorje Lingpa's *Tawa Longyang,* the *Vast Expanse of the View*; the *Könchok Chidü,* the *Embodiment of the Three Jewels*, revealed by Jatsön Nyingpo; and *Gongpa Zangtal*, the *Unimpeded Realization of Samantabhadra,* revealed by Rigdzin Gödem. There have been countless others. A little more than one hundred years ago, Jamyang Khyentse Wangpo revealed the *Chetsün Nyingtig*, the *Heart Essence of Chetsün*, while Chokgyur Lingpa revealed the *Kunzang Tuktig,* the *Heart Essence of Samantabhadra*. Thus, the Dzogchen lineages are continuously renewed by the discovery of new termas.

One might ask, what is the purpose of heaping up stacks upon stacks of Dzogchen scriptures? There is a very important point involved here: namely, the purity of transmission. As teachings are passed down from one generation to the next, it is possible that some contamination or damage of samaya may creep in, diminishing the blessings. To counteract this, Padmasambhava in his immeasurably skillful wisdom and compassion gives us fresh hidden treasures. There is nothing of greater profundity than the Three Sections of Dzogchen: the Mind Section, Space Section, and Instruction Section. The distance from the Buddha to the practitioner is very short when a revelation is fresh and direct; there is no damage to the line of transmission. The purity or lack thereof lies not in the teaching itself but in how long the line of transmission is. That is why there is a continuous renewal of the transmission of Dzogchen teachings.

The chief disciples of Padmasambhava and Vimalamitra are known as the king and twenty-five disciples. They all attained a rainbow body, the dissolution of the physical body at death into a state of rainbow light. Such practitioners leave behind only their hair and fingernails.

From these practitioners onward, for many, many generations, like the unceasing flow of a river, numerous disciples also left in a rainbow body. Among the three kayas—dharmakaya, sambhogakaya, and nirmanakaya— sambhogakaya manifests visually in the form of rainbow light. So, to attain a rainbow body in this lifetime means to be directly awakened in the state of enlightenment of sambhogakaya. A disciple of the great Tibetan translator Vairotsana named Pang Mipham Gönpo attained a rainbow body. His disciple attained a rainbow body, and for the next seven generations, each disciple's disciple in turn left in a rainbow body. In the Kham region of eastern Tibet, there were four great Nyingma monasteries: Katok, Palyul, Shechen, and Dzogchen. At Katok Monastery, eight generations of practitioners achieved a rainbow body, beginning with its founder and continuing through the succeeding seven generations of disciples. There has been an unceasing occurrence of practitioners departing from this world in the rainbow body up until the present day.

5

GUIDANCE MANUALS

Tulku Urgyen Rinpoche

Apply the three degrees of knowledge resulting from study, reflection, and meditation practice, as well as your theoretical understanding, experience, and realization, to the Dzogchen teachings and you will possess the instructions necessary to reach the state of Samantabhadra in one lifetime.

The most effective style of teaching for a practitioner in this dark age is not a lengthy scholarly explanation but a direct guidance manual. A guidance manual *(triyig)* is a short, comprehensive teaching. The Dzogchen tantras themselves were written down in a style that shrouds and conceals the meaning so that only a master who is extremely well versed in oral instructions and treatises would be able to clarify the tantric statements. A guidance manual, on the other hand, is written down using oral instructions, so as to be clear and simple. An excellent summary of the Dzogchen teachings can enable a worthy practitioner to reach the state of primordial enlightenment in this very life.

Trekchö and Tögal are the two main topics in Dzogchen. Trekchö is the main view in all the Eight Practice Lineages. Through Trekchö all the masters of the past attained enlightenment. Without the view of Trekchö, one doesn't reach the core of Tögal practice. The Tögal visions are manifestations of awareness, *rigdang*, but without the correct view of recognizing rigpa, they become nothing but manifestations of the karmic wind known as *lungdang*, which are merely expressions of dualistic fixation. So recognizing rigpa is the key point in Trekchö.

Adapted from Tulku Urgyen Rinpoche, "Introductory Teachings," in *Circle of the Sun* by Tsele Natsok Rangdröl (Boudhanath: Rangjung Yeshe Publications, 1990).

When one engages in Tögal practice after having mastered awareness, all manifestations will appear as *rigdang*. The kayas and wisdoms are the maturation of rigpa, not of dualistic mind (*sem*).

As Tilopa said, recognition of rigpa occurs through gathering the accumulations and purifying obscurations and through the blessings of a qualified master. Depending on other means should be known as delusion. Have you heard of anyone who recognized nondual awareness simply by reading books? Aside from receiving blessings, gathering the accumulations, and purifying obscurations, no other technique exists for recognizing rigpa.

Devotion is more important than scholarship. One could possibly gain impressive skill in debate and in analytical thought yet still find fault in the Dzogchen teachings, calling them the erroneous view of the Hashang followers.

"Receiving blessings" refers to a moment of deep devotion. Recognizing rigpa through mere intellectual speculation is indeed very difficult. The Kagyü and Nyingma schools emphasize the simple resting meditation of a kusulu, as opposed to the analytical meditation of a pandita. Through the single method of devotion, receiving the blessings and focusing on meditation, countless practitioners of the past have reached accomplishment.

The Kagyü and Nyingma are known more for a long line of realized masters than for great scholars. Although there have been several learned masters, for the most part their followers were male and female lay practitioners. The fact that countless of these practitioners died while sitting up in undistracted wakefulness is because of this tradition of simple, direct teachings. You can read about this yourself in the wondrous histories of the followers of the Nyingma school as well as of the various Kagyü lineages.

To mention one example, the siddha Seltong Shogom, together with a gathering of his disciples, left more than thirty clear footprints in solid rock. When I was young, my father took me to see them in eastern Tibet. In several places they had molded the rock like dough. Amazing!

On the fifteenth day of the month, the moon sets simultaneously with the sun's rising—there is no gap. A garuda bird can fly instantaneously upon hatching from its egg, its wing power being fully perfected at birth. In the same way, a Dzogchen practitioner attains complete enlightenment simultaneously with the death of the physical body. At the moment of death, an experienced yogi does not lose consciousness but reaches enlightenment!

6

SONG OF ENCOURAGEMENT TO READ THE SEVEN TREASURIES

The excellent words of omniscient Longchen Rabjampa

Paltrul Rinpoche

NAMAH SARVAJNANAYA
Homage to the Omniscient One.

Utterly at peace from the beginning, intrinsic, all-pervasive realm,
Forever unmoved, wisdom space of dharmakaya,
Possessing realization's greatest strength, perfection's light,
Omniscient master, at your feet I bow.

Listen here about the virtues, the most eminent of all,
That you cannot generate unless you follow in the footsteps of the noble beings.
The finest pearls are found within the ocean's deepest waters,
So how can they be found in any lesser place?

Like sunlight, the realized state of wakefulness
Springs from a master's pith instructions, from a line of blessings unimpaired.
Dull-minded meditators, cultivating vacant states,
Will rarely reach authentic levels on the perfect path.

Though lack of learning is the greatest failing in this world,
Distorted learning is a greater evil.
So now, while you have leisure to peruse a learned master's books,
Why don't you open your eyes of learning?

From Paltrul Rinpoche, "Song of Encouragement to Read the Seven Treasuries, The Excellent Words of Omniscient Longchen Rabjampa," in *Crystal Cave: A Compendium of Teachings by Masters of the Practice Lineage* (Boudhanath: Rangjung Yeshe Publications, 1990).

Resembling the unique and wish-fulfilling jewel,
There is no other buddha to be found within this world
Like the precious scriptures of the Omniscient Master.
Who can avoid finding great delight in them?

The ultimate summit of vehicles, the supreme vajra essence,[15]
Is a precious treasury of the realization of 100,000 tantras
Which contains the vast—the words that express the meaning—and the
    profound—the expressed meaning itself.
To see it is to meet Samantabhadra in person.

By reading it you will comprehend the meaning of the 64,000,000 tantras;
You will understand the nature of all of existence and peace, samsara and
    nirvana;
And you will realize the special qualities of the intent of the profound path,
    the summit of vehicles.
Therefore, persevere in reading this scripture.

Beyond the observance of precepts, the natural state of dharmakaya[16]
Is the treasury of Samantabhadra's realization, beyond cause and effect.
Without cutting through mental constructs by means of such an excellent
    scripture,
Who can destroy the wicked clinging of the vehicles of assumption?

The essence of all oral instructions, concise and condensed,[17]
Fully contains the sacred Dharma in each six-line teaching.
Wouldn't it be difficult to receive such an excellent path, all at once,
Even if you met the Victorious One in person?

The precious *Treasury of Philosophical Views*[18]
Is an exposition in which all teachings are complete within one treatise.
I swear such an eminent scripture has not appeared in India or in Tibet
In the past, nor will it appear in the future.

The *Wish-Fulfilling Treasury* of learning, reflecting, and meditating on the
    entire body of teachings[19]
Excellently shows all that should be adopted or avoided.
By reading it, you will comprehend the nature of all the teachings
And so become well versed in a hundred scriptures.

The single treasury of the key points on practicing the oral instructions,
The intent of the summit of vehicles, complete and concise,
Fully contained in the meanings of eleven words,[20]
Is the only solace truly cutting the root of samsara in this world.

In particular, the most profound and precious *Treasury of Dharmadhatu*[21]
Is the core of the Omniscient Master's realization.
It fully and directly shows wakefulness beyond accepting and rejecting—
The dharmakaya nature of your intrinsic mind-essence.
This text is the true dharmakaya, manifest in physical form.
Such an excellent text is the Buddha in person.
It fulfills the deeds of the victorious ones in this world.
This text shows the buddha-mind directly.
I swear there is nothing higher, even if you met the Buddha!

Such an excellent text is a treasury of all the sacred Dharma,
The ultimate meaning expressed by all the teachings.
It directly shows the dharmakaya wisdom;
I swear there is nothing higher, even if you compare all the teachings.

Such an excellent text is the heart of the noble sangha.
It is unsurpassed by the wisdom of realization
Of all the noble buddhas' offspring throughout the three times.
I swear that the wisdom of noble beings is not superior to this.

This relic-vessel of dharmakaya, the complete Triple Gem,
Is the unexcelled path of all the victorious ones.
A replica of the Omniscient Master's realization—
Whoever meets it has attained the end of rebirth.

Simply hearing one line of such an excellent text
Can bring your samsaric experience to a halt.
Having had the chance to read it entirely,
How will you feel if you throw it away?

Pay heed! The Tripitaka and the teachings of the nine vehicles
Are mostly intended for energetic people.
Claiming to be liberated by meditating, practicing, and striving
Will not make you see the wisdom beyond acceptance and rejection.

This effortless vajra pinnacle, transcending conceptual mind,
Is uncultivated buddhahood, the naked space of empty awareness.
Through this, when free from clinging to the idea of meditation, practice,
    and effort,
Even a lazy person can realize the dharmakaya.

In this world and that of the gods,
Only the omniscient dharmakaya master teaches such a path.
Among all the existing dharmakaya teachings,
This *Dharmadhatu Treasury* is the essence of the Dharma.

In this world, such an eminent text
Is liberation through seeing, as well as through hearing and recollecting.
Whoever connects with it is a future buddha.
If you realize it, you are a buddha of the present.

As the power of the blessing lineage is unbroken,
You will receive the wisdom of the true lineage through his entrusted
    intention.
Sealed with his entrustment to future disciples,
It is equal to meeting the Omniscient Master in person.

Though you may not understand the exact meaning of the words,
If you have devotion you will receive the wisdom of the blessing lineage.
The precious word empowerment is received by reading this text
And it grants the empowerment of awareness display.

When weary, fearful, or tormented by sorrow,
If you read this text the wisdom of great joy will arise.
Delighted and joyful, your mind will be clear and bright,
And your confused perception will immediately collapse.

If you read this text when your delight expands and great bliss blazes forth,
Your clinging to joyfulness will collapse.
All-pervasive, intrinsic space is free from distinctions like accepting.
Thus you are taught the profound realization of the Omniscient Master.

When the striving and clinging to this life torments you,
Read this text and your fixation on solid reality will fall apart.
With a wide-open mind, whatever you do is fine.
Free from the ties of hope and fear, your meditation is spontaneous.

It is the Middle Way; it is also the paramitas.
It is the Cutting as well as the Pacification of suffering.[22]
It is Mahamudra and also Dzogchen.
Embodying all teachings, it surpasses them all.

If you are a child who follows the Omniscient Master,
Never separate yourself from this excellent text.
It is sufficient to rely only on this permanent companion of awareness.
I swear there is no lasting shelter superior to it.

For now, your mind will be at ease, and in the end you will achieve
    buddhahood.
Unhurt by striving, your mind's ties will come undone.
Calming you in elation and consoling you in sorrow,
Such an excellent text never deceives.

Put it into a melody; sing it as a song.
It is composed in verse, so read it until you can chant it freely.
If you never part from it,
Your deluded samsaric experience will collapse.

When you receive the blessed lineage, the vital point of realization,
Indescribable wakefulness will dawn within you.
When you see the true face of the Omniscient Dharmakaya Master,
Your happiness will be unceasing in the state of basic bliss.

Besides reading this text, you need no other practice,
As it is the essence of both meditation and sadhana.
As long as you read this excellent text,
The realization of dharmakaya arises spontaneously.

Therefore, do not harbor a lot of restless striving—
Just read these eminent texts with a free and easy mind.
Decide that nothing is more profound than the meaning they express,
Then rest in the state of naturalness.

You need not struggle and concentrate, seeking the meaning of the words,
As in scholars' treatises, which are so hard to understand.
Just mingle your mind with the text in the state of naturalness,
And naked openness will occur unimpededly.

This is the pointing-out instruction. This is your innate wakefulness!
This is the instruction of the Omniscient Master!
It is the expressed meaning, as well as the true empowerment.
It will also suffice as the essential practice.

Whether or not you comprehend the definitions and connotations,
Whether or not you understand the profound meaning,
Whether or not you discover the final and innermost intent,
Cut your hope and fear, and read in the state of nondistraction.

Read it again and again; read while mingling it with your experience.
Mingle the text with your mind and seal your mind with these scriptures.
Chant with a joyful melody in this state of unity.
The power of devotion will blaze forth and the wisdom of realization will
    dawn.

Pay heed! This is the essence of the essence.
There is no "deepest of the deep" apart from this.
It is a treasury of blessings, the essence teaching.
It is the teacher in person—the Buddha placed in the palm of your hand.

Even if I were to extol its virtues for eons,
The inspiration of my narrow mind would not be exhausted.
It is needless to mention the eloquence of other wise beings.
There is no excellent path superior to this that delights the noble ones.

Pay heed! Such a precious gemstone!
Now while you have the fortune of leisure in which to read it,
Why feel sad even if you have to remain in samsara!
Is it not sufficient to have devotion and a wide-open mind?

Dear friend, when reading this text,
Resolve your mind on this in a free and easy state.
Right here, relax your striving and restless mind.
Right here, cut your striving for many other teachings.

What is the use of so many interesting philosophies?
What is the use of so many profound instructions?
What is the use of so many elaborate practices?
What is the use of so many dry explanations?

This itself is the free meditation of simple rest!
This itself is the carefree happiness of self-liberation!
This itself is the good book of "knowing one that frees all"!
This itself is the instruction of "one bridge to cross a hundred rivers"!

Don't leave this at home and search for it elsewhere!
Don't throw away the core and gather the peels!
Don't abandon the effortless to accomplish it through striving!
Don't cast away nonaction to busy yourself with activity!

Once you take birth in the bloodline of the Omniscient Master,
This excellent text is your deserved legacy.
This is the eminent path laid down by your forefather.
If you want to feel at ease—this is where you should do it!

Pay heed! Pay heed! Thanks to the three lineages!
What good fortune to meet this excellent text!
What a boon to be able to practice this eminent path!
The Buddha is within you—how true that is!

On this eminent path that gladdens the victorious ones,
Mingle your mind with the Dharma, dear friend!
This is my heart advice—imprint it in the core of your heart!
If you keep it there, it will be of some use.

I, the careless and useless Uncle Tatter,
Have no wish to explain mere words I haven't realized myself.
But for sure, I have gained confidence and a little experience
In the writings transmitted by the Omniscient Master.

Ablaze with the five poisons, I roam about enslaved by distraction!
But even for someone like me with evil karma, whose delusions are hard to
    conquer,
Samsaric experiences fall to pieces
When I hear and read an excellent text like this.

Therefore, when you and someone with good fortune and pure samaya
    like yourself,
Who are stable-minded and have but a few of the five poisons,

Read this text, you will surely attain the supreme wisdom of the blessing
    lineage.
Arouse confidence again and again!

Whoever is touched by the blessed brilliance
Of the Omniscient Master, a perfect buddha,
It is true, and one can directly perceive,
That understanding and liberation are simultaneous.
Thus, the Omniscient Master is the ancestor of hundreds of siddhas.

The Great Lhatsün, the lord of realized ones,
Rigdzin Jigmey Lingpa who attained spontaneous realization,
And the Great Treasure Master, the king of the teachings,
Obtained the blessing lineage through the writings of the Omniscient One.

Keep this in your mind, my dear friend!
In the same way, may you have true regard
For the eminent writings of the Omniscient One, receive the wisdom of
    the true lineage,
And attain liberation in the expanse of his realization, the space of
    suchness.

SARVA MANGALAM

7

THE ASPIRATION FOR ALL THE WRITINGS OF THE GREAT OMNISCIENT ONE AND FOR THE SEVENTEEN TANTRAS OF THE DEFINITIVE GREAT SECRET

Khenpo Ngakchung, Ngawang Palzang

Emaho!
Samantabhadra dharmakaya, sambhogakaya Vajradhara,
Twelve teachers of the mind transmission of the true perfection,
Garab Dorje and four knowledge holders of the sign transmission,
Tingdzin Zangpo, Dangma Lhüngyal, and so forth,
Guru knowledge holders of the hearing lineage, please pay heed to me!
Especially, victorious Longchen Rabjam,
Protector, please bear witness to this aspiration!

From today and during all my lives
May the *Seventeen Tantras* of the Luminous Essence, the innermost, refined,
The *Seven Treasuries* and the *Threefold Secret Essence*—
And all the words and meaning of these secret topics, deep and vast,
Arise within my mind by means of perfect recall.
May I open the door of Dharma for all beings with an ocean of courageous
    eloquence,
And may the realization of dharmata be unceasing!

Flawless Light Ray who was Vimala in person,
Please accept me, in your wisdom body,

From the collected writings of Khenpo Ngakchung Ngawang Palzang (Boudhanath: Rangjung Yeshe Publications, 2005). This little text contained the legend: "These are the Words of the Vajra Holder Ngagi Wangpo."

And transmit to me the ultimate, the realization lineage,
So that I become like you, omniscient master.

When the rise and fall of Dharma is completed in this realm,
And when the Dzogchen teachings' Triple Portents pass on to the
    buddhafield of Beautiful Array,[23]
May I then study and reflect there.
Through meditation training, may I hold the teachings of the greatest secret,
So that the doors of Dharma may swing open for sentient beings.

And after that, within Immense Protection's northern realm,
In Utpala Flower Buddha's noble presence,
May I take birth among the first assembly of his retinue.

May I serve the sugata in the most perfect way.
May I taste his sweetest nectar, ripening and liberation,
And assist in working for the teachings of the Buddha.

And then, when to the west the Triple Sources of the teachings soar,
Descending on the world known as the Space Sublime,
Where the teachings will remain for 700,000 years,
From the time of Buddha Krakuchanda,
May I at first become his main disciple
And next the regent of this conqueror.

Finally, may I single-handedly establish in both ripening and liberation
Everyone there is to tame, without a single exception,
And deliver them to the island of sublime emancipation.

From this present rebirth throughout all my future lives,
May I gain a free command of recall, wisdom, and courageous eloquence.

Among the secret of all secrets, the *Seventeen Tantras of the Luminosity,*
The *Tantras of Self-Manifest, Self-Liberated,* and the *Tantra of No Letters*—
Just like a sovereign and his close retinue assembled,
May I embrace the essence of the tantras in my mind with perfect recollection
And use courageous eloquence to shower every being with the rain of
    Dharma.

The *Tantra of Studded Jewels,* the *Mirror of the Heart,*
The *Tantra of the Mirror of the Mind of Vajrasattva,*
May I embrace this threefold essence of the tantras, lucid and exceptional,

Within my mind with perfect recollection,
And use courageous eloquence to shower every being with the rain of Dharma.

The *Tantra of the Garland Pearls*, the *Tantra of Perfected Lion*,
The *Tantra of Graceful Auspiciousness*—
May I embrace these three within my mind with perfect recollection
And use courageous eloquence to shower every being with the rain of
    Dharma.

The single summary, the *Self-Existing Tantra of Perfection*,
The *Tantra of the Pointing-out Instructions* that perfects the visions from
    within,
The *Tantra of the Sun and Moon in Union*, victorious in the battlefield of
    wisdom,
The *Tantra of the Pile of Gems* to mend deficiencies,
And the two segments of the *Tantra of the Shining Relics,*
May I embrace them within my mind with perfect recollection
And use courageous eloquence to shower every being with the rain of
    Dharma.

The *Tantra of the Blazing Lamp,* the total liberation,
The *Tantra of the Sixfold Spheres,* resemblance of the heart,
The *Root Tantra, the Dra Talgyur*, the secrecy in itself,
And then the *Tantra of the Wrathful Black* that crushes all adversity—
May I embrace them within my mind with perfect recollection
And use courageous eloquence to shower every being with the rain of
    Dharma.

The secret *Seven Treasuries,* disclosing all in detail,
The *Fourfold Nyingtig*, mothers and their children, instructions in the most
    profound,
May I never be apart from these, the teachings of the *Vajra Essence of the
    Greatest Secret*
In this rebirth and all my future lives,
And may I be taught in person by the Omniscient Master.

May I achieve the light of wisdom, the six limits and the fourfold modes
That reveal the deepest tantras and instructions.
May I obtain the eyes of insight of the triple perspicacity
And be a master of the complete threefold reason.

Having thus attained your view and realization, Flawless Light Ray,
Together with your samadhi and conduct, complete and exact,
May I then secure the happiness and welfare of all beings.

I have harbored this supplication from my heart to the Omniscient Master [Flawless Light Ray, also known as Longchen Rabjam] in my mind for a long time. And then, with the thought that these aspirations may be of benefit for a few other people in this dark age who are of the same level as me, this was written down by Ösel Rinchen Nyingpo Pema Leydrel Tsal. May it be virtuous!

8

The Dzogchen Scriptures

Khenpo Ngakchung, Ngawang Palzang

The Great Perfection is the ultimate of all the 84,000 profound and extensive sections of the Dharma. It is the realization of Buddha Samantabhadra, exactly as it is.

In terms of tantric scriptures, there are 6,400,000 tantras of the Great Perfection, which can be divided into the Three Sections of Mind, Space, and Instruction. The *Kulayaraja Tantra (All-Creating King)* is the chief tantra of the Mind Section, the *Tantra of Infinite Vastness* is the chief tantra of the Space Section, and the *Dra Talgyur Root Tantra* is the chief tantra of the Instruction Section.

All these Dzogchen tantras were compiled by Vajrasattva, who is the manifestation of the bliss and emptiness of the mind of Samantabhadra. Vajrasattva then taught the tantras to the three main bodhisattvas who spread the teachings in the three worlds: Manjushri taught the devas, Avalokiteshvara taught the nagas, and Vajrapani taught human beings. Thus, countless sentient beings were brought to the primordial ground of liberation.

In order to spread the Dzogchen teachings in our world, the Jambu continent, Vajrasattva emanated from his heart the deva prince Noble Spirit, who then incarnated in the human world in the family of King Indrabhuti as the child Garab Dorje, also known as Rolang Deva. Garab Dorje received all the tantras, scriptures, and oral instructions of Dzogchen from Vajrasattva in person and thus became the first human vidyadhara in the Dzogchen lineage.

A summary of the teachings of Vimalamitra, Longchenpa, and Khenpo Ngakchung as recorded in the Nyingtik Yabzhi and its related commentaries, as well as in extracts from oral teachings of Kyabje Dilgo Khyentse and Tulku Urgyen Rinpoche (Boudhanath: Rangjung Yeshe Publications, 1990).

Garab Dorje entrusted these teachings to his main disciple, Manjushri-mitra, who then classified them into the *Three Sections of the Great Perfection*.

Manjushrimitra's chief disciple, the great master Shri Singha, divided the Instruction Section into *The Four Cycles of Heart Essence* (*Nyingtig*): the Outer, Inner, Secret, and Innermost Unexcelled Cycles.

Three great masters brought these three sections of Dzogchen to Tibet: Padmasambhava, Vimalamitra, and Vairotsana.

The Innermost Unexcelled Cycle consists of seventeen tantras. There are eighteen when adding the *Tantra of the Wrathful Black Protectoress of Mantra*, which is focused on the protective rites of Ekajati. According to the system of Padmakara, there are nineteen when including the *Tantra of the Blazing Sun of the Brilliant Expanse* (*Longsal*).

These tantras teach all the requirements for a person to practice and attain complete buddhahood within a single lifetime. No tantra is dependent upon the others; all are complete in themselves.

1. The *Dra Talgyur Root Tantra*, which resembles the gateway and key to the Luminous Essence, the supreme vehicle, explains how to attain the level of nirmanakaya and how to accomplish the welfare of others through practices related to sound.

2. The *Tantra of Graceful Auspiciousness*, which resembles a wheel, teaches how to establish the nature of awareness and how to identify the basis of confusion and the unmistaken wisdom.

3. The *Tantra of the Heart Mirror of Samantabhadra*, which resembles a sword, shows how to identify and cut through pitfalls and errors and how to establish what is intrinsic.

4. The *Tantra of the Blazing Lamp*, which resembles a radiant gemstone, teaches how to identify the "lamps" related to awareness, their terminology, analogies for how wisdom arises, the unity of awareness, and how to clear misconceptions about self-cognizance and how to practice.

5. The *Tantra of the Mind Mirror of Vajrasattva*, which resembles the sun, teaches how the lamps are the self-display of awareness. By means of twenty-one pointing-out instructions, the different types of people recognize wisdom. It further teaches the four key points and how to practice.

6. The *Tantra of Self-Manifest Awareness*, which resembles the ocean, teaches how to resolve the view, meditation, and action.

7. The *Tantra of Studded Jewels*, which resembles refined gold, shows how to eliminate the defects and sidetracks connected to the view and the practice of meditation, conduct, and fruition.

8. The *Tantra of the Pointing-Out Instructions*, which resembles showing a mirror to a maiden, describes, through various indications, how to apply the essence of awareness in one's practice.

9. The *Tantra of the Six Spheres of Samantabhadra*, which resembles a great garuda, teaches how to purify and prevent rebirth in the six realms and how to manifest the pure realms of self-display.

10. The *Tantra Beyond Letters*, which resembles the King of Mountains, describes the actual means of practice, how to abandon activities and live in places free from defects, the four ways of freely resting, how to sustain naturalness, as well as the undefiled method of the main part of practice.

11. The *Tantra of the Perfected Lion*, which resembles a lion, explains the degrees of progress and the signs that occur, how to stabilize awareness, and how to increase the level of experience.

12. The *Pearl Garland Tantra*, which resembles a garland ornament, is taught for the sake of preventing awareness from straying by means of bringing it to maturation. It teaches how to practice and reach familiarity and liberation.

13. The *Tantra of Self-Liberated Awareness*, which resembles a knotted snake that uncoils by itself, teaches how awareness is uncreated but is liberated by itself, how to control appearances, how to grow familiar with the vajra chain, and how to naturally free all of samsara and nirvana.

14. The *Tantra of Piled Gems*, which resembles a king's treasury, explains how the manifest qualities are all the essence of space and awareness.

15. The *Tantra of Shining Relics*, which resembles a king taking control of his land, describes the outer and inner signs of awareness reaching maturity that are manifest before and after the time of death in order to inspire and instill confidence in others.

16. The *Union of Sun and Moon Tantra*, which resembles a child climbing onto its mother's lap, shows which experience a person undergoes in the intermediate state, the bardo, after passing away. It teaches how to resolve one's master's oral instructions during the bardo of this life, how to stabilize awareness during the bardo of dying, how to attain enlightenment through recognizing awareness during the bardo of dharmata, and, if necessary, how to be assured of a rebirth in a natural nirmanakaya

realm during the bardo of becoming and there attain buddhahood without further rebirths.

17. The *Tantra of Self-Existing Perfection*, which resembles a river, teaches how to prepare to be a suitable recipient of the teachings by means of the four empowerments.

18. The *Tantra of the Wrathful Black Guardian Shri Ekajati*, which resembles a sharp razor, describes how to protect the practitioner against harms inflicted by others.

Vimalamitra united the two aspects of the Innermost Unexcelled Section: the explanatory lineage with scriptures and the hearing lineage without scriptures, which he then concealed to be revealed in the future. These teachings became renowned as *Vima Nyingtig*, and also as the *Secret Heart Essence* of Vimalamitra. Longchenpa later clarified them in his fifty-one sections of *Lama Yangtig*.

Padmasambhava concealed his teachings on the Innermost Unexcelled Cycle to be revealed in the future as the *Heart Essence of the Dakinis* (*Khandro Nyingtig*). Longchenpa also clarified these teachings in his *Quintessence of the Dakinis* (*Khandro Yangtig*).

These four exceptional sets of Dzogchen instructions are contained, together with Longchenpa's additional teachings *Profound Quintessence* (*Zabmo Yangtig*), in his collection famed as the *Heart Essence in Four Branches* (*Nyingtig Yabzhi*).

PART TWO
THE GROUND

9

The Prayer of Kuntuzangpo

Samantabhadra

Ho!
Everything—appearance and existence, samsara and nirvana—
Has a single ground, yet two paths and two fruitions,
And magically displays as awareness or unawareness.

Through Samantabhadra's prayer, may all beings become buddhas,
 completely perfected in
The abode of the dharmadhatu.

The ground of all is uncompounded,
And the self-arising great expanse, beyond expression,
Has neither the name "samsara" nor "nirvana."

Realizing just this, you are a buddha;
Not realizing this, you are a being wandering in samsara.

I pray that all you beings of the three realms
May realize the true meaning of the inexpressible ground.

I, Samantabhadra, have realized the truth of this ground,
Free from cause and condition,
Which is just this self-arising awareness.

It is unstained by outer (expression) and inner (thought), affirmation or
 denial, and is not defiled
By the darkness of unmindfulness;
Thus, this self-manifesting display is free from defects.

[I, Samantabhadra,] abide as intrinsic awareness:

From *The Root Tantras That Directly Reveals Samantabhadra's Mind*, a rediscovered
terma treasure by Rigdzin Gödem (unpublished manuscript).

Even if the three realms were to be destroyed,
There is no fear.

There is no attachment to the
Five desirable qualities (of sense objects).

In self-arising consciousness, free of thoughts,
There is neither solid form nor the five poisons.

In the unceasing clarity of awareness,
Singular in essence, there yet arises
The display of the five wisdoms.

From the ripening of these five wisdoms,
The five original buddha families emerge,
And through the expanse of their wisdom
The forty-two (peaceful) buddhas appear.

Through the arising power of the five wisdoms,
The sixty (wrathful) herukas manifest.

Thus, the ground awareness is never errant or wrong.

I, [Samantabhadra] am the original buddha of all,
And through this prayer of mine
May all you beings who
Wander in the three realms of samsara
Realize this self-arising awareness,
And may your great wisdom spontaneously increase!

My emanations will continuously manifest
In billions of unimaginable ways,
Appearing in forms (to help) you beings
Who can be trained.

Through my compassionate prayer,
May all you beings who
Wander in the three realms of samsara
Escape from the six life forms!

From the beginning you beings are deluded
Because you do not recognize
The awareness of the ground

And are thus unmindful and indecisive,
Which is the very state of unawareness,
The cause of going astray.

From this (delusive state)
Comes a sudden fainting away and then
A subtle consciousness of wavering fear.

From that wavering there arises
A separation of self
And the perception of others as enemies.

Gradually, the tendency of separation strengthens,
And from this the circle of samsara begins.

Then the emotions of the five poisons develop;
The actions of these emotions are endless.

You beings lack awareness because you are unmindful,
And this is the basis of your going astray.

Through my prayer, may all you beings
Recognize your intrinsic awareness!

Innate unawareness means
Unmindfulness and distraction.
Imputing unawareness means
Dualistic thoughts toward self and others.
Both kinds of unawareness are
The basis for the delusion of all beings.

Through Samantabhadra's prayer,
May all you beings wandering in samsara
Clear away the dark fog of unmindfulness,
Clear away the clinging thoughts of duality!
May you recognize your own intrinsic awareness!

Dualistic thoughts create doubt.
From subtle attachment to this dualistic turn of mind,
Dualistic tendencies become stronger and thicker.

Food, wealth, clothes, home, and friends,
The five objects of the senses,

And your beloved family—
All these things cause torment
By creating longing and desire.

These are all worldly delusions;
The activities of grasping and clinging are endless.

When the fruition of attachment ripens,
You are born as a hungry ghost,
Tormented by coveting and desiring,
Miserable, starving, and thirsty.

Through Samantabhadra's prayer,
May all you desirous and lustful beings
Who have attachments
Neither reject longing desires
Nor accept attachment to desires.

Let your consciousness relax in its own natural state;
Then your awareness will be able to hold its own.
May you achieve the wisdom of perfect discernment!

When external objects appear,
The subtle consciousness of fear will arise.
From this fear, the habit of anger
Becomes stronger and stronger.

Finally, hostility comes, causing violence and murder.
When the fruition of this anger ripens,
You will suffer in hell by boiling and burning.

Through Samantabhadra's prayer,
You beings of the six realms,
When strong anger arises for you,

Neither reject nor accept it.
Instead, relax in the natural state
And achieve the wisdom of clarity!

When your mind becomes prideful,
There will arise thoughts of competition and humiliation.

As this pride becomes stronger and stronger,
You will experience the suffering of quarrels and abuse.

When the fruition of this karma ripens,
You will be born in the god realm and experience
The suffering of change and falling (to lower births).

Through Samantabhadra's prayer,
May you beings who develop pride
Let your consciousness relax in the natural state;
Then your awareness will be able to hold its own.
May you achieve the wisdom of equanimity!

By increasing the habit of duality,
By praising yourself and denigrating others,
Your competitive mind will
Lead you to jealousy and fighting,
And you will be born in the jealous god realm,
Where there is much killing and injury.

From the result of that killing,
You will fall into the hell realm.

Through Samantabhadra's prayer,
When jealousy and competitive thoughts arise,
Do not grasp them as enemies:
Just relax in ease; then consciousness can
Hold its own natural state. May you achieve the wisdom of unobstructed
    action!

By being distracted, careless, and unmindful,
You beings will become dull, foggy, and forgetful.

By being unconscious and lazy, you will
Increase your ignorance,
And the fruition of this ignorance will be
To wander helplessly in the animal realm.

Through Samantabhadra's prayer,
May you beings who have fallen into the
Dark pit of ignorance
Shine the light of mindfulness

And thereby achieve
Wisdom free from thought.

All you beings of the three realms
Are actually identical to buddhas,
The ground of All;
But your misunderstanding of the ground
Causes you to go astray,
So you act without aim.

The six karmic actions are a delusion, like a dream.

I am the primordial buddha
Here to train the six kinds of beings
Through all my manifestations.

Through Samantabhadra's prayer
May all you beings without exception
Attain enlightenment in the state of dharmadhatu.

Ah ho!
Hereafter, whenever a very powerful yogi
With his awareness radiant and free from delusion
Recites this very powerful prayer,
Then all who hear it
Will achieve enlightenment
Within three lifetimes.

During a solar or lunar eclipse,
During an earthquake, or when the earth rumbles,
At the solstices or the new year,
You should visualize Samantabhadra.

And if you pray loudly so all can hear,
Then beings of the three realms will be
Gradually liberated from suffering
Through the prayer of the yogi
And will finally achieve enlightenment.

This prayer was taken from the nineteenth chapter of the Dzogchen Teachings of the Gongpa Zangtal, the Northern Treasures.

10

ATI YOGA

Padmasambhava & Jamgön Kongtrül

Having stabilized the experience of bliss and emptiness in your being, ⚬
Now, for the ultimate path, by means of the supreme true
    empowerment, ⚬
The Great Accomplishment of the resultant Ati Yoga, ⚬
You should resolve the unexcelled vajralike samadhi, ⚬
The natural Great Perfection. ⚬

In the outer, the intent of the Mind Section, ⚬
Regard all external objects to be like dreams. ⚬
Within, invalidate the sense faculties to be unreal like magical illusions. ⚬
In between, the cognitions are devoid of arising, dwelling, and ceasing. ⚬
The innermost, the all-ground, is a cognizant and nonconceptual state. ⚬
This view is the all-doer, the original awakened mind. ⚬

With a meditation that is free of effort, leave whatever occurs without
    contriving. ⚬
Utilize the conduct and realize the fruition. ⚬

    The path connected to the fourth empowerment, the Ati Yoga train-
ing in the union of awareness and emptiness, has two parts: a brief statement connecting the previous words with the following and the extensive
explanation.

Adapted from Padmasambhava and Jamgön Kongtrül, *The Light of Wisdom*, *Vol. IV*
(Boudhanath: Rangjung Yeshe Publications, 2001), "Ati Yoga."

Brief Statement

The *Lamrim Yeshe Nyingpo* root text says:

> Having stabilized the experience of bliss and emptiness in your being, ࿒
> Now, for the ultimate path, by means of the supreme true
>   empowerment, ࿒
> The Great Accomplishment of the resultant Ati Yoga, ࿒
> You should resolve the unexcelled vajralike samadhi, ࿒
> The natural Great Perfection. ࿒

When, by means of the gradual stages of the Anu Yoga path that are the practices of the secret empowerment and knowledge empowerment, the unified experience of great bliss as the means and emptiness as the knowledge has fully arisen and been stabilized in your being, you should enter the ultimate destination of all the gradual vehicles of the path, the supreme or ultimate of all yogas, the Great Accomplishment of the effortless and resultant vehicle of Ati Yoga, by practicing the wisdom of the fourth—the empowerment of awareness display—that directly reveals the true original wakefulness.[24]

That is to say, you should resolve the vajralike samadhi—the original wakefulness at the *end of the stream* not excelled by any other samadhi—which is composed of the path without impediment, the final point of the four paths of training.[25] It is called this because it destroys the most subtle defilements that are difficult to destroy, and it possesses the seven qualities such as being indivisible, indestructible, unhindered, and so forth.[26] Thus, you should resolve all the paths of means and liberation and the entire fruition of the path within realizing the nature of the original basic state, the luminous Great Perfection. To quote the *Tantra of the All-Creating King*:

> As being, it is no more than one.
> As teaching, it is taught as two kinds.
> As appearance, it appears as nine vehicles.
> As inclusion, they are included within the Great Perfection.

The same text says:

> I resolve the points of all teachings.[27]

In this context, the general key points of the extraordinary perspective of the Great Perfection are described in this way: what the natural state of the ground is like, how sentient beings were deluded from it, how luminosity is present during delusion, the methods of practice, and how the final fruition is accomplished. In particular, these are definitely topics belonging to the innermost cycle of the Instruction Section:

> The ground, the way of delusion, and the way it is present,
> The abode, the pathways, the gate and the fields,
> The practice, the measure, and the intermediate states,
> The state of liberation; thus eleven points.[28]

Even though it is essential to know the meaning of these points, I am afraid of using too many words here. They are exclusively to be understood from the tantras, statements, and instructions in general and from the writings of the ever-excellent Drimey Özer in particular.

Detailed Explanation

This has three parts: describing the methods of training in the outer Mind Section, the inner Space Section and the innermost Instruction Section.

The Outer Mind Section

This has four points: deciding through the view, resolving through the meditation, clearing the dangerous passages through the conduct, and relinquishing hope and fear through the fruition.

Deciding through the View

First, the *Lamrim Yeshe Nyingpo* root text says:

> In the outer, the intent of the Mind Section, ⚕
> Regard all external objects to be like dreams. ⚕
> Within, invalidate the sense faculties to be unreal like magical illusions. ⚕
> In between, the cognitions are devoid of arising, dwelling, and ceasing. ⚕
> The innermost, the all-ground, is a cognizant and nonconceptual state. ⚕
> This view is the all-doer, the original awakened mind. ⚕

The path of the natural Great Perfection—the summit of the vehicles that transcends effort and striving, something to be discarded and its antidote, sidetracks and obscurations—is the domain of worthy ones with extremely sharp faculties whose different levels of capacity bring forth three distinct perspectives.

The first of these is the bodylike Outer Cycle, the intent of the Mind Section, the meaning of which is stated in tantras and scriptures such as the *All-Creating King,* the *Eighteen Marvels of Mind,* and others.

For this, regard all external perceived objects, which include all that appears and exists, samsara and nirvana, to be the expressions of your own mind and as having no existence whatsoever besides being your own mind—just like the perception of objects in dreams.

The perceiver within is no different. Consequently, since the six sense faculties supported by the body are imaginary phenomena within deluded experience, and therefore as unreal as the sense faculties of a person in a magical illusion, understand them to be so by invalidating them through intelligent investigation.

In between, the six cognitions that become involved with objects are originally devoid of an origin of arising, at present a place of dwelling, and finally a location of ceasing. If you examine and explore these places, you find that, just like space, they are devoid of any basis for such labels and are therefore all experienced as the play of the mind itself.

The innermost, the all-ground and basic condition of mind, is by nature cognizant and in essence a nonconceptual and self-existing wakefulness. Within this indescribable and unconditioned state, view all conditioned phenomena as perfected.

Decide that this view of the fully established—the all-creator of samsara and nirvana—is the nature of the totally unfabricated, original awakened mind. As the *All-Creating King* mentions:

> The buddha kayas and wisdom qualities,
> The actions and tendencies of sentient beings, and so forth,
> Everything comprising the worlds and beings, all that appears and exists,
> Is from the beginning the essence of awakened mind.

Resolving through the Meditation

Second, the *Lamrim Yeshe Nyingpo* root text says:

> With a meditation that is free of effort, leave whatever occurs
>   without contriving. §

After having so decided through the view beyond limitations and categories, now comes how to practice the meditation. While sitting in the sevenfold posture of Vairochana in a secluded place, loosely relax your present mind free of any striving or effort of your three doors, in the state of original emptiness that is like the sky. As objects are fundamentally freed and the perceiver is primordially freed, leave whatever occurs without contriving by means of a remedy to re-free them and resolve this within the great natural resting. The *All-Creating King* mentions:

> Within the great bliss of simplicity, as it is,
> Do not force your three doors; neither contrive nor focus;
> Do not create mentally; do not pursue attributes;
> Remain in the blissful nature of self-existing wakefulness.

Clearing the Dangerous Passages through the Conduct

Third, the *Lamrim Yeshe Nyingpo* root text says:

> Utilize the conduct ... ౄ

No matter which desirable object you may perceive, let it be an adornment for the subject—the self-liberated nature—and look into the identity of the five poisons. That they are consequently experienced as wakefulness that is freed upon arising is the conduct of naturally freeing emotions.

The very moment thoughts connected to the six types of cognition arise, to recognize that they are perfect as the threefold uncreated mandalas of spontaneous presence is the conduct of mastering perceptions.

When all the conceived objects of accepting and rejecting, affirming and denying, are naturally freed into nonduality by means of the transformative training that promotes equal taste, the conduct of utilizing courageous discipline is to be liberated from the dangerous passages of hope and fear.

Utilize these three and thus bring forth enhancement in your view and meditation.

Relinquishing Hope and Fear through the Fruition

Fourth, the *Lamrim Yeshe Nyingpo* root text says:

> ... and realize the fruition. ౄ

Since the basic space of your present mind—the originally free essence-body beyond ground and root—is primordially free from meeting and separation, and complete within yourself without being sought for, there is no other buddhahood (of fruition) to be accomplished elsewhere.[29] You should therefore realize this very fact by training in the view and meditation. As the *All-Creating King* mentions:

> Do not accomplish anything other than your essence itself.
> It is your own nature, so do not seek it elsewhere.
> The basic space of the victorious ones is not found by seeking.

11

THE SPONTANEOUS VAJRA MANIFESTATION OF AWARENESS AND EMPTINESS

An aspiration of the Great Perfection of Manjushri, the inseparable nature of the ground, path, and fruition

Jamgön Mipham Rinpoche

You assume the nondual form of being the wisdom body
Of the sugatas and their sons throughout the ten directions and the
    four times.
Ever-Youthful Manjushri, within your state of equality,
May we be spontaneously perfected in the nature of nonaction.

By devotion to the Primordial Lord, the glorious master,
And regarding him as the dharmakaya of equality,
May we obtain the great empowerment of awareness display
Through the blessing of the realization of the ultimate lineage being
    transmitted to our hearts.

Present since the beginning, it is not dependent upon being
    cultivated,
Nor upon such things as differences in one's capacity.
May this vital point of mind, not trusted since it seems too easy,
Be recognized through the power of the master's oral instructions.

To elaborate or to examine is nothing but adding concepts.
To make effort or to cultivate is only to exhaust oneself.
To focus or to meditate is but a trap of further entanglement.
May these painful fabrications be cut from within.

From the collected works of Jamgön Mipham Rinpoche (Boudhanath: Rangjung Yeshe Publications, 1988).

Because it is beyond thought or description, not a thing is seen.
There is, however, nothing extra remaining to be seen.

That is the profound meaning of resolving one's mind.
May this nature, hard to illustrate, be realized.

Because it is primordially pure of all constructs, the extreme of
    existence has been discarded.
As the manifestation of awareness is spontaneously present, it is free
    from the extreme of nonexistence.
Although described as two aspects, these are but the labor of
    conceptual mind.
May we perceive this inseparable nature of equality, beyond description.

Although it is initially grasped through intellectual statements,
Just like a finger pointing to the moon,
The natural state of dharmata lies beyond the reach of assumptions.
May we take this to heart and perceive it ourselves.

In this there is nothing seen to be discarded,
Nor is there anything to be kept or established.
May this state of dharmata, unspoiled by acceptance and rejection,
Be perceived as the spontaneously present nature.

Although attaching attributes, the ground to be known,
The path to be journeyed, and the fruition to be attained
Are but like levels in space in the actual nature.
May we spontaneously abide in the nature of nonaction.

Samsaric impure phenomena, imputed through confusion,
As well as its opposite, pure perception,
Are but constructed attributes, named in dependence.
May we perceive their nonexistence in the unfabricated essence.

In its way of being, the nonconceptual essence of dharmata
Is only obscured by concepts or spoiled by having a view and meditation.
Looking into the ordinary essence, while being free from a view and
    meditation,
May we spontaneously rest in the genuine nature.

Whatever one is focused on is poison for the view.
Whatever is embraced by effort is a fault of meditation.

Whatever is adopted or abandoned is a defect of action.
May we perceive the nature free from all shortcomings.

If we are not trapped in the mire of mental constructs,
The manifestation of awareness is directly seen, free from concepts.
Without tying knots in the air with the rope of speculation,
May we be skilled in spontaneously resting in the genuine nature.

At that very moment, may the light from the lamp of self-existing
    knowledge,
The wisdom aspect of the self-cognizant Youthful Vase Body,
Manjushri of Natural Cognizance,
Overcome the dense darkness of the obscurations.

Since the unfabricated and uncompounded dharmata
Has nothing new to be obtained through the path of fabrications,
May the nature of the ultimate fruition, which does not result from a
    cause,
Be perceived as being primordially present within us.

Being covered up by words of speculation is the path of confusion.
Whatever is expressed is but a web of concepts.
May the profound instruction to be individually cognized, which
    does not result from statements,
Be practiced within our hearts.

The mind that holds subject and object is, by nature, mistaken.
It is never exactly like what one imagines.
May the self-existing wisdom body that does not result from dualistic
    mind,
The buddhahood of true meaning, be accomplished.

Within the cognizant space of awareness and emptiness,
All phenomena are in a state of equality.
In this single sphere the hopes and fears of samsara and nirvana have
    collapsed.
May we, in this nature, attain the kingdom of nondwelling dharmakaya.

Whatever is perceived as one's body or as a sense object
Appears like a visual aberration produced by conceptual thought.
By the natural radiance of the great nonconceptual wakefulness,
May it be purified in the primordial space of exhausted dharmas.

The wisdom body, equal to the sky,
Is a wish-fulfilling jewel yielding well-being and happiness.
May we obtain this unobscured and ultimate fruition
For all beings, in all times and directions, till the end of existence.

This was undertaken at the command of Jetsünma Dekyong Yeshe Wangmo, who is renowned as being an incarnation of the dakini Varahi, at the fortunate time of the fourth day in the third month, accompanied by an auspicious scarf and the precious ornament of a crystal rosary. The composition was completed on that very day by the one called Mipham Jampal Gyepa Ösel Dorje. By the virtue of uttering these independent and unique words of the doctrine of the Great Perfection, as they naturally arose, may all beings attain the state of the Primordial Lord, the Ever-Youthful Manjushri.

12

THE FOURTH DHARMA
OF GAMPOPA

Tulku Urgyen Rinpoche

Now let's look at the fourth Dharma of Longchenpa and Gampopa, letting confusion dawn as wisdom. All sentient beings, without a single exception, have buddha nature, from the dharmakaya buddha down to the tiniest insect. There is no real difference between individuals in the quality or size of this enlightened essence. However, buddhas and fully enlightened bodhisattvas have cut the movement of dualistic mind at the very beginning. That is how they are different from sentient beings. Buddhas and bodhisattvas' expression of mind takes the form of compassionate activity. This activity, through emanations and re-emanations, appears in all samsaric realms in order to teach other beings.

Sentient beings, on the other hand, have fallen under the power of dualistic thinking. An ordinary person's attention strays according to any movement of mind. Suddenly there is the confusion of believing in self and other, subject and object, and this situation goes on and on, repeating itself endlessly. This is samsaric existence. The buddhas and bodhisattvas were successful in getting up on the dry land of enlightenment. But we sentient beings became bewildered and are now drowning in the unsuccessful, unsatisfactory state we all find ourselves in. We are still in the ocean of samsara; we have not yet gotten our heads fully out of the water. We have roamed about in one confused state of experience after another, endlessly. At the same time, we haven't lost our buddha nature. Our buddha nature is never separate from our minds. Though we are not apart from it, we do not know it, and thus we wander in samsaric existence.

From Tulku Urgyen Rinpoche, *As It Is, Vol. 1* (Boudhanath: Rangjung Yeshe Publications, 1999), and *Repeating the Words of the Buddha* (Boudhanath: Rangjung Yeshe Publications, 1991), "The Four Dharmas of Gampopa."

"Confusion arising as wisdom" means realizing that the buddha nature pervades all sentient beings. We have not lost it; it has never been apart from our mind for even a single instant. This buddha nature is always present, and the only thing that conceals it is our own thinking. Nothing else obscures it. The essence becomes obscured by the expression. The expression of our own attention takes the form of the confused thinking that obscures us. In other words, *we* are obscuring our own buddha nature, and now is the time to clear up this confusion.

Now is the time to free ourselves from samsara. Unless we do it in this lifetime, it is not going to happen all by itself. The Buddha not only appeared in this world, he imparted the precious instructions on how to realize our own buddha nature. And these teachings on how to realize our enlightened essence have been made available through an unbroken lineage of great masters.

Confusion here means believing something to be what it is not. To be confused is the same as to be mistaken. How do we turn confusion into wisdom? First we need to understand what confusion is. Confusion is taking what isn't for what is. It's the opposite of knowing what is to be as it is. In Tibet there is a drug called *datura*, which, when you take it, makes other people appear as if they had fifty heads or thirty hands. We know that this is not possible in this world; this is an example of confusion.

Within our buddha nature are three qualities of enlightened body, speech, and mind. The unchanging quality that is like the openness of space is called vajra body. The unceasing quality is called vajra speech. The unmistaken quality, the capacity to perceive even without thought, is called vajra mind. These three—vajra body, speech, and mind—are inherently present as the nature of all sentient beings. All we need to do is recognize this. Even though we have the three vajras, we don't know it, and thus we continue to wander in samsara. Ordinary confusion covers up our innate three vajras. Our physical body of flesh and blood covers the vajra body. The words and sounds we utter, which are interrupted and intermittently created, obscure the unceasing quality of vajra speech. And our train of thoughts that comes and goes and endlessly arises and ceases from moment to moment, day after day, life after life, is exactly what obscures the unmistaken quality of vajra mind. What is necessary now is to recognize our own nature instead of going on being confused.

To explain this fourth Dharma of Longchenpa and Gampopa in a more detailed way, then, confusion dawning as wisdom refers to the completion stage. The former mention[30] of the completion stage is defined by and dependent upon a visualization that is either dissolved into emptiness or reappears from emptiness; thus it is called completion stage with attributes. The true completion stage involves recognizing our buddha nature. When pure gold is covered by dirt, it is not obvious that it is gold, even though this dirt is temporary. But once the dirt is removed, we realize that the gold is gold. In the same way, when our confusion is purified, the wisdom that is our basic wakefulness is made manifest.

At present the state of ordinary people is like pure gold covered with dirt. Our buddha nature is covered by temporary obscurations. One of the main obscurations that need to be purified is our fixation on duality, on solid reality. Once it is purified, then gold is just pure gold. As long as our mind is confused, bewildered, deluded, and mistaken, our buddha nature continues to be dragged through the realms of samsara. But when the mind is unconfused, unmistaken, and undeluded, it is the buddha nature itself. It is not that the buddha nature is one thing and our mind is another separate thing. They are not two different entities. The undeluded mind itself is the pure gold, the buddha nature. Sentient beings do not have two minds. When the mind is deluded, it is given the name *sentient being*. When the mind is undeluded, unmistaken, is called *buddha*.

It is said, "There is no buddha apart from your own mind." We do not have two minds. There is just one mind that is either deluded or undeluded. The buddha nature is exactly the originally unmistaken quality of our mind, also called the dharmakaya buddha Samantabhadra.

There is a difference between being deluded and undeluded, between recognizing and not recognizing our nature. The primordially unmistaken quality is called enlightenment, buddhahood, or the awakened state of dharmakaya. The primordially deluded aspect is called ignorance, or the deluded experience of sentient beings. Although we have the essence of buddhahood within us, it is temporarily obscured.

The essence of the Buddha's teachings is the method on how to let confusion dawn as wisdom. The most vital point here is the introduction to and recognition of the buddha nature, the innate wisdom of dharmakaya that is already present within oneself. This fourth Dharma is a teaching on how to recognize, train in, and stabilize this recognition of the buddha nature. Understanding it is called the view, practicing it is called samadhi, and stabilizing it is called buddhahood. Buddhahood is not outside. It is not something else that all of a sudden is absorbed into ourselves and magically transforms us into a buddha.

We have one mind, but we need to distinguish between its two aspects: essence and expression. Understand this analogy for the relationship between the two. The essence is like the sun shining in the sky. The expression is like its reflection upon the surface of water. The sun in the sky is the real sun. The reflection of the sun appearing on the surface of water looks like the sun but is not the real sun. Let's call the sun in the sky the buddha nature, the unmistaken, undeluded quality, the essence itself. The reflection of the sun upon the surface of water is an analogy for our normal deluded thinking, the expression. Without the sun in the sky, it is impossible for a reflection of the sun to appear. Although there is actually only one sun, it looks like there are two. That is what is called one identity with two aspects. The essence, the buddha nature, is like the sun shining in the sky. The expression is our thinking, compared to the sun's reflection.

The state of being a buddha is unconfused and undeluded, just like the sun shining in the sky. The state of mind of sentient beings is like the reflection of the sun on water. Just as the reflection is dependent upon water, our thoughts are dependent upon objects. The object is what is thought of, and the subject is the perceiving mind. Subject-object fixation is the cause for continuing in deluded samsaric existence, day and night, life after life. The fixation upon subject and object, the perceiving subject and the perceived object, is solidified again and again each moment and thus recreates samsaric existence. Right now we have the five sense objects of sights, sounds, smells, tastes, and textures. In between, as the gates, we have the five senses, and there are also the various consciousnesses that continuously apprehend these different sense objects.

Can the reflection of the sun on the water illuminate the whole world? Can it even shine over the whole lake? Can it make things grow? No, because it does not have the qualities of the real sun. In the same way, the aspect of mind known as expression, our thinking, lacks the qualities of the real state of buddhahood. But the sun in the sky by itself is able to shine and spread its warmth throughout the whole world, illuminating all darkness. To put it simply, the mind of the buddhas is unobscured, while the mind of sentient beings is obscured. What is the obscuration? It is our own reoccurring fixation on subject and object.

Buddha nature is continuously present in us as well as in everyone else, without any exception whatsoever. It is in essence forever unobscured. It doesn't increase or decrease. It is not sometimes covered or uncovered. It is totally beyond mental constructs. It does not change in size. It is not that someone has a big buddha nature and somebody else a small one. There is no difference in quality either. It is continuously present to the same extent in everyone.

To recognize the buddha nature present in oneself is called the view. To sustain the continuity of that correctly is called meditation or training. To mingle that with daily activities and act in accordance with the Dharma is called action or conduct. And to realize it as totally unobscured, like the sun shining with unchanging brilliance in the sky, is called fruition. We need to recognize the view; we need to recognize our buddha nature. Although it is something we already have, we need to acknowledge what we possess. The preliminary practices, the development stage, and so forth are all meant to enable us to recognize the buddha nature. They are like helpers, assistants.

To say "Recognize your own nature, the buddha nature!" does not mean that we have to produce something that does not exist, like trying to squeeze gold out of a piece of wood, which is impossible. We must simply recognize what we already possess. But humans, who are the most clever and capable of all the different types of sentient beings, seem to be bent on totally throwing away this most precious wish-fulfilling jewel. The normal state of a human being is like someone who has found a precious wish-fulfilling jewel but ignores it, thinking that a fake piece of jewelry is more valuable. There is nothing sadder or more wasteful than this.

Think very hard about this. Try to understand that the situation we are in now is like holding a wish-fulfilling jewel right in our hand. It is not easy to take rebirth as a human being, and it is definitely not easy to gain a precious human body with its opportunity to practice the Dharma. The precious human body is something extremely rare. If we do not use the opportunity we have right now, there is no guarantee whatsoever that we will be human in our next life. In fact, it is almost certain that we will not, because the habitual negative karmic patterns are so strong. This short opening right now will soon be covered up again for eons and eons before we have another chance to be a human. Please think sincerely about this. Is there any greater waste than throwing away a wish-fulfilling jewel when you finally find one?

If we didn't already have this wish-fulfilling jewel, it would be difficult to find. But, as a matter of fact, through all our beginningless lifetimes we have never been without it. If we were told, "You must possess a wish-fulfilling jewel!" then we would be in trouble because we would suddenly have to come up with something we don't possess. But the wish-fulfilling jewel of buddha nature is already present in us. It is because of our ignorance and delusion that we do not recognize it and continue life after life among the six classes of sentient beings. How sad that people throw away what is really valuable and instead chase after food, wealth, a good reputation, and praise. But if we do not take hold of what is truly valuable in this lifetime, we will just continue endlessly in samsaric existence. I'm not asking you to understand this, because of course you already do; I'm simply reminding you.

The buddha nature, the *sugata-garbha,* is already present as the nature of our own mind, just like the unchanging brilliance of the sun shining in the sky. But due to our ordinary dualistic thinking, this sun of the buddha nature is not evident; we don't see it. Not even a fraction of the innate qualities of buddhahood are manifest in the state of mind of a normal person. The conceptual thoughts we have day and night obscure our buddha nature, just like the sun in the sky is momentarily covered by clouds and seems to be obscured. Due to the passing clouds of ignorance, we do not recognize the buddha nature.

The ever-present buddha nature is like the unhindered sun shining in the sky, but sunshine never reaches inside a cave facing north. This cave is an analogy for misunderstanding, wrong view, or partial understanding.

From primordial time until this very moment, the main actions we have performed have been the activities of the three poisons—attachment, anger, and dullness. We have continuously engaged in liking, disliking, and remaining indifferent, not just in one or two lives but throughout countless lifetimes.

"Mind beyond concepts" refers to the situation of being free of the three poisons. A normal person is totally engrossed in the three poisons throughout his or her whole lifetime. To attain liberation from samsara, we need to leave behind the three poisons. How can we be free from them? We cannot bury them underground, flush them away, burn them, blow them up, or even throw a nuclear bomb at them and expect the three poisons to disappear. Our continuous involvement with them is like an evil machine. The perfect Buddha described samsaric existence as an ocean of endless suffering, or like the continuous revolving of an evil machine, like a vicious circle. We need to apply a method to liberate ourselves and all other sentient beings from the ocean of samsara. That method is recognition of buddha nature, which can clear away and eradicate the three poisons in our mind. Self-existing awareness is itself the path followed by all the buddhas of the three times. The buddhas of the past followed the path of self-existing wisdom, *rangjung yeshe*, and attained enlightenment. The buddhas of the present follow the path of self-existing wisdom, and in the future anyone who attains enlightenment will do so only by recognizing self-existing wisdom. There is not even an atom of any other path that leads to true enlightenment.

Let's take another example. Imagine a room that has been completely sealed off and has remained in total darkness for ten thousand years. The ignorant state of mind of a normal person who does not recognize the nature of mind, the buddha nature, is like the dense darkness inside that room. The moment of recognizing self-aware wisdom is like pressing the switch to turn on the light in the room that has been dark for ten thousand years. In that instant all the darkness is gone, right? Ten thousand years of darkness are dispelled in one moment. In the same way, the wisdom of recognizing one's nature dispels eons of ignorance and negative actions. When you press the switch to turn on the light in a room that has been dark for ten thousand years, the darkness disappears at once.

If all the windows and the doors in the room were closed, we would be unable to see anything, but when the light comes on we can see everything perfectly clearly. It is possible to purify countless eons of negative karma and attain the state of complete enlightenment in this very lifetime because self-existing wisdom is so potent, so effective.

Now I will give a name to our buddha nature. It is called *empty and cognizant self-existing wakefulness*. The empty aspect, the essence, is like space that pervades everywhere. But inseparable from this empty quality is a natural capacity to cognize and perceive, which is basic wakefulness. Buddha nature is called self-existing because it is not made out of anything or created by anyone. *Self-existing* means uncreated by causes in the beginning and undestroyed by circumstances in the end. This self-existing wakefulness is present in all beings without a single exception. Our thinking and self-existing wakefulness are never apart. The thinking mind is called expression, while the basic wakefulness is called essence. Thus there are actually two names for the mind. In the case of an ignorant sentient being, the mind is called empty cognizance with a core of ignorance (*marigpa*). The mind of all the buddhas is called empty cognizance with a core of awareness (*rigpa*).

In order to enable us to recognize or know our own essence, the teacher, the vajra master, gives what is called the pointing-out instruction. It is for that single purpose. And yet, what he points out is not something we don't already have. We already possess the buddha nature.

First, we must recognize our own nature, our essence. Next, we must endeavor with great diligence to continuously sustain that recognition, which is called training. Finally, reaching the state where not even an iota of conceptual thinking remains, when conceptual thinking is totally purified, is called the attainment of stability. This stability is also known as the complete enlightenment of buddhahood.

Another analogy is the seed of a flower. Knowing it's a seed corresponds to recognizing our buddha nature. After it has been planted and watered and starts to sprout leaves, a stamen, and petals, that is called training. When the flower is finally fully grown, with beautiful multicolored blossoms, that corresponds to the attainment of stability. The seed of a flower does not look like a flower in full bloom. But a seed that is the unmistaken seed of a beautiful flower can be planted and it will grow into one.

Although when we see a flower it is amazingly beautiful, we wouldn't find the seed of that flower spectacular at all. In the same way, do not expect the recognition of mind-essence to be something spectacular. But when the recognition has been stabilized, as in the case of a buddha, the state of complete enlightenment contains many great qualities like the fourfold fearlessnesses, the ten powers, the eighteen unique qualities, and so forth. The state of buddhahood also contains the capacity to transform an instant into an eon and an eon into an instant. The qualities of buddhahood are inconceivable, and all these qualities are inherently present in the buddha nature. They are not some new qualities that are achieved later on. There are not two different types of buddha nature—it is not that the buddhas have one type of buddha nature and we sentient beings have another type.

Humans are as numerous as stars at nighttime, but those with precious human bodies are like stars in the morning. Although I needn't ask you to treasure this teaching, to regard it as really important, still it is necessary to repeat that the practice of recognizing buddha nature should continue throughout our lives. We must equalize life and practice. In other words, we should not practice only for a short time and then abandon the Dharma. We should train for as long as we live.

PART THREE

THE PATH

13

POINTING THE STAFF
AT THE OLD MAN

Padmasambhava

While the great master Padmasambhava was staying in Great Rock Hermitage at Samye, Sherab Gyalpo of Ngok, an uneducated sixty-one-year-old man who had the highest faith and strong devotion to the master, served him for one year. All this while Ngok didn't ask for any teachings, nor did the master give him any. When after a year the master intended to leave, Ngok offered a mandala plate upon which he placed a flower of one ounce of gold. Then he said, "Great master, think of me with kindness. First of all, I am uneducated. Second, my intelligence is small. Third, I am old, so my elements are worn down. I beg you to give a teaching to an old man on the verge of death that is simple to understand, can thoroughly cut through doubt, is easy to realize and apply, has an effective view, and will help me in future lives."

The master pointed his walking staff at the old man's heart and gave this instruction:

Listen here, old man! Look into the awakened mind of your own awareness! It has neither form nor color, neither center nor edge. At first, it has no origin but is empty. Next, it has no dwelling place but is empty. At the end, it has no destination but is empty. This emptiness is not made of anything and is clear and cognizant. When you see this and recognize it, you know your natural face. You understand the nature of things. You have then seen the nature of mind, resolved the basic state of reality, and cut through doubts about topics of knowledge.

From Padmasambhava, *Advice from the Lotus-Born* (Boudhanath: Rangjung Yeshe Publications, 1994), "Pointing the Staff at the Old Man."

This awakened mind of awareness is not made out of any material substance; it is self-existing and inherent in yourself. This is the nature of things that is easy to realize because it is not to be sought for elsewhere. This is the nature of mind that does not consist of a concrete perceiver and something perceived to fixate on. It defies the limitations of permanence and annihilation. In it there is no thing to awaken; the awakened state of enlightenment is your own awareness that is naturally awake. In it there is no thing that goes to the hells; awareness is naturally pure. In it there is no practice to carry out; its nature is naturally cognizant. This great view of the natural state is present in yourself. Resolve that it is not to be sought for elsewhere.

When you understand the view in this way and want to apply it in your experience, wherever you stay is the mountain retreat of your body. Whatever external appearance you perceive is a naturally occurring appearance and a naturally empty emptiness; let it be, free from mental constructs. Naturally freed appearances become your helpers, and you can practice while taking appearances as the path.

Within, whatever moves in your mind, whatever you think, has no essence but is empty. Thought occurrences are naturally freed. When remembering your mind-essence, you can take thoughts as the path and the practice is easy.

As for the innermost advice: no matter what kind of disturbing emotion you feel, look into the emotion and it tracelessly subsides. The disturbing emotion is thus naturally freed. This is simple to practice.

When you can practice in this way, your meditation training is not confined to sessions. When you know that everything is a helper, your meditation experience is unchanging, the innate nature is unceasing, and your conduct is unshackled. Wherever you stay, you are never apart from the innate nature.

Once you realize this, your material body may be old, but awakened mind doesn't age. It knows no difference between young and old. The innate nature is beyond bias and partiality. When you recognize that awareness, innate wakefulness, is present in yourself, there is no difference between sharp and dull faculties. When you understand that the innate nature, free from bias and partiality, is present in yourself, there is no difference between great and small learning. Even though your body, the support for the mind, falls apart, the dharmakaya of awareness wisdom is unceasing.

When you gain stability in this unchanging state, there is no difference between a long and a short life span.

Old man, practice the true meaning! Take the practice to heart! Don't mistake words and meaning! Don't part from your friend, diligence! Embrace everything with mindfulness! Don't indulge in idle talk and pointless gossip! Don't become involved in common aims! Don't disturb yourself with the worry of offspring! Don't excessively crave food and drink! Intend to die an ordinary man![31] Your life is running out, so be diligent! Practice this instruction for an old man on the verge of death!

Because of his pointing the staff at Sherab Gyalpo's heart, this is entitled The Instruction of Pointing the Staff at the Old Man. Sherab Gyalpo of Ngok was liberated and attained accomplishment. This was written down by the Princess of Kharchen for the sake of future generations. It is also known under the name The Instruction of Pointing the Staff.

14

A Dear Treasure
for Destined Disciples

Dudjom Rinpoche

Homage to the Guru.

Padmakara, the Great Master of Uddiyana, said:

Do not resolve the Dharma,
Resolve your mind.
To resolve your mind is to know the one which frees all.
Not to resolve your mind is to know all but lack the one.

When engaging in the actual practice of the nature of mind, keep your body erect, let your breath flow naturally, and with your eyes half open gaze directly into the sky before you. Think, "For the sake of all sentient beings who have been my mothers, I will look into the natural face of self-awareness, Samantabhadra!" Wholeheartedly supplicate your root teacher, who is inseparable from Padmakara, the Lotus Master of Uddiyana. At the end, mingle your mind with his and rest in equanimity.

When resting in this way, your mind will not remain in the state of empty and cognizant awareness for long but will become restless, disturbed, or un-settled and will move about like a monkey. This is not the mind-essence. It is called *thinking*. If you indulge in it, this thinking will recall, make thoughts about, or plan to carry out anything! In the past, this is exactly what has thrown you into the ocean of samsara. For sure, it will throw you there again. Now, wouldn't it be better to stop this insidious, deluded thinking?

Adapted from Dudjom Rinpoche, "A Dear Treasure for Destined Disciples" in *Crystal Cave: A Compendium of Teachings by Masters of the Practice Lineage* (Boudhanath: Rangjung Yeshe Publications, 1990).

In the context of trying to stop this thinking, what is meant by awareness?[32] Awareness is utterly empty, totally open, spacious, and blissful. It is never made of something with substantial attributes, and it pervades all the phenomena of samsara and nirvana. From the beginning, it has been intrinsic to yourself, without any separation whatsoever, and lies beyond effort and the domain of concepts.

Well, if that is so, what happens when you recognize the natural face of self-awareness? When you recognize the natural face of self-awareness, it is just like the dream of a mute person. It is impossible to separate yourself, the sustainer, from the awareness to be sustained.

When you rest nakedly and naturally in the great openness of this awareness, do not be concerned with your old archenemy, the thinking that reflects, has myriad attributes, and has never given you a moment's rest in the past. Instead, in the space of awareness, which is like a cloudless sky, the movement of thoughts has vanished, disappeared, collapsed. All the power of thinking is lost to awareness. This awareness is your intrinsic dharmakaya wisdom, naked and fresh!

Well, then, who points out this awareness? What is decided upon? How does one gain confidence?

Awareness is first pointed out by your master. Thereby, you recognize your natural face, by yourself, and are introduced to your own nature. All the phenomena of samsara and nirvana, however they may appear, are none other than the expression of awareness itself. Thus, decide on one thing—*awareness!*

Just as waves on the ocean subside again into the ocean, gain confidence in the liberation of all thoughts, whatever may arise. Confidence is beyond the object of meditation and the act of meditating. It is free from the conceptual mind that fixates on meditation.

If that's the case, you may say, "It's sufficient to not meditate!" No, that's ridiculous! You haven't arrived at the state of liberation simply by recognizing awareness. For beginningless lifetimes, we have been enveloped within the cocoon of deluded tendencies. Up until now, we have been spending our lives deep under the shit of this conceptual thinking.

At the time of death, you aren't certain where you will go, but you must follow your karma and undergo more suffering. Therefore, you should now practice sustaining the continuity of the awareness that you have recognized, and nothing other than that.

The great omniscient master Longchenpa said:

> You may have recognized your nature,
> But unless you become familiar with it,
> The enemy, thinking, will carry you off
> Like an infant on a battlefield.

Generally speaking, the word *meditation* means to sustain the continuity of awareness with natural and innate mindfulness, resting in undistracted nonfixation and growing accustomed to the innate nature.

As for growing accustomed, when you are meditating and a thought arises, just let it arise—there is no need to regard it as your enemy. Relax in its arising. If no thought arises, don't try to make it do so—just rest in its nonarising.

When meditating, it is very easy to recognize a coarse thought as it suddenly arises, but after a few subtle thoughts have arisen you don't notice anything. This is called an undercurrent of thought. This undercurrent acts as a sneak thief during your meditation, so it is essential to place mindfulness on guard. If you can keep continuity through mindfulness in all situations—whether you are eating, sleeping, walking, or sitting, in meditation or in postmeditation—then that itself is sufficient.

The great master Padmakara said:

> Whether explained a hundred or a thousand times,
> There is only one thing to understand—
> Knowing the one that frees all,
> Sustain the natural face of self-awareness!

Once again, if you don't meditate, you won't gain certainty. If you do meditate, certainty will be attained.

What kind of certainty should be attained? If you meditate with strong diligence, the uptight fixation on solid duality will gradually grow more relaxed. Your constant ups and downs, hopes and fears, efforts and struggles will gradually diminish as a natural sign of having become fully acquainted. Devotion to your guru will grow stronger and you will feel confidence in his oral instruction from the very core of your heart.

At some point, the conceptual mind that solidly fixates on duality will naturally vanish. After that, gold and stone are equal, food and shit are equal, gods and demons are equal, good and evil are equal, buddha realms and hell realms are equal—you will find it impossible to choose. But until that happens, according to the perception that fixates on duality, there is virtue and evil, there are buddhafields and hells, and there are joys and sorrows—the effects of karma are all unfailing. This is why Padmakara, the great master, said:

> My view is higher than the sky,
> But the cause and effect of karma is finer than powder.

Therefore, it won't do just to proclaim, "I'm a Dzogchen practitioner. I'm a meditator!" while sleeping the time away, reeking from the mouth with the acrid smell of wine and from the crotch with the pungent stench of fornication.

Lay your foundation with pure faith, devotion, and samaya, and follow the main flow of practice with strong, unwavering diligence. If you are able to meditate after completely setting aside all the pointless activities of this life, it is certain that you will capture the primordial stronghold within this very lifetime without having to depend upon a result in a subsequent life. This is the special quality of the profound path of the Great Perfection.

This dear treasure for worthy disciples, the direct oral instructions placed in the palm of one's hand, was uttered by Jñana (Jigdral Yeshe Dorje).[33]

My own guru said to me:

I have no thought besides the guru.
I have nothing to chant besides supplication to him.
I have nothing to practice besides nonaction.
I simply rest in that way.
Now, I am in a happy state—open, spacious, and free from reference point.

For accomplishing the permanent goal of one's wishes,[34]
The profound instruction of Dzogchen is enough in itself.
This oral instruction that is easy to understand
Was composed by the crazy Dudjom and given to you.

May it be virtuous.

15

TEN PROFOUND POINTS
OF ESSENTIAL ADVICE

Shri Singha

Self-existing, self-occurring, natural state of freedom—
Homage to Samantabhadra's vast expanse.

Abiding in the state of indivisible luminosity,
The nature of all buddhas,
In identity undivided from Samantabhadra,
This Lotus-Born master of Uddiyana
Paid respectful homage to Guru Shri Singha
And made this request.

Emaho,
Precious guru, what is the meaning of buddha?
What is the dividing line between samsara and nirvana?
What is the dividing line between unknowing and knowing?
What is the dividing line between mind and mind-essence?
How does a person apply this meaning to his stream-of-being?

So he asked. Samaya. Seal, seal, seal.

Guru Shri Singha replied in these words:
Emaho, *buddha* (*sang-gye*) is used when unknowing is purified (*sang*) and
wisdom is perfected (*gye*). When applying this to your own stream-of-being,
look into your mind-essence, and when you see and realize that mind does not
consist of any identity, that it is empty and cognizant, and that any occurring
thought is personal experience, you have recognized mind to be buddha.

From *Gongpa Zangtal*, the cycle of teachings on *Directly Revealing Samantabhadra's Mind*
(Boudhanath: Rangjung Yeshe Publications, 2005).

Samsara is being caught up in unwholesome action and circling among the six classes of beings from one state to another. *Nirvana* is having recognized the nature of mind and thereby having totally cut through samsaric attachment. When applying this to your own stream-of-being, see that the basic state of your mind-essence is a nonarising self-existence, untainted by flaws of materiality.[35] This, the primordial purity within samsaric states, is called nirvana.

Unknowing (*marigpa*) is not knowing the nature of mind. *Knowing* (*rigpa*) is the knowing of the original wakefulness that is personal experience. When applying this to your stream-of-being, look into and seek the mind. Through this, you fail to find an observer and something observed. Let be—clearly, vividly, and awake—in simply that state of not finding. Then look, and you will see that it is simply so. That is known as the key point of unknowing dissolving into itself.

Mind (*sem*) is formative thinking. *Mind-essence* (*semnyi*) is free of thinking and mental doing. When applying this to your stream-of-being, mind-essence is not changed by thinking, so let it be, uncontrived and as it naturally is. This vividly awake state, free of any mental doing whatsoever, is known as the key point of mind dissolving into itself.

Again, he asked:

Great master, what is the dividing line between the dharmakaya and the all-ground?

What is the dividing line between the other shore and this shore?

What is the dividing line between dullness and wakefulness?

What is the dividing line between pain and pleasure?

How does a person apply the meaning of this to his stream-of-being?

So he asked. The master replied:

All refers to a repose within not conceptualizing form.[36] Ground is mingled with dharmakaya and therefore is the vessel for good and evil habitual tendencies. The mind of the all-ground stirs toward *all* and gives rise to thinking.[37] When applying this to your own stream-of-being, your ground—the uncontrived and true nature of things, which remains awake, relaxed, and nonconceptual without producing thoughts—is present while being totally unhindered by any delusion. Look into the *all* and this ultimate nature, which is not composed of relative mental objects, is an emptiness that is not composed of anything whatsoever. That is known as the key point of the relative naturally dissolving into the ultimate.

This shore is samsaric phenomena. *The other shore* is beyond samsara. If you want to apply this to your own stream-of-being, look into the normal thinking mind belonging to this shore and thereby see that it is utterly insubstantial, a cognizance that cannot be apprehended. That is known as reaching the other shore.

Dullness (*timug*) is failing to comprehend anything because of a dense mental habit. *Wakefulness* (*yeshe*) clears the obstruction for seeing it as it is. If you want to apply this to your own stream-of-being, look into this unknowing, uncomprehending mind itself and hereby the very absence of questioning whether mind understands or doesn't is known as the key point of dullness dissolving into wakefulness.

Pain is the mind bound by dualistic concepts. *Pleasure* is the ease of having realized nonduality. If you want to apply this to your own stream-of-being, look into the very identity of the pain or the pleasure, and it is seen to be an emptiness that is not composed of anything whatsoever. That is known as the natural dissolving of pain.

Again, he asked:

What is the dividing line between hate and love?

What is the dividing line between desire and joy?

What is the dividing line between self and other?

What is the dividing line between good and evil actions?

How does a person apply the meaning of this to his stream-of-being?

So he asked. The master replied:

Hate is loathing another object. *Love* is adoring another object. When applying this to your own stream-of-being, look into the object of hate as well as your own mind that feels it and see that they have no identity but are empty. The hated enemy is therefore your mind. When you look into the object of love, it is also seen to be mind. Since this empty mind is not composed of either enemy or friend, that is the key point of hate and love naturally dissolving.

Desire is when a thought moves toward an object and the mind is attached to and yearns for a certain thing. *Joy* is a delighted frame of mind. When applying this to your own stream-of-being, look into the mind that feels desire and see that it is mind that perceives the attractive object, person, or property. It is also the mind that feels joy and delight. Since both instances are one in being mind, and since this mind is not made out of any identity whatsoever, desire and delight naturally dissolve.

Self is a perception that unequivocally clings. *Other* is a one-sided discrimination. When applying this to your own stream-of-being, look into self and see that it does not consist of a self to which you can cling. Look into other and see that it does not consist of a one-sided category or type to which you can cling. That which clings to self and other is itself the empty mind-essence. Look into this very mind and see that this empty mind-essence that is not composed of any identity whatsoever is the key point of self and other naturally dissolving, free from duality.

A *good action* is what is wholesome and the well-being of both self and others. An *evil action* is what is unwholesome and harms both self and others. When applying this to your own stream-of-being, look directly into the mind that clings to an action as being either good or evil, and [see that the mental states essentially] are one in being awakened mind. Since the awakened mind is utterly pure from the beginning, untainted by the flaws of wholesome or unwholesome actions, and since empty mind-essence does not accumulate karmic ripening, this is the key point of naturally dissolving the clinging to good and evil actions.

Samaya.

Again, he asked:

What is the dividing line between the mind of buddhas and that of sentient beings?

What is the dividing line between the perception of gods and demons?

What is the dividing line between valuable and worthless?

What is the dividing line between the perceiver and the perceived?

How are they applied to one's stream-of-being?

So he asked. The master replied:

The *buddha-mind* is the ground that is not composed of any identity whatsoever and yet is totally unhindered in its radiance. The *mind of a sentient being* is manifold thought occurrences involved in clinging. When applying this to your own stream-of-being, look directly into this very mind of a sentient being with its manifold thought occurrences involved in clinging, and see that it is an evanescent wakefulness produced by neither causes nor conditions. This itself is the uncontrived natural mind-essence that is not composed of any identity whatsoever. To let it be in the state of great self-existence itself is the utterly pure buddha-mind. This is also the single key point that embodies the mind of buddhas and sentient beings.

A *god* is one who has abandoned ill will. A *demon* is one who retains ill will. When applying this to your own stream-of-being, the dualistic perception of gods and demons is itself your thinking mind. Look directly into this very thinking and see that it does not have any identity whatsoever but has an empty nature. In fact, benefit and harm, pleasure and pain, being empty, are also of the same taste. Thus, to cut through the thought's clinging is known as the natural dissolving of gods and demons.

Valuable means to be bound by miserliness while clinging. *Worthless* means to be uninvolved in attachment and clinging. When applying this to your own stream-of-being, look directly into your miserly clinging and understand that the perception of an object of greed as being pleasant and agreeable is also your mind's thinking. When you understand that the perception of something being filthy muck is also your mind, you can resolve that the perceiver and the perceived are both your mind. This fact that gold and dirt are equal is the key point of realizing the valuable and the worthless as being indivisible.

The *perceived* means to regard external material objects to be permanent. The *perceiver* means to regard the inner mind as existent. In applying this to your own stream-of-being, by looking into the external perceived objects you realize that appearances are empty in themselves. By looking into the inner perceiving mind, you see that mind is intangible. To realize this is the key point of establishing that perceiver and perceived, appearance and emptiness, are indivisible.

Again, he asked:

What is the dividing line between accepting and rejecting?

What is the dividing line between cause and effect?

What is the dividing line between shamatha and vipashyana?

What is the dividing line between means and knowledge?

How are they applied to one's stream-of-being?

So he asked. The master replied:

Accepting is to mentally embrace and not reject. *Rejecting* is to mentally discard and not utilize. When applying this to your own stream-of-being, acknowledge that samsara's suffering is dualistic mind, and by that understand its futility and be free from the impulse to cling. By turning your mind away from samsara, you are freed into not needing anything whatsoever. Thus, to realize this complete nonduality is the key point of naturally dissolving accepting and rejecting.

The *cause*—the accumulation of merit—refers to the actions of the six paramitas, including development stage, recitation and chanting, offerings, torma, giving alms, and so forth. The *effect*—the accumulation of wisdom—refers to the training in concentration and insight, and in the nature of dharmadhatu as being indivisible appearance and emptiness. This training is the resultant accumulation of wisdom when you give it the seal of not conceptualizing. No matter what you train in, to seal it with the absence of conceptualizing the doer and the deed is the key point of perfecting cause and effect into wisdom.

Shamatha is when thought activity totally subsides and your attention remains unmoving. *Vipashyana* is when you let be in the nature of dharmata.[38] To vividly experience the basic nature, in whatever you see and whatever you think, is to realize the nonduality of shamatha and vipashyana.

Skillful *means* is to be ingenious and discerning. *Knowledge* is to know and perceive reality. When applying this to your own stream-of-being, since mind is nonarising, its emptiness—not being composed of any identity whatsoever—is realized through skillful means. Through knowledge you realize that this very knowing is empty and without cause. Thus, this indivisibility of nature and knowledge is known as the key point of realizing the nonduality of means and knowledge.

Again, he asked:

What is the dividing line between meditation and postmeditation?

What is the dividing line between space and wakefulness?

What is the dividing line between dharmata and dharmas?

What is the dividing line between the view and the viewer?

How are they applied to one's stream-of-being?

So he asked. The master replied:

Meditation is leaving your body, speech, and mind in composure, to calm your restless attention, and to stabilize this calm. *Postmeditation* is putting this meaning to use and further enhancing it. When applying this to your own stream-of-being, during the meditation state you train in being free from conceptualizing all phenomena. During the postmeditation you attain stability and gain mastery in it. That is the key point of the nonduality of meditation and postmeditation.

Space (ying) is the nature of mind, the pure essence of dharmata revealed to its depth. *Wakefulness (yeshe)* is knowing that this space is in yourself. When applying this to your own stream-of-being, the nature of mind-essence is a pure wakefulness that does not consist of any materiality and is hard to fathom. To see this nature of things by means of self-knowing wakefulness is dharmata revealed to its depths.

Dharmas (*chö*) are wholesome phenomena, unwholesome phenomena, and neutral phenomena—everything that can be described and indicated in this way. *Dharmata* (*chönyi*) means that they are all empty in essence, empty by nature, and empty of characteristics. When applying this to your own stream-of-being, dharmata is that all phenomena (*chö*) arise from this mind that is emptiness. That is the key point of the nonduality of dharmas and dharmata.

The *view* is the undistorted buddha-mind. The *viewer* is a sentient being's mind. When you apply this experientially to your stream-of-being, it is not the case that the view is elsewhere, so let your mind-essence be uncontrived—an unbiased and vast pervasiveness, free from center and edge; that is the view. While your mind looks into that, do not see it as "other" but instead that it is primordially present in yourself; that is realizing the nonduality of viewed and viewer.

Again, he asked:

What is the dividing line between training and trainer?

What is the dividing line between conduct and application?

What is the dividing line between the fruition to be attained and the attainer?

What is the dividing line between the samayas to be observed and the observing?

How are they applied to one's stream-of-being?

So he asked. The master replied:

Training is placing yourself in the uncontrived natural state of thought-free dharmata. The *trainer* is, when you, the yogi, apply this to your stream-of-being, relaxing body and mind into the unfabricated state of your ordinary mind-essence and let be in the self-existing, self-cognizant state that is unspoiled by thoughts. Since, in this, there is no other object of training to be gained, it includes the key point of the nonduality of object, training, and the act of training.

The *conduct* is doing whatever you do. The *application* is to make use of whatever you do for practice. When applying this to your own stream-of-being, embrace whatever you do—such as walking, lying down, sitting, and so forth—with the guard of watchfulness. Do not get caught up in [mindless] normality. Embrace your conduct and the application of it with dharmata. In this way, your conduct and application are not separate.

The *fruition to be attained* is the three kayas. The *attainer* is the mind that intends to realize them. When you apply this to your own stream-of-being, the three kayas are not elsewhere. The nature of mind and the nature of things, being empty and indivisible, is dharmakaya. Experiencing this as unconfined cognizance is sambhogakaya. Manifesting in manifold ways beyond categories is nirmanakaya. To recognize that the fruition to be attained is present in yourself without being something to be accomplished elsewhere is known as perfecting the fruition within yourself.

The *samayas to be observed* are all included within the root and branches. The *observing* of them is nothing other than guarding your body, speech, and mind against violations. When you apply this to your own stream-of-being, all the root and branch samayas to be observed and their observance are nothing other than the continuity of your mind that is in no way something to be accomplished. To recognize that your mind is immaculate is known as the nonduality of samayas and their observance.

> Emaho!
> How wonderful that someone like myself, Padmasambhava,
> Lived in the presence of Shri Singha,
> A nirmanakaya emanated from the heart of Samantabhadra,
> And that I respectfully supplicated and made aspirations.
>
> I requested this pointing-out instruction of Essential Advice,
> Wrote it down for the benefit of future generations,
> And concealed it within a brown rhino casket.
> In the future, there will be a destined son of Padma,
> Wrathful, with a three-pointed mole,
> Maintaining an uninhibited conduct.
> May it meet with this destined son!
> Samaya
>
> SARVA MANGALAM.

16

THE INHERITANCE

Tulku Urgyen Rinpoche

We think, we remember, we plan—and the attention thus exerted moves toward an object and sticks to it. This mental movement is called thinking, or conceptual mind. We have many different expressions in Tibetan to describe the functioning of this basic attitude of mind, this extroverted consciousness unaware of its own nature. This ignorant mind grabs hold of objects, forms concepts about them, and gets involved and caught up in the concepts it has created. This is the nature of samsara, and it has been continuing through beginningless lifetimes up to the present moment.

All these involvements are merely fabricated creations; they are not the natural state. They are based on the concepts of subject and object, perceiver and perceived. This dualistic structure, together with the disturbing emotions and the karma that is produced through them, are the forces that drive us from one samsaric experience to another. Yet all the while, there is still the basic nature, which is not made out of anything whatsoever. It is totally unconstructed and empty, and at the same time it is aware: it has the quality of being able to cognize. This indivisible unity of being empty and cognizant is our original ground that is never lost.

What we are missing is the recognition that our natural state is the indivisible unity of emptiness and cognizance. We miss that recognition because our mind is always searching somewhere else. We do not acknowledge our actual cognizant presence, and instead we are always preoccupied by looking elsewhere, outside of ourselves. And we perpetuate this process continuously. Shantideva said, "Unless you know the secret key point, whatever

From Tulku Urgyen Rinpoche, *As It Is*, *Vol. 2* (Boudhanath: Rangjung Yeshe Publications, 2000), "The Inheritance."

you do will miss the mark." The secret key point of mind is that its nature is a self-existing, original wakefulness. To identify the key point we need to receive the pointing-out instruction, which tells and shows us: "The nature of your mind is the buddha-mind itself." Right now we are like the dim-witted person who lost himself in Asan Tol (in downtown Kathmandu), who runs around wailing, "I've lost myself! Where am I?" The pointing-out instruction is just like telling him, "You are *you!*" Throughout beginningless samsara, sentient beings have never found themselves until somebody says, "You are right here." This is a metaphor for introducing the secret key point of mind.

If it weren't for the buddhas' teachings, all sentient beings would be totally lost, because they need to be pointed toward that basic ground that is always present but never acknowledged. That is the purpose of the pointing-out instruction, literally, the "instruction bringing you face-to-face with your own essence." This instruction is given great, impressive names like Mahamudra, the Great Middle Way, or the Great Perfection. All of these teachings point toward the same basic nature. They are the exact opposite of the conceptual thinking that holds a subject and object—the dualistic frame of mind that is unaware of its own nature.

It doesn't have to be this way. We *can* know our own nature. We can realize it by applying the pith instructions of Mahamudra, the Great Middle Way, and the Great Perfection. Even though our nature is primordially enlightened, we are oblivious to that fact. Therefore we need to become re-enlightened. First we need to recognize; next, train in that recognition; and finally, attain stability. Once we are re-enlightened, we no longer need to wander in samsara.

The buddha nature is the very identity within which the body, speech, mind, qualities, and activities of all buddhas are complete. It is out of the expression of these that the body, speech, and mind of all beings appear. In fact, the body, speech, and mind of any sentient being have the same origin as the body, speech, and mind of the awakened ones. Body, speech, and mind cannot come from earth or stone or matter. The unchanging quality is called the vajra body, the unceasing quality is called the vajra speech, and the undeluded quality is called the vajra mind. The indivisible unity of the three is exactly what is meant by buddha nature.

Not recognizing in our own experience the unchanging quality of this buddha nature, we entered into the encasement of a physical body of flesh and blood. Our speech became wrapped within the movement of breath to become voice and words. It appears and disappears. Consciousness began to hold a perceiver as separate from the perceived. In other words, it became a fixation on duality, a stop-and-start process that arises and ceases each moment. Thoughts come continuously, one after the other, like an endless string. This endless string of thought has continued from beginningless time and just goes on and on. That is how the normal state of mind is. If we don't now recognize our own nature in this lifetime, we fail to capture our natural seat of unchanging, self-existing wakefulness. Instead, we chase after one perishing thought after the other, like chasing after each new bead on the string. This is how samsara becomes endless. While we are governed by this involvement in thought, we are truly helpless.

Who can stop samsara for us? There is nobody but ourselves. Even if all the sentient beings of the six realms were lined up and you cried, "Please, help me, so I can stop being overpowered by my own thinking!"—even then, not a single one of them could help. How sad that we are controlled by this involvement in thought, day and night, life after life! We could try to blow up a nuclear bomb to stop samsara, but it still wouldn't help. Nuclear bombs can destroy cities, even countries, but they cannot stop the mind from thinking. Unless we become free of conceptual thinking, there is absolutely no way to end samsara and truly awaken to enlightenment.

Great peace comes when conceptual thinking subsides, calms down. There is a way for that to happen. Thoughts are actually an expression of the buddha nature. They are expressions of our natural face. If we truly recognize buddha nature, in that very same moment, any thought will vanish by itself, leaving no trace. This is what brings an end to samsara. There is a supreme method to do this. Once we know that method, there is nothing superior we need to know. This way is already at hand in ourselves. It is not something that we need to get from someone else—it is not something we need to buy, bribe, or search for and finally achieve. Such effort is not necessary at all. Once you recognize your own natural face, you have already transcended the six realms of samsara.

What is the method? It is what one asks for when requesting a master to give instructions on how to recognize mind-essence and train in it. Our mind-essence is incredibly precious. It is the natural inheritance we possess right now. Receiving teachings on how to recognize the essence of mind and correctly applying those teachings is like the Buddha being placed in the palm of your own hand. That analogy means that at the moment of being introduced and recognizing, you don't have to seek for the awakened state somewhere else. Line up all the money, all the wealth in the whole world in one big heap and put it on one side. On the other side put the recognition of buddha nature, the nature of your own mind. What is most valuable? If you are going to somehow compare the two, I can promise you that recognizing mind-essence, the "amazing buddha within," is a billion times more valuable.

If instead we continue to fool ourselves, we're simply doing what we have been doing for so long. How much trouble and misery have we gone through in samsara, among the six realms? Do we want to continue like that? How much more misery won't we go through again while traveling through the eighteen hells and the neighboring hells? Buddha taught that any sentient being has drunk more red-hot liquid metal in the hells than could fill an entire ocean. That is an example of the suffering we have endured. It's only because we are dull, ordinary beings that we have forgotten all about it. If we don't realize this natural state, there is no way to stop wandering about in the six realms of samsara. No one else is going to prevent you from rambling on, and it certainly won't stop by itself.

What is of true value? We need to think about this for ourselves. When we do business and make a profit, we rejoice. If we have a loss, we fall into despair. Let's compare our business capital to our buddha nature, which is like a wish-fulfilling jewel. If we don't use this wish-fulfilling jewel, endless samsara lies ahead of us. Isn't it just incredibly stupid to throw away our fortune—and troublesome as well? We need to think about this. I am not reciting this from memory. It is not a lie either. This is the real, crucial point. If we didn't have a buddha nature, nobody could blame us. But we do have buddha nature, a buddha nature that is the identity of the three kayas of all buddhas. However, as Jamgön Kongtrül said:[39]

> Although my mind is the Buddha, I don't recognize it.
> Although my thinking is dharmakaya, I don't realize it.
> Although nonfabrication is the innate, I fail to sustain it.
> Although naturalness is the basic state, I am not convinced.
> Guru, think of me. Quickly, look upon me with compassion!
> Bless me so that natural awareness is liberated into itself.

We need to understand what mind essentially is. As I have often said, in this world, mind is the most important, for the simple reason that it is mind that understands and experiences. Besides mind, nothing else perceives anything. The five outer elements of earth, water, fire, wind, and space—do they feel anything? In truth, there is nothing other than mind that experiences.

The whole universe is made out of the five major elements, which in themselves are insensate; they don't know anything. Likewise, the physical bodies of sentient beings are made out of the five minor elements. In their properties, the bones and flesh are the same as the element of earth. Blood and the other liquids resemble the element of water. The heat of our body is essentially the same as fire. Our breath is wind, while the vacuities in the body, the different openings and hollow places and so on, are in essence the same as space. These five elements don't experience, they don't perceive anything whatsoever. Unless there is a mind in that body, the body itself doesn't feel anything.

The outer major elements and the inner minor elements are also similar in structure. Our body with its flesh and bones can be compared to the surface of this earth, with its soil and rocks. The greenery and shrubs growing on the hillside can be likened to our pores and small hairs. There are forests outside, and we have hair growing on our heads. Whenever you dig into the ground, you usually find water at some point. Similarly, if we ever make a hole in our body, some liquid will start pouring out. The heat of our body has the same property as heat found anywhere else outside. The wind that moves through our lungs is the same as the wind or air outside. The vacuities are the same as empty space. There is a very strong resemblance between inner and outer elements. In a sense, they are identical, in that the elements by themselves do not perceive.

We also have five senses, five sense doors—eyes, ears, nose, tongue, and skin, with its ability to perceive texture through touch. However, these five senses really don't experience anything in themselves. If there is not a mind or consciousness connected with the five senses, the sense organs by themselves do not experience. A corpse has eyes, ears, nose, tongue, and skin, but if you show something to a corpse, even if the eyes are open, it doesn't see anything, nor does it perceive sound. A corpse has no ability to smell or taste, and if you press the body it doesn't feel the touch either.

Then there are the five sense objects, the impressions we get of physical forms seen through the eyes, sounds heard through the ears, the different flavors we can taste by means of the tongue, the fragrances sensed through the nose, and the textures we can feel through the body. These objects of the five senses are also not cognizant. They don't experience anything at all. Unless there is a mind to perceive them, the objects by themselves don't perceive. A sentient being is basically made out of nothing other than mind. Apart from this mind, no thing in this world experiences anything at all. Without mind, this world would be utterly empty: there would be nothing known, nothing experienced. Matter would exist, of course, but matter doesn't know anything; it is totally empty of consciousness.

In this world, nothing is more essential than mind, except for one thing: the nature of this mind, buddha nature, sugata-garbha. All sentient beings, without a single exception, have this nature. This buddha nature is present in everyone, from the dharmakaya buddha Samantabhadra down to the tiniest insect, even the smallest entities you can only see through a microscope. In all of these beings, the buddha nature is identical. There is no difference in size or quality—not at all. Buddha nature never differs in terms of quality or quantity. It is not like Samantabhadra has a large buddha nature and a small insect has a small one, or that the Buddha has a superior buddha nature and a fly an inferior one; there is no difference at all.

So we need to distinguish between mind and mind-essence. The mind-essence of sentient beings and the awakened mind of the buddhas is the same. Buddhahood means being totally stable in the state before dualistic thought occurs. A sentient being like ourselves, not realizing our essence, gets caught up in our own thinking and becomes bewildered. Still, the essence of our mind and the very essence of all awakened buddhas is primordially the same. Sentient beings and buddhas have an identical source, the buddha nature. Buddhas became awakened because of realizing their essence. Sentient beings became confused because of not realizing their essence. Thus there is one basis or ground and two different paths.

Mind is that which thinks and remembers and plans all these different thoughts that we have. *Thought* in Tibetan is called *namtok*. *Nam* means the object, what is thought of. *Tok* means to make ideas and concepts about those objects. Namtok is something that mind churns out incessantly, day and night. A buddha is someone who has recognized the essence itself and is awakened through that. A sentient being is someone who hasn't and who is confused by his or her own thinking. Someone who has failed to recognize the essence of mind is called a sentient being. Someone who has realized the nature itself and becoming stable in that realization is called a buddha.

Isn't it true that this mind here thinks a lot? It remembers, it plans, it thinks, it worries. It has been doing so for countless lifetimes, day and night, without stop. Moment by moment, this mind is creating thoughts of one thing after another, and not just during this lifetime. Thinking takes place because of not seeing the essence of this mind itself. It thinks of something, makes thoughts and emotions about it—the process goes on and on. It is like beads on an endless string, life after life in endless succession. This is called samsara.

It is the thinking that perpetuates samsara. Samsara will go on endlessly unless the thinking stops. As I mentioned many times before, mind is not a thing that has physical form, sound, smell, taste, or texture. Mind is empty. Space is also empty. No matter where you go in space, there is no limit, no boundary, no edge. If you were to travel in a spaceship in a single direction for a hundred billion years, you would not reach the end of space. Even if you could go all the way through the earth and come out the other side, you would not find the bottom of space. And were you to travel another hundred billion years, you still wouldn't find the bottom anywhere. It's the same with the other directions—you can travel forever and you'll still never reach a place where space ends.

Now, how can something without limits have a center? It can't, can it? That is why it is taught that space has no center and no edge. The Buddha used space to point at how mind is. He said that mind is empty like space: that just as space has no limits in any direction, mind has no center or edge. As a matter of fact, wherever there is space, mind is present. And Buddha taught that throughout space, wherever space reaches, there are sentient beings. And wherever there are sentient beings, there are disturbing emotions and the creation of karma. And wherever there is the creation of disturbing emotion and karma, there is also buddha nature. The awakened mind of the buddhas is all-pervasive. In short, the nature of this mind is empty in essence; it is like space. Because it has no form, no smell, no taste, sound, or texture, it is completely empty. It always was, primordially. In being empty, mind seems like space. But there is a difference: space is not conscious; it doesn't feel pleasure or pain. Our mind is spacious, wide open and empty, yet it still feels pleasure and pain. It is sometimes called the "ever-knowing, ever-conscious mind." Whatever is present is known by mind.

When this mind is put to work, it can invent any possible thing, even nuclear bombs. Mind creates all these amazing gadgets—voice recorders, airplanes that can fly through the sky. These inventions don't think, but they were created by the thinking mind. Sentient beings create the samsara that we have right now. The creation of samsara will not ultimately help us in any way.

Mind is invisible and intangible. That is why people don't know it. That is why they wonder, "Have I really recognized this nature of mind?" If it were a concrete thing, scientists would have figured it out a long time ago. But it isn't, so scientists don't necessarily know what mind is. If they did, all scientists would be enlightened! But have you ever heard of scientists becoming enlightened through science? Sure, they know a lot of other things. They can make telephones that let you instantly talk to anybody anywhere in the world. And they can make machinery that flies hundreds of people together through the sky. They can drive trains directly through mountains. All this is possible. If mind is put to work, it is an inexhaustible treasure, but that still doesn't mean enlightenment. When the mind is put to use for something and gets caught up in it, this does not lead to enlightenment. We need to know the essential nature of mind.

It is mind that right now thinks of all these different things. As long as thinking does not dissolve, we do not attain enlightenment. Being caught up in thoughts is exactly what is meant by spinning in samsara, just like a wheel in machinery. With wheels on a car, you can drive all over the world, right?

What is the way to dissolve thoughts, to totally clear them up and let them vanish? The Buddha had the technique for clearing up thinking. That's what the pointing-out instruction from a qualified master is for. When you go to school, you have to recite the ABC's so that the teacher can tell whether you know the alphabet or not. Until one knows, one needs to be taught, to be shown. Until one fully knows mind-essence, one needs a teacher. It's as simple as that.

Otherwise, our thinking spins like the wheels on a car. When the wheels on a car move, they drag the car around. Like the spinning wheels of a car, our thinking has never stopped, through so many lifetimes. Even when we try to stop it, it gets worse. Thinking is like the shadow of our own hand—just try to shake it off! You can order the thoughts to stop, but they won't listen. Wherever mind goes, thoughts follow, like the shadow of our body. But as long as this thinking is not exhausted, samsara does not stop. Samsara means spinning, circling, continuing to circle around. Apart from recognizing mind-essence, there is no other way to stop the mind from thinking.

The operating system of this spinning around is called the twelve links of dependent origination, the head of which is ignorance, the lack of knowing. This ignorance of unknowing means not recognizing what our nature really is. Ignorance forces the five *skandhas* to be perpetuated—the physical forms, sensations, conceptions, formations, and cognitions that make birth follow death, again and again. Mind doesn't die. When it remains ignorant of its own nature, again it perpetuates the arrangement of the five skandhas to create a new body in one of four ways—through a womb, as in the case of a human being; through instantaneous birth; through heat and moisture; or through an egg. These are the four different ways of taking rebirth in the three realms and among the six classes of beings.

Try to check how many sentient beings there are living on just one mountainside. See how many insects live in just one lake. They are all sentient beings. If you were to count the insects here on the slopes of the Shivapuri Mountain behind my hermitage, you would probably find that they outnumber the human beings in the whole world. Human bodies are very few compared to the number of other sentient beings. Even though we happen to be human, if in this life we don't attain realization by recognizing our own nature, we will continue again in some other state within samsara. The Buddha taught that if we were to collect the blood that has spilled from each death we have experienced, there would be more blood than the ocean could hold; not from the deaths of all sentient beings, but merely from one sentient being. That is how many lives we have had before.

If we continue to spin around in the realms of samsara, will this process somehow stop by itself? Not at all! Right now we have attained what is described as a precious human body. We're at a point that is like a fork in the road: one road leads higher, the other one lower. We are right at that point now. If we recognize and realize our buddha nature, we can go upward to enlightenment. If we are careless and ignore it, we don't have to try to go deeper in samsara—it happens automatically. Negative karma doesn't require much effort. The normal mind thinks mainly in terms of being against something, being attached to something, or being simply dull and not caring about anything. This automatically creates negative karma, further perpetuating samsara.

True virtue, real goodness, is created through recognizing our buddha nature, our natural state. Recognizing our own nature is itself the path of enlightenment. Not recognizing buddha nature is itself the path of samsara. There are these two roads. The basis for these two is the same: it is buddha nature. There are two choices, two paths. One is the path of knowing, the wakefulness that knows its own nature. One is the path of unknowing, of not recognizing our own nature, and being caught up in what is being thought of, through the consciousness connecting with sense objects via the senses. This process continuously puts the wheel of samsara in motion. That is why a famous statement goes:

> To recognize is the path of nirvana;
> Not to recognize is the path of samsara.

When ordinary people see an object, for instance, a rosary, they think, "This is a rosary." Next they wonder, "Are there a hundred beads? Where is it made? Maybe in China, or maybe India, I don't know." It will be one thought after the other. This conceptualizing an object is namtok. The object is the rosary, and all the ideas we have about it are the concepts. "It is yellow, it is Indian, maybe it is Chinese, I like it, it is quite neat." One thought continues after another. For the ordinary person there is the object observed, the rosary. The subject is the mind, that which knows. A yogi practitioner, on the other hand, does not dwell on the object but recognizes the nature of the subject.

There is knowing. The mind of any sentient being is both empty and cognizant, and it is the cognizance that can recognize its own nature. In the very moment of recognizing, you see the empty essence. This empty essence is called the dharmakaya of the buddhas. The cognizance is called the sambhogakaya of the buddhas. These two are actually indivisible, and this indivisibility is nirmanakaya. This indivisibility of emptiness and cognizance is a natural quality, just like water's liquidity or the heat of a flame. They are a union. You cannot take the heat away from a flame. Moreover, the recognizing of one's natural face is called *svabhavikakaya*. This is to be face-to-face with the three kayas of the buddhas, and we cannot find anything superior to that in the entire world.

Recognize your mind, and in the absence of any concrete thing, rest loosely. After a while we again get caught up in thoughts. But, by recognizing again and again, we grow more and more used to the natural state. It's like learning something by heart—after a while, you don't need to think about it. Through this process, our thought involvement grows weaker and weaker. The gap between thoughts begins to last longer and longer. At a certain point, for half an hour there will be a stretch of no conceptual thought whatsoever, without having to suppress the thinking.

The essence of mind that is primordially empty and rootless is unlike holding the *idea* of emptiness in mind, and it is not the same as the sustained attempt to feel empty. Neither of these helps much. By growing used to this natural, original emptiness again and again, we become accustomed to it. Then there will be a stretch throughout the whole day from morning to evening, which is only empty awareness untainted by notions of perceived objects or the perceiving mind. This corresponds to having attained the bodhisattva levels, the bhumis. When there is never a break throughout day and night, that is called buddhahood, true and complete enlightenment.

From the perspective of mind-essence, the interruptions of thoughts are like clouds in the sky. The empty essence itself is like the space of the sky. Our cognizance is like sunshine. The sky itself never changes whether it's sunny or cloudy. Similarly, when you realize the awakened state of the buddhas, all cloudlike thoughts have vanished. But the qualities of wisdom, meaning original wakefulness, are fully developed, fully present, even now, when thoughts are present. We need to train in slowly growing more and more used to the recognition of mind-essence. This will dissolve our negative karma and disturbing emotions. In this recognition it is impossible to be tainted by karma and emotions, just like midair cannot be painted.

I would like to give you a famous quote from the *Hevajra Tantra*:

> All sentient beings are buddhas,
> But they are covered by temporary obscurations.

This temporary obscuration is our own thinking. If we didn't already have the buddha nature, meaning a nature that is identical to that of all awakened ones, then no matter how much we tried we would never be enlightened. The Buddha used the example of churning milk into butter. Sentient beings contain within themselves the butter-yielding milk, in the sense of this basic material of enlightenment. It is not like we are water—

you could churn water for a billion years and still never get butter from it. All sentient beings have the essence of buddhahood within themselves. But if you ignore this most precious essence inside yourself, you will continue spinning around in the three painful realms of samsara.

Samsara is painful because of impermanence. There is the unavoidable pain of death, for example. There is nothing in the world you can do to avoid dying. If we never died, it would be just fine! Or if the mind died when the body dies, well, that wouldn't be so bad either. But actually what happens is the body dies at the end of every life, and the mind experiences this and continues on. We just keep on experiencing. Even when we lie down to take a rest, we keep on dreaming the whole night long. It's like that; it just goes on and on. Recognizing that the essence of mind is empty cognizance and realizing this will enable us to cross the bardo.

Having received the pointing-out instruction, we need to resolve it—not merely recognize it but make up our minds that this is how to solve the basic problem of samsara. To have that kind of trust and also the diligence to practice is like the famous proverb, "The son of a rich father naturally receives his inheritance." Where the father is rich and has a son, there is no question that the son will inherit the wealth. We missed the chance to be primordially enlightened like all the buddhas, bodhisattvas, dakas and dakinis, and Dharma protectors with the eye of wisdom. Nevertheless, if we recognize our nature and train in that diligently, we have the chance to be re-enlightened, just like the son of a rich father taking hold of his inheritance.

17

THE DZOGCHEN PRELIMINARIES

Tulku Urgyen Rinpoche

There are two arrangements for the Dzogchen preliminary practices. The sequence in *The Light of Wisdom, Lamrim Yeshe Nyingpo,* is slightly different from the order in the *Triyig Yeshe Lama* and the *Neluk Rangjung*. In those texts, the practices are called the outer, inner, and secret *rushen*. The outer is the enactment of the experiences of beings of the six realms. The inner is the purification of the six syllables within one's body. The secret is the vajra posture; the four speech yogas; the examination of the coming, staying, and going of thoughts; resting in naturalness; and sustaining freshness. According to *The Light of Wisdom*, the vajra posture, the four speech yogas, examining the coming, staying, and going of thoughts, resting in naturalness; and sustaining freshness comprise the preliminaries for Trekchö. Only the preliminaries for Tögal, the enactment of the experiences of beings of the six realms and the purification of the six syllables, are named *rushen*.

In the past, Vimalamitra used to practice the rushen six months out of every year on Vulture's Peak of Rajgir. He spent half the year on this practice. Attaining the rainbow body actually comes down to the preliminaries. "The preliminaries are the vital point," it is said. This is probably because all the habitual patterns and obscurations are purified through the preliminaries. The Ati Yoga practices of separating samsara and nirvana are extremely powerful and purifying. The closer one gets to mind, the greater the blessings get and the more profound the teachings become.

Adapted from Tulku Urgyen Rinpoche, unpublished teachings, and his introduction to *The Light of Wisdom*, *Vol. IV* (Boudhanath: Rangjung Yeshe Publications, 2001), "Endnotes."

You can begin with the practices of separating the three doors. The first is the vajra posture for the body. Next are the four speech yogas: sealing, developing strength, making pliant, and taking to the road. After that you practice the examination of the coming, staying, and going of thoughts. Finally, there is resting in naturalness and sustaining freshness.

According to Dzogchen, unfabricated shamatha begins when you remain in the natural state after you have resolved that mind is without a place where it comes from, abides, or goes to. After that, the practice of sustaining freshness is to mingle this naturalness with your daily activities. You engage in the path of action, not moving away from the natural state, free from both distraction and fixation. Most people, even if they are undistracted, still fixate and identify objects: "This is a carpet, this is a window," and so on—they are continuously fixating or thinking. But, when distracted, you are completely unaware and do not notice what is being thought of; you are totally dissipated. It is said that on the path of distraction, Mara's robbers lie in ambush.

If you have recognized awareness, there is absolutely no point in being distracted. Once you have recognized awareness, the most important point is not to wander. It does not help anything to think, "Oh, I am undistracted, so why should I look to see whether I am distracted or not? To check is just fixation, so there is no need to look." If you think like that, then everything is lost. Mindfulness is lost.

Sometimes students might wonder whether the practitioner is introduced to the essence at the time of resting in naturalness and sustaining freshness. If one practices these correctly, then resting in naturalness is remaining in awareness, and sustaining freshness is not losing its continuity during any activity. In the Mahamudra system of shamatha and vipashyana, the first steps are called one-pointedness and simplicity. In one-pointedness, one mainly practices shamatha; in simplicity, mainly vipashyana. In both of these, there is still some involvement in conceptual mind. The practice of Dzogchen is a bit different. Resting in naturalness refers to shamatha and sustaining freshness to vipashyana. However, they are not called shamatha and vipashyana here, as they are in the Mahamudra system. If they were, there would be some concepts involved. But from the very beginning, the Dzogchen practice is without concepts, without conceptual mind. So why shouldn't the essence be introduced from the very first?

You might ask, "How come the *Three Words Striking the Vital Point*[40] are placed afterward?" There is nothing wrong with this arrangement. The three vital points are under the rubric of the view, whereas resting in naturalness and sustaining freshness are preliminaries. In the Dzogchen system, shamatha and vipashyana are called preliminaries. To reiterate, resting in naturalness means nonfabrication, and sustaining freshness means not losing the continuity of naturalness. If one has been introduced to the essence in Dzogchen without naturalness, one won't be able to accomplish anything. There is a saying about this in Kham: "The inside is showing from outside." If the door is open, then even if you are standing outside, you can still see the innermost part of the room with all the images there. Although naturalness is placed as a preliminary according to the sequence of chapters, it does not mean that one should abandon it and try to get to something higher or more profound. The essence is being introduced because there is a use for it in the very beginning. If one hasn't been introduced, it is still possible to get the teachings on the three vital points and not recognize, isn't it?

In short, one is introduced to the nonfabrication, to the naturalness that in general refers to the shamatha and then vipashyana. It is said that sometimes the preliminaries are more profound than the main practice. Somebody who is going to be introduced will have recognized already at this point. If one is somebody who is supposed to recognize, the view is quite remarkable. There is a tradition of pointing it out right away. Sometimes you hear strange stories about unusual circumstances in which a student recognized mind-essence.[41] If one has the karmic potential, recognition doesn't always fit the traditional sequence. There are some people who are introduced during the preliminaries. Resting in naturalness and sustaining freshness belong to the preliminaries in Dzogchen, whereas the main part is the *Three Words Striking the Vital Point*.

18

Songs of Examining

Lama Shabkar

Emaho!
Now listen once again, fortunate and noble children of my heart!

No matter which spiritual practice you may perform,
It can't reach the crucial point
Unless you resolve your own mind.
It would be like standing directly in front of a target
And shooting your arrows far away.
It would be like letting a thief stay inside your house
While frantically searching for him outside of it.

It would be like having a demon at the eastern door
And placing a ghost-trap in the western entrance.
It would be like a beggar who does not know that a stone in his
    fireplace is made of gold
And goes around begging alms from others.
For this reason, examine your mind to its root
In the following way, my heart-children.
This so-called mind thinks, and knows this and that,
And moves to and fro.
If you pursue it, it isn't caught but vanishes, elusive as mist.
If you try to settle it, it won't stay
But moves here and there and then disperses.
You cannot pin it down by saying, "That's it!"
Rather, it is an insubstantial emptiness.

From Lama Shabkar Tsokdrug Rangdröl, *The Flight of the Garuda* (Boudhanath: Rangjung Yeshe Publications, 1984), "Song 3 and Song 4."

First, examine the source of your mind, this knower of happiness and
    sorrow.
Where does it come from?
Does it come from external phenomena like mountains, rocks, water
    and trees, or the wind in the sky?
From something solid or from something immaterial?
Where can you find its source?
If you think it comes from the semen and blood of your father and
    mother, how did that happen?

After analyzing in this way and finding no source,
Next examine the upper and lower body,
Then the sense organs, heart, and so forth.
At this very instant, where is the mind?
If it's in the heart, is it in the top or the bottom?
What kind of shape and color does it have?

When you haven't found the dwelling place of mind after precise
    examination,
Try, finally, to determine where the mind goes when it moves.
Through which door of the sense organs does it leave?
When it reaches outer objects in split seconds,
Does the body go, or is it only the mind that goes?
Or do the body and mind go together?
In this way examine and analyze.

When an emotion or a thought first arises,
Find the place from which it arose.
Then, in the present moment, look at where it remains
And whether or not it has color and form.
Finally, when it spontaneously vanishes,
Find out where it went when it disappeared.

Investigate how the mind leaves at the time of death.
Analyze this precisely until you have established with certainty
That it is inexpressible and utterly empty,
Intangible, beyond birth and death, beyond coming and going.

It brings no benefit to parrot the examples and statements of others
By just saying, "It is emptiness!"

For example, people may say that there aren't any tigers
In a place where they are rumored to be,
But you may not feel convinced that this is true.
Instead, you may be disturbed by doubts about it.

But when you yourself have traced the root of mind
And have arrived at certainty about it,
It is as if you had gone to a place where tigers are said to live
And had explored the whole region from top to bottom
To see for yourself if there were any tigers.
When you don't find any, you are certain,
And from then on have no doubt about whether or not tigers are there.

Emaho!
Once again pay attention, my fortunate children!

So now you have examined and analyzed in this manner
And haven't found even an atom of substantial matter
That you can point to and say, "This is the mind!"
It is this not finding anything that is the supreme discovery.

First of all, mind has no place from which it arises.
Empty since the beginning, it has no tangible essence.
Second, it has no dwelling place, no color, no form.
Finally, there is no place to which the mind goes,
Nor is a trace left that shows where it went.
Its moving is an empty movement;
Its being empty is an appearing emptiness.

To begin with, this mind was not produced through causes,
And in the end it will not be destroyed by outer conditions.
Knowing neither decrease nor increase,
It neither gets filled nor gets emptied.
Since it embraces the whole of samsara and nirvana,
It is beyond partiality.

Since it manifests as everything without limitation,
It is not defined by your saying, "This is it!"
Since it does not possess any substantial existence,
It is beyond the extremes of being and nonbeing.

Beyond being obscured or cleared,
Without coming and going, it is beyond both birth and death.

The qualities of the mind are like those of a stainless sphere of crystal.
Its essence is empty, its nature is luminous,
And its expressive quality is vivid, beyond limitation.
Without being tainted by the defects of samsara even in the slightest,
The mind itself is surely the enlightened state since the very
    beginning.

This was the song indicating how to ascertain the character of basic mind in its natural state.

19

Taking Direct Perception as the Path

Thrangu Rinpoche

The Paths of Reasoning and Direct Perception

Sometimes the Buddha taught at length about past and future lives, the consequences of karmic actions, and so on, and at other times on the importance of developing loving-kindness, compassion, and bodhichitta. He also gave detailed teachings on meditation training, on how to develop insight. While involved in samsara's confusion, we automatically have erroneous ways of perceiving, and this confusion needs to be cleared up. Buddhism presents two major ways to go about this: reasoning and direct perception.

Reasoning refers to employing our intelligence to find out exactly how individuals and phenomena are devoid of an independent identity, how all things are empty, and so on. We use inference to understand and gain some conviction about the way things are. This is the basic Sutra approach. Direct perception, on the other hand, refers to Vajrayana practice. It does not involve any intellectual speculation. One employs a more direct experience of the absence of a personal identity and the emptiness of phenomena, and continues to train in this insight until it is fully realized.

The nature of all things is already emptiness. By nature, any given phenomenon is insubstantial and devoid of an independent identity. This is how it is; it is a natural fact. Not understanding this, we get involved in worries, hope, and fear. However, there is no real need to, because in reality things in themselves are devoid of any entity to which we may cling if it is pleasant or which we need to avoid if it is unpleasant. This becomes obvious

Adapted from Thrangu Rinpoche, *Crystal Clear* (Boudhanath: Rangjung Yeshe Publications, 2003), "Taking Direct Perception as the Path."

once we investigate intelligently. Therefore, we can use reasoning to deduce how things actually are and, upon gaining some conviction, train in seeing things as we have understood them to be. This is called taking the path of reasoning.

The pivotal difference between these two paths consists in whether our attention faces out, away from itself, or whether the mind faces itself, looks into itself. The path of reasoning is always concerned with looking at something "out there"; it is to examine using the power of reason, until we are convinced that what we are looking at is by nature empty, devoid of an independent identity. Whether on a coarse or subtle level, it is definitely empty. However, no matter how long and how thoroughly we convince ourselves that things are by nature empty, every time we stub our toe on something, it hurts. We are still obstructed; we cannot move our hands straight through things, even though we understand their emptiness. The path of reasoning alone does not dissolve the habitual mental tendency to experience a solid reality that we have developed over beginningless lifetimes.

No particular practice transforms into emptiness the five skandhas—the aggregates of forms, sensations, perceptions, formations, and consciousnesses; instead, it is a matter of acknowledging how all phenomena are empty by nature. This is what the Buddha taught in the sutras. A person presented with such a teaching may understand the words and trust the teachings but often does not personally experience that this is how it really is. Nagarjuna kindly devised the Middle Way techniques of intellectual reasoning in order for us to understand and gain conviction. By analyzing the five aggregates one after the other, one is eventually convinced: "Oh, it really is true! All phenomena actually *are* empty by nature!"

While we use many tools to reach such an understanding, the reasoning of dependent origination is very simple to understand. For example, when standing on one side of a valley, you say that you stand on "this" side, and across the valley is the "other" side. However, if you walk across the valley, you will again describe it as "this" side, though it was the "other" side before. In the same way, when comparing a short object to a longer one, we agree that one is shorter and the other longer. Nevertheless, that is not fixed because if you compare the longer one to something even longer, it is then the shorter one. In other words, it is impossible to pin down a reality for such values; they are merely labels or projections created by our own minds.

We superimpose labels onto temporary gatherings of parts, which in themselves are only other labels superimposed on a further gathering of smaller parts. Each thing only *seems* to be a singular entity. It appears as if we have a body and that there are material things. Yet, just because something appears to be, because something is experienced, does not mean that it truly exists. For example, if you gaze at the spectacle of the ocean when it is calm, on a clear night you can see the moon and stars in it. But if you sent out a ship, cast nets, and tried to gather up the moon and stars, would you be able to? No, you would find that there is nothing to catch. That is how it is: things are experienced and seem to be, while in reality they have no true existence. This quality of being devoid of true existence is, in a word, emptiness. This is the approach of using reasoning to understand emptiness.

The use of reasoning is not the same as seeing the emptiness of things directly and is said to be a longer path. In the framework of meditation, the intellectual certainty of thinking that all things are emptiness is not convenient to use as the training and takes a long time. That is why the *Prajñaparamita* scriptures mention that a buddha attains true and complete enlightenment after accumulating merit over three incalculable eons. Yet, the Vajrayana teachings declare that in one body and one lifetime you can reach the unified level of a vajra holder; in other words, you can attain complete enlightenment in this very life. Though these appear to be contradictory, both are true. Using reasoning and accumulating merit, it does take three incalculable eons to reach true and complete enlightenment. Nevertheless, by being pointed out the nature of mind directly and taking the path of direct perception, you can reach the unified level of a vajra holder within this same body and lifetime.

Taking direct perception as the path, using actual insight, is the way of mind looking into itself. Instead of looking outwardly, one turns the attention back upon itself. Often we assume that mind is a powerful and concrete "thing" we walk around with inside of us, but in reality it is just an empty form. When looking into it directly to see what it is, we do not need to think of it as being empty and infer emptiness through reasoning. It is possible to see in actuality the emptiness of this mind directly. Instead of merely thinking of it, we can have a special experience, an extraordinary experience, and discover, "Oh, yes, it really is empty!" It is no longer just a conclusion we postulate; we see it clearly and directly. This is how the great masters of India and Tibet reached accomplishment.

Instead of inferring the emptiness of external phenomena through reasoning, the Mahamudra tradition taught by Tilopa, Naropa, Marpa, and Milarepa shows us how to directly experience emptiness as an actuality. Since we habitually perceive external objects as always having concrete existence, we do not really experience them directly as being empty of true existence. It is not very practical to become convinced of the emptiness of external objects such as mountains, houses, walls, trees, and so on. Instead, we should look into our own minds. When we truly see our mind's nature, we find that it has no concrete identity whatsoever. This is the main point of using direct perception: look directly into your own mind, see in actuality that it is empty, and then continue training in that.

This mind, the perceiver, *does* experience a variety of moods. Sometimes there is a feeling of being happy, sad, exhilarated, depressed, angry, attached, jealous, proud, or closed-minded; sometimes one feels blissful, sometimes clear or without thoughts. A large variety of different feelings can occupy this mind. However, when we look into what the mind really is and use the instructions, it is not very difficult to directly perceive its true nature. Not only is it quite simple to do, but it is extremely beneficial as well. We usually believe that all these different moods are provoked by a material cause in the external environment, but this is not so. All these states are based on the perceiver, the mind itself. Therefore, look into this mind and discover that it is totally devoid of any concrete identity. You will see that the mental states of anger and attachment, all the mental poisons, immediately subside and dissolve—this is extremely beneficial.

To conclude this section, I will repeat my previous point. On one hand, we hear that to awaken to true and complete enlightenment, it is necessary to perfect the accumulations of merit through three incalculable eons. Then on the other hand, we hear that it is possible to attain the unified level of a vajra holder within this same body and lifetime. These two statements appear to contradict one another. In truth, there is no way one could be enlightened in one lifetime if one had to gather accumulations of merit throughout three incalculable eons. However, if one could be enlightened in a single lifetime, then there would seem to be no need to perfect the accumulation of merit throughout three incalculable eons. Actually, both are right, in that it does take a very long time if one takes the path of reasoning, whereas it *is* possible to attain enlightenment within a single lifetime if one follows the tradition of the pith instructions for using direct perception as the path.

Establishing the Identity of Mind and Perceptions

In his explanation of taking direct perception as the path, Dakpo Tashi Namgyal starts out by giving us two tasks: gain certainty about the identity of mind and about the identity of its expression, including thoughts and perceptions. In other words, he tells us to investigate three aspects. One he simply calls mind, second is thought, and third is perception. The first of these—mind—is when one is not involved in any thoughts, neither blatant thought states nor subtle ones. Its ongoing sense of being present is not interrupted in any way. This quality is given the name *cognizance,* or *salcha* in Tibetan. *Salcha* means that there is a readiness to perceive, a readiness to think, to experience that does not simply disappear. Since we do not turn to stone or into a corpse when we are not occupied by thinking, there must be an ongoing continuity of mind, an ongoing cognizance.

Next are thoughts, or *namtok* in Tibetan. There are many different types of thoughts, some subtle like ideas or assumptions, and others quite strong like anger or joy. We may think that mind and thoughts are the same, but they are not.

The third one, perceptions, or *nangwa*, actually has two aspects. One is the perception of so-called external objects, for example, sight, hearing, smell, taste, and touch. But let us set those aside for the time being, as they are not the basis for the training at this point. The other aspect of perception deals with what occurs to the sixth consciousness, what may be called mental images. These mental impressions are not perceived through the senses but somehow occur to the mind in the form of memories, something imagined or thought of, a plan taking form; yet each of them does feel as if it is sight, sound, smell, taste, or texture. Usually, we do not pay attention to any of this; it just happens, and we are caught up in it, for example, when daydreaming or fantasizing.

It is important to become clear about what mind, thoughts, and perceptions actually are, not in a theoretical way but in actuality. Up to now, we may not have paid a lot of attention to our mind's way of being when unoccupied with thoughts or perceptions. We may not have looked into what the mind itself, that which experiences or perceives, actually consists of, and, therefore, we may not be certain. When there are thoughts, mental images, or perceptions, the usual habit is simply to lose control and be caught up in the show. We continually get absorbed in what is going on instead of taking a good, clear look at the perceiving mind. We tend not to be aware that we are thinking or daydreaming; we tend to be in a rather vague, hazy state. Now, the meditation training lets these thoughts and mental images become quite vivid. They can become as clear as day. At this point, we should take a good look and establish experientially what their actual nature or identity is.

In these instructions, Dakpo Tashi Namgyal uses the word *examine* repeatedly. When you establish the nature of things by means of reason, examining refers to intellectual analysis, but that is not what is meant here. Unlike an intellectual investigation, *examine* should be understood as simply looking at how things actually are.

Establishing the Identity of Mind—the Basis

When following the path of reasoning, one gives these topics a lot of thought, closely scrutinizing them before concluding that, taking everything into account, this is how it must be. Through intellectual examination one comes to an understanding of what the mind is. The Mahamudra training in vipashyana is entirely different.

First, Dakpo Tashi Namgyal tells us to assume the sevenfold posture of Vairochana and look straight ahead without blinking or shifting position. It may sound as if you are not supposed to blink during this practice, but that is not really the central issue. The important point is not to be concerned with whatever might enter your field of vision. Instead you should concern yourself with mind—the perceiver.

The labels "my mind" and "my consciousness" are simply words, and when we think of them, we have a vague idea of what is meant. However, that is not the actual mind but merely an idea, a vague concept of what mind is. The Mahamudra notion of vipashyana does not mean to examine concepts but to look into what the mind actually is, namely, a sense of being awake and conscious, continuously present and very clear. Whenever we do look, no matter when, we cannot help discovering that mind does not have any form, color, or shape—none at all. Then we may think, "Does that mean that there is no mind? Does the mind not exist?" If there were no consciousness in the body, then the body would be a corpse and not alive. Yet we can see and hear, and we can understand what we are reading—so we are not dead, that's for sure. The truth is that while mind is empty—it has no shape, color, or form—it also has the ability to cognize; there is a knowing quality. The fact is that these two aspects, being empty and being able to know, are an indivisible unity.

Mind does exist as a continuing presence of cognizance. We are not suddenly extinct because there are no thoughts; there is something *ongoing*, a quality of being able to perceive. What then is this mind actually? What does it look like? If mind exists, then in what mode does it exist? Does the mind have a particular form, shape, color, and so on? We should simply take a close look at what it is that perceives and what it looks like, in an attempt to find out exactly what it is.

The second question is, where is this mind, this perceiver, located? Is it inside or outside of the body? If outside, then exactly where? Is it in any particular object? If it is in the body, then exactly where? Does it pervade the entire body, the head, arms, legs, and so on? Or is it in a particular part—the head or the torso, the upper part or the lower part—exactly where? In this way, we investigate until we become clear about the exact shape, location, and nature of this perceiving mind. Then if we do not actually find any entity or location, we may conclude that mind is empty. There are different ways in which something can be empty. It could simply be absent, in the sense that there is no mind. However, we have not totally disappeared—we still perceive; there is still some experience taking place—so you cannot say that mind is simply empty. Though this mind is empty, it is still able to experience. So what then is this emptiness of mind?

By investigating in this way, we do not have to find some thing that is empty or cognizant or that has a shape, color, or location. That is not the point. The point is simply to investigate in order to see it for what it is—however that might be. Whether we discover that the perceiver is empty, cognizant, or devoid of any concreteness, it is fine. We should simply become clear about how it is and be certain, not as a theory but as an actual experience.

If we look into the perceiver, we won't find any perceiver. We do think, but if we look into the thinker, trying to find that which thinks, we do not find any thinker. Yet, at the same time, we do see and we do think. The reality is that seeing occurs without a seer and thinking without a thinker. This is just how it is; this is the nature of the mind. The *Heart Sutra* sums this up by saying that form is emptiness; because whatever we look at is, by nature, devoid of true existence. At the same time, emptiness is also form; because the form only occurs as emptiness. Emptiness is no other than form and form is no other than emptiness. This may appear to apply only to other things, but when applied to the mind, the perceiver, one can also see that the perceiver is emptiness and emptiness is also the perceiver. Mind is no other than emptiness; emptiness is no other than mind. This is not just a concept; it is our basic state.

This—the reality of our mind—may seem very deep and difficult to understand, but it may also be something very simple and easy, because this mind is not somewhere else. It is not somebody else's mind; it is your own mind. It is right here. Therefore, it is something that you can know. When you look into it, you actually *can* see that not only is mind empty, it also knows; it is cognizant. All the Buddhist scriptures, their commentaries, and the songs of realization by the great siddhas express this as *the indivisible unity of emptiness and cognizance* or *undivided empty perceiving* or *the unity of empty cognizance*. No matter how it is described, this is how our basic nature really is. It is not our making; it is not the result of practice; it is simply the way it has always been.

The trouble is that, since beginningless lifetimes, we have been so occupied with other things that we have never really paid any attention to it; otherwise, we would have already seen that this is how it is. Now, due to favorable circumstances, you are able to hear the Buddha's words, to read the statements made by sublime beings, and to receive a spiritual teacher's guidance. As you have started to investigate how the mind is, when you follow the advice you have received, you *can* discover how mind really is.

20

SHAMATHA AND VIPASHYANA

Tulku Urgyen Rinpoche

The traditional phrase is: *cultivate shamatha; train in vipashyana*. Buddhism never says that shamatha and vipashyana are superfluous and should be ignored or totally set aside. Nor would I ever teach that. But there are times when I seemingly put down shamatha a little bit. There is a reason for that, and that reason is found only in a particular context.

The context of the general teachings is one of talking to a sentient being who is experiencing uninterrupted bewilderment—one thought or emotion after another like the surface of the ocean in turmoil, without any recognition of mind-essence. This confusion is continuous, with almost no break, life after life. To tell such a person that shamatha is unnecessary is definitely not the correct way of teaching, because that person's mind is like a drunken elephant or a crazy monkey; it simply won't stay quiet. Such a mind has grown used to the habit of following after what is thought of, without any insight whatsoever. Shamatha is a skillful means to deal with this state. Once confused thoughts have subsided to some extent, it is easier to recognize the clear insight of emptiness. It is therefore never taught that shamatha and vipashyana are unnecessary.

Teaching styles are adapted to the two basic types of mentality: one oriented toward perceived objects, the other toward the knowing mind. The first mentality pursues sights, sounds, smells, tastes, textures, and mental objects and is unstable in buddha nature. This is the situation with the threefold bewilderment—the bewilderment of object, sense faculty, and sense perception, which causes rebirth in an ordinary body. Due to this deep-

Adapted from Tulku Urgyen Rinpoche, *As It Is, Vol. 2* (Boudhanath: Rangjung Yeshe Publications, 2000), "Shamatha and Vipashyana."

seated habit of getting caught up in one thought after another, we traverse through endless samsara. To stabilize such a mind, the first teachings need to show that person how to calm down, how to attain or resolve upon some steadfast quality within the turmoil. It's like the example of muddy water: unless and until the water is clear, you can't see the reflection of your face. Likewise, instructions on shamatha are essential for the individual who gets carried away by thoughts.

Thoughts come out of our empty cognizance. They don't come only from the empty quality. Space doesn't have any thoughts, nor do the four elements. Sights, sounds, and other sensations do not think. The five sense doors do not think. Thoughts are in the mind, and this mind, as I have mentioned so often, is the unity of being empty and cognizant. If it were only empty, there would be no way thoughts could arise. Thoughts come only from the empty cognizance.

The general vehicles hold that the method of shamatha is necessary in order to abide peacefully. To counteract our tendency to constantly fabricate, the buddhas taught us how to rely on a support. By getting accustomed to this support, our attention becomes stabilized, able to remain steady. At this point it is much easier to have pointed out that the attention's nature is empty cognizance. But please remember that merely abiding, merely resting in the stability of shamatha practice, does not guarantee the recognition of the naked state of self-existing wakefulness.

Generally speaking, mind has many different characteristics—some good, some bad, some calm, some untamable. Some people grasp with desire, some are more aggressive; there are so many different kinds of worldly attitudes. If you want your mind to become quiet and still, it will become quiet and still, provided you train long enough. It will indeed—but that is not a liberated state.

The process of becoming quiet is like a person learning how to sit down instead of roaming about bewildered and confused. Still, looking at him from a distance while he sits doesn't necessarily give any indication of his true character. And, as you know, people have different personalities. One person may be very gentle, disciplined, and kind—but while he is just sitting there, you won't know that. Another one may be very crude, short-tempered, and violent, but you won't know that either. These characteristics only show themselves once a person's thoughts begin to move again. When thoughts move, we usually become caught up in delusion. At the same time, our nature is primordially free of the obscuration of emotions and thoughts. Thoughts and emotions are only temporary. The actual *character* of mind is one of self-existing wakefulness, the state realized by all buddhas.

The instructions of Dzogchen, Mahamudra, and the Middle Way all explain how whatever thought arises is free of form, sound, taste, touch, and so on. All movement is empty, empty movement. Though an emotion is empty, it still seems to arise. Because our nature is empty cognizance, thought movement *can* occur. To get carried away by a thought is the state of a sentient being. Rather than that, recognize your basic state as being the essence, nature, and capacity that are the three kayas of the buddhas. Remain in uncontrived naturalness for short moments, repeated many times. You *can* become accustomed to this. The short moment *can* grow longer. In one instant of remaining in unfabricated naturalness, a kalpa of negative karma is purified. An instant of naturalness transforms a kalpa of negative karma.

You need to simply *allow* the moment of uncontrived naturalness. Instead of meditating upon it, meaning focusing upon it, simply allow it to naturally be. As you train like that—and the words for *training* and *meditating* sound the same in Tibetan, so to play on that word—it is more a matter of familiarization than meditation. The more you grow familiar with mind-essence, and the less you deliberately meditate upon it, the easier it becomes to recognize and the simpler to sustain.

The glimpse of recognizing mind-essence that in the beginning lasted only for a few seconds gradually becomes half a minute, then a minute, then half an hour, then hours, until eventually it is uninterrupted throughout the whole day. You need that kind of training. I mention this because, if the goal of the main training is to construct a state in which thoughts have subsided and which feels very clear and quiet, that is still a training in which a particular state is deliberately kept. Such a state is the outcome of a mental effort, a pursuit. Therefore it is neither the ultimate nor the original natural state.

The naked essence of mind is not known in shamatha, because the mind is occupied with abiding in stillness; it remains unseen. All one is doing is simply not following the movement of thought. But being deluded by thought movement is not the only delusion; one can also be deluded by abiding in quietude. The preoccupation with being calm blocks recognition of self-existing wakefulness and also blocks the knowing of the three kayas of the awakened state. This calm is simply one of no thought, of the attention abiding in itself while still not knowing itself.

The root of samsara is thought. The *owner* of samsara is thought. Nevertheless, the very essence of thought is dharmakaya, isn't it? We need to train in recognizing this essence of thought—the "four parts without the three." Training in this is not an act of meditating on something, but a "getting used to." Yet it is not like memorizing either, as in learning verses by heart.

Meditation generally means paying attention. But in this case, we need to train in being free of the watcher and what is watched. In shamatha there is an observer and an object observed. So, honestly, shamatha is also a training in blocking off emptiness. Shamatha makes the mind used to and occupied with being quiet. Something is always maintained. That kind of state is a product of a technique. One applies a lot of effort to fabricating a certain mind-made state. And any state that is a product of training is not liberation. Simply being able to remain quiet does not cause confusion to collapse.

The ocean may look totally still if you could somehow force the waves to subside, but inside the water, all sorts of sediment is still floating around. The water may be free of waves, but it is not free of debris. In the same way, during a sustained state of stillness, the habitual tendencies for the eighty innate thought states, the fifty-one mental events, and all the virtuous and unvirtuous emotions are all latently present. They may not be obvious; they may not be active; but still, they are not liberated.

What I am criticizing here is the idea that the stillness of mind free of thought is ultimately preferable or a goal in itself. The Buddha's teaching is that it is not; stillness in itself is *not* liberation. By pursuing it, one can attain long, long stretches of complete tranquility, but this is not the same as true liberation.

The awakened state of rigpa, on the other hand, is wide open. Nothing is fixated upon, like the ocean in which no sediment remains. When you mix earth into water, it makes the water dirty. In the same way, you don't attain enlightenment by shamatha alone. You need the vipashyana, the quality of clear seeing, which is inherent in the emptiness beyond conceptual mind.

At all levels of Buddhist practice, these two have to go together: stillness and insight, shamatha and vipashyana. In beginning shamatha practice, one may use either a pebble or the breath as the object of attention, but in this case there is always duality: the split between the object of attention and the attentive mindfulness itself—that which keeps an eye on that from which one should not be distracted. In Dzogchen, on the other hand, one is introduced to the naked state of dharmakaya from the very beginning. In the Dzogchen context it is sometimes said that stillness is not absolutely necessary. This is only meant for the person of the highest capacity; it is not meant for everybody. It is not a general Dzogchen teaching to dispense with shamatha, not at all. In Dzogchen, Mahamudra, and the Middle Way, it is never taught that you don't need shamatha; it is only the above-mentioned shortcoming of shamatha that needs to be avoided.

So, you begin with shamatha and continue until you are able to remain acceptably steady. At this point it is much easier to see your naked essence. It's like wanting to see your face reflected in a pool of water—it doesn't help to continuously stir the surface of the water. Rather, you need to allow it to become still and placid. In order to gain the insight of vipashyana, it is first necessary to allow the mind to settle so that your essence can be seen clearly. In the general system of Buddhism, this is indispensable.

As you progress further through the vehicles, you uncover more depth to the meanings of shamatha and vipashyana. There are, for instance, the ordinary and extraordinary shamatha and vipashyana. Ultimately it is said that buddha-mind is the unity of shamatha and vipashyana, but that kind of shamatha and vipashyana is not the ordinary, conceptual type of induced stillness followed by an achieved insight. The name used at that point is the *shamatha and vipashyana that delights the tathagatas*. In other words, they are pleased with that kind because it is flawless. Similar words, different meanings: the ordinary and extraordinary shamatha and vipashyana are as different as sky and earth.

Once more, don't think that shamatha and vipashyana are unnecessary. In rigpa, the intrinsic steadiness is shamatha and the awake quality is vipashyana. The steadiness free of thought is the ultimate shamatha. Being free of thought while recognizing your essence is the indivisible unity of shamatha and vipashyana that delights the tathagatas.

Dzogchen as well uses the words *shamatha* and *vipashyana,* but at that point they do not refer to an outcome of practice. The *Treasury of Dharmadhatu* by Longchenpa says:

> The original nature, totally free of all thoughts, is the ultimate shamatha.
> Natural cognizance, spontaneously present like the radiance of the sun,
> Is the vipashyana that is utterly uncontrived and naturally present.

From this Dzogchen perspective, shamatha is the unchanging quality of innate steadiness, while the natural sense of being awake is the vipashyana aspect. Neither of these is produced or fabricated in any way. Saying that shamatha is not needed refers to the stillness of mind-made fabrication. When I told you before to not meditate, it was to not meditate in the sense of mind-made meditation. It was that kind of shamatha I told you to stop.

Clear seeing, vipashyana, is your empty cognizance, your naked awareness beyond waxing and waning. This sentence has incredible meaning. In Dzogchen it refers to the true recognition of rigpa, while in Mahamudra it is called the innate suchness. This is when the *real* is recognized. It can be called many things, but in short it is the seeing of mind-essence simultaneously with looking. "Seen the moment you look. Free the moment it's seen." There is not a single thought that can stick to that state. However, after a bit of time you discover that you are again looking at something seen. That is when thought has arrived. Then you need to apply "remindfulness," and once again, immediately, the looker is dropped. Relax into uncontrived naturalness!

When remaining without doing anything whatsoever, there is total letting go. In the same moment there is also a sense of being wide awake; there is an awake quality that is unproduced.

Simultaneous with the disappearance of thought, there is an awake quality that is like the radiant flame of a candle, which exists all by itself. That awake quality doesn't need to be supported through meditation, because it is not something that is cultivated. Since its recognition lasts for only a short while, it is necessary to remind yourself again. But honestly, how far away is it to get to that moment? When you put your finger out in the air to touch space, how far do you need to move your hand forward before you connect with space? In the same way, the very moment you recognize mind-essence, it is seen the very moment you look. It is not that at some later point you will see it or that you have to continuously look, look, look for it. There are not two different things going on here.

The recognition of emptiness is accomplished the moment you look. "Seeing no thing is the supreme sight." When seeing emptiness, you don't need to do anything whatsoever to it. The key word here is *uncontrived,* which means you don't have to alter it in any way; just leave it as it naturally is. At that moment, you are totally out of a job; there is nothing you need to do to it. In other words, no act of meditating is necessary at this point. That is what I meant by "Don't meditate." Because at that moment whatever you do to try to keep or prolong the natural state only envelops it in more activity and complexity, which is not really what we need. We have been doing that nonstop anyway, for countless lifetimes.

The perfect dharmakaya is when thought has been allowed to subside. Ordinary beings have fallen under the influence of thought. It is a matter of either recognizing or not. In Dzogchen, the essence is seen the moment you look. Yet, dharmata is not a thing to be seen. If it were, it would be a product of mind.

Sentient beings hold on to this moment. In the present moment, the past has ceased and the future has not arrived. Be free of the three times; then there is nothing except being empty. Trekchö is like cutting through a string; there is no thought conceptualizing past, future, or present. Free of the thoughts of the three times, your present, fresh wakefulness is rigpa.

The shamatha I told you to be free of, in the sense of not meditating, is mind-made peace. It is extremely good that you have dropped it. Mind-made peace is not the perfect path to liberation. Existence and peace, samsara and nirvana—we need to be free of both of these. *That* is the perfect state of enlightenment.

The natural state of totally naked awareness has the quality of being unimpeded; that is true freedom. Recognize the moment of totally open and unimpeded awareness, which does not hold or dwell on anything whatsoever. This is not the mere absence of thought activity, as in induced serenity. That is one major difference. That is also the main reason that shamatha is not by itself the true path of liberation; it needs to be conjoined with the clear seeing of vipashyana on every level, all the way to complete enlightenment.

The ultimate achievement through shamatha practice, with partial but not the full and clear seeing of vipashyana, which is the recognition of mind-essence, is to attain the nirvana of an arhat, but not the nondwelling true and complete enlightenment of a buddha. We should always aspire toward the complete enlightenment that dwells neither in samsara nor in nirvana.

It is also possible to have a sustained meditative state of serenity and yet not be liberated. Here is a story about that. Once I was with my father at a benefactor's house. The man who brought in the tea was a meditator. While carrying the tea in through the door, he somehow suddenly froze, the teakettle lifted in midair. One of the boys wanted to call him, but my father said, "No, let him be—if he drops the pot of boiling tea, it will make a mess; simply leave him be." He stood there for hours, and as the sun was about to set, my father gently called his name into his ear. He slowly regained his senses. Someone said, "What happened?" He replied, "What do you mean what happened? I am bringing the tea." They told him, "That was this morning. Now it is afternoon." He said, "No, no, it is right now, I just came in with it." He was interviewed more about what he experienced, and he said, "I didn't experience anything at all—it was totally vacant, with nothing to express or explain, just totally quiet." When he was told that so many hours had gone by, he was quite surprised, because to him it didn't feel as if any time had passed.

The key point in this context is *don't meditate*. That doesn't mean you have to frown upon all the years of training you have put into meditation. That training was beneficial in that there are far fewer thoughts. However, it is not beneficial to continuously pursue a special, thought-free mental state. Rather, simply allow yourself to be in naturalness free of any fabrication. This uncontrived naturalness is its own remedy for thoughts or emotions.

Mind is something amazing. It is said to be like a wish-fulfilling treasury, a treasure chest of any possible thing. Whatever you put mind to; it can produce that. The true way to go beyond stillness is, whenever you experience the quietude of an absence of thoughts and emotions, recognize the experiencer—what it is that feels the quietness, what it is that abides. At that moment it becomes transparent; in other words, the fixation on stillness disintegrates.

When shamatha is destroyed or disintegrates, then there is true emptiness, an uncultivated emptiness, a natural emptiness. This primordial emptiness is dharmakaya indivisible from sambhogakaya and nirmanakaya. It is the nature of the three kayas—one instant of the essence of mind. Shamatha taints the three kayas with work. The three kayas in themselves are totally effortless.

Our aspiration should be, "Not bewildered in samsaric existence, nor dwelling in the quiescent peace of nirvana, may we liberate all beings." Through recognizing mind-essence, we are of course free from disturbing emotions that create further samsara. But attaining the peace of no disturbing emotions is not enough to be beyond nirvana. So form the resolve to go beyond both.

154

There is one way to make 100 percent sure that your spiritual practice goes in the right direction, and that is simply the three excellences. Always remember, no matter what level of practice you are doing, to start with refuge and bodhichitta. It doesn't matter how much you are able to practice while being totally free of concepts; just train to the best of your ability for the main part of the session. Always complete by dedicating the merit to all sentient beings and making pure aspirations. Embracing your spiritual practice with these three ensures that you are proceeding in the right direction.

Otherwise, one can easily be "meditating" in a way that doesn't necessarily lead near true liberation. There are certain states within samsara called the formless realms. Many people regard the causes for the formless realms as being the true meditation practice. Cultivating these, however, will lead to nothing but a prolonged visit to such a state. Whenever something is deliberately kept in mind, it becomes easier as one goes along because the mind assumes the habit of doing so. Eventually one comes to believe that it is totally effortless.

One could exert sustained effort on dwelling on the idea of emptiness, or just dwelling on feeling clear and quiet. One then "attains" such a state, but because this state is a product, it eventually wears off. Fading from a formless god realm, you awaken after a long, beautiful stay in that meditation realm and discover that your body died at some point, way back in the past. You now realize, "I am dead, I am not liberated in spite of everything, and all of this meditation was for nothing." At that moment the resentment you feel due to the futility of your efforts becomes a direct cause for rebirth in one of the lower realms. Thus, it makes a tremendous difference what you currently identify as being the meditation state and with which motivation you practice.

For many people, shamatha can be a way of preparing for the formless realms. It can also simply be quieting down the mind or imagining a state of emptiness. One repeatedly tries to quiet the mind, to calm down and keep the idea of emptiness in a sustained way, without the real knowing of what it is that sustains. What we need is to combine shamatha with the clear seeing of mind-essence itself. In this context such seeing is called vipashyana, and it is totally beyond anything that dwells and anything to be dwelled upon. That is the moment when shamatha and vipashyana are a unity. Understanding this point is extremely important.

The Buddha himself described the path as a progression through stages of meditation practice:

> Just like the steps of a staircase,
> You should train step by step
> And endeavor in my profound teachings.
> Without jumping over any steps, proceed gradually to the end.
>
> Just as a small child
> Gradually develops its body and strength,
> My teachings are also in this way—
> From the beginning steps of entering
> Up until the complete perfection.

Some teachers have explained that the phrase *complete perfection* here means the Great Perfection, the Dzogchen teachings. This quote also means that the teachings are dependent upon the recipients. Because people are of different types and can be of sharp, mediocre, or lesser capacity, a buddha wanting to benefit them has to teach according to their own level. A teacher may want to teach Dzogchen to everyone, but that is only possible if every single person is of the highest capacity. That would be wonderful, but it is not realistic. Even a fully enlightened buddha cannot avoid having to teach nine gradual vehicles. It doesn't help to give the teachings on a level that people are not actually at. In the same way, you don't give low teachings to someone of higher capacity. That is why it is indispensable to have nine different levels of vehicles.

> Amazing: this unmade, present wakefulness
> Is the true Samantabhadra
> From which you have never been apart for even an instant.
> While recognizing, let be in naturalness.

This is a very important verse, and I will discuss it line by line. It begins with the exclamation *ema*, which means "amazing." The first line is: "This unmade, present wakefulness." The word for *wakefulness (shepa)* here is the same as the word for *consciousness* or *mind;* it is simply what experiences right now. *(Rinpoche snaps his fingers.)* You hear that sound, right? There is no question about that. There is a hearing of sound. That is because there is present wakefulness in these bodies. There is a mind in the body right now, and that is why it is possible to hear through our ears. When mind, the wakeful quality, leaves your body—in other words, when it becomes a corpse—I can snap my fingers a hundred times in front of your ears but there still won't be any hearing. There is no consciousness that hears, no cognition of sound, because mind has departed. That which experiences is not the body, it is that which is *in* the body right now, which is in this moment, right now—not in the past and not in the future, but just in this present moment.

When somebody snaps his fingers like I just did, an immediacy of hearing readily takes place. That is only possible because of present wakefulness. Nothing else can hear sound. The ears by themselves cannot hear, as in the case of a corpse. The five elements and so forth don't hear, the sense organs by themselves don't hear, it is only mind that hears. This unmade, present wakefulness—*unmade* means natural—should be left as it naturally is.

I have often—maybe too often!—given a very simple analogy for naturalness. When wood grows as a tree in the mountain, it is natural but if it is cut down and shaped into a table, it is not the natural form of wood anymore. The word *unmade* here means that you are to leave your present moment of wakefulness exactly as it is, without doing anything to it. There is nothing adopted or avoided, nothing to be held, accepted, or rejected, nothing to be examined at all. Without any hope or fear whatsoever, simply allow present wakefulness to be as it is. That is the first line: "This unmade present wakefulness."

The second line is: "Is the true Samantabhadra." Samantabhadra is the full mastery of the nature that is present throughout all samsaric and nirvanic states; it is your buddha nature, which is all-encompassing but fully realized. The true Samantabhadra is the realization of your own present wakefulness.

The third line is: "From which you have never been apart for even an instant." At no point in time, never, has your nature been lost. Mind and its essence are never separate, like the example of the sun and its rays not being separate. This is called *rangjung yeshe*, self-existing wakefulness. The buddha nature is like the sun; the rays of light are like the thoughts of sentient beings' mind.

Mind and its essence are not separate, just like the sun and its rays are not separate. Coemergent wisdom and coemergent ignorance are also as inseparable as fire and smoke. We have never been separate from this essence for even a moment. Our true nature is Samantabhadra—the nature pervading both nirvana and samsara. Even though it's always been present, this alone doesn't help, because it hasn't been recognized. We need to recognize it.

The fourth line is: "While recognizing, let be in naturalness." You need to go beyond dualistic intelligence. Go beyond viewer and what is viewed; go beyond duality. Right now our intelligence is an act of thinking *of* something. This moment of original, self-existing wakefulness is thought-free. We need to recognize this, train in it and attain stability in the recognition. Recognizing is like the example of an infant who grows up into a twenty-five-year-old man. From infancy, the training is to recognize and continue recognizing until full mastery.

Whether you are Buddha Samantabhadra or a tiny insect, there is no difference in the quality or size of the buddha nature itself. Here's what makes the difference: in the case of a sentient being there is no knowing of itself, and therefore the cognizant quality grasps at what is experienced. In other words, out of ignorance emerges a bewilderment that is endlessly repeated.

The paths and levels toward enlightenment describe degrees of stability in recognition. We need to recognize empty cognizance—what this present moment of unmade wakefulness really is. Allow that to simply be *as it is*; let be in naturalness. That is the whole teaching in a nutshell. Having recognized this, train in it through uncontrived naturalness. Finally attain stability. To repeat these four lines:

Amazing: this unmade, present wakefulness
Is the true Samantabhadra
From which you have never been apart for even an instant.
While recognizing, let be in naturalness.

Every sentient being is cognizant. Cognizance is incessant, as is our nature. It is the nature of mind to cognize. Wakefulness is present always, at any moment. If the present moment of wakefulness is left without being altered, that is the very essence of naked mind. The past has ceased, the future has not come, and the present is not conceptualized in any way whatsoever. The present moment of unfabricated wakefulness is seen the moment we look. Sometimes it is called present mind, ordinary mind, naked mind. Ordinary mind means that it is neither worsened nor improved. Ordinary means that unceasing wakefulness is present in all beings from Samantabhadra down to the tiniest insect. This unceasing wakefulness is the true Samantabhadra.

Usually we contrive our present wakefulness through hope and fear, accepting and rejecting. At this moment, after having recognized its nature, however, you don't need to do anything more to it. It is not something that has to be kept or maintained in any way whatsoever, because it is *naturally so* by itself. If we simply leave it as it is, without doing anything to it, it is beyond improvement or ruin.

Honestly, it's not as if there is a good buddha nature in Samantabhadra and a bad one in an insect. The minds of every single one of us possess the same quality of buddha nature. It is so close and easy that we don't believe it. It is so close and so easy that most people find it impossible to trust that simply letting be is sufficient! But the difference between samsara and nirvana is simply a matter of either recognizing or not recognizing. The very moment you recognize, there is nothing simpler than that. In the moment of seeing mind-essence, it is already recognized; there is nothing more that needs to be done. At that very moment it is not necessary to meditate even a speck. Shamatha needs to be meditated, cultivated. This emptiness does not possess an atom of anything to meditate on.

After recognizing, of course, we lose the continuity. We get distracted. Losing the continuity, becoming distracted, is itself the state of delusion. Meditating on buddha nature as if it were an object is the work of conceptual mind. This conceptual mind is exactly what keeps us spinning through samsara.

"The immediacy of your present wakefulness" means no longer thinking of the past and not planning the future. The past thought has gone, and the future thought hasn't come yet. Although a gap may appear in the present, sentient beings continuously close it up; we reconnect to thoughts, instead of allowing a gap that is free of concepts. Instead of hurrying to do that, simply let be in present wakefulness. Naked ordinary mind, *what naturally is*, is present. You don't have to do anything to bring it forth. That going beyond thoughts of the three times is the essential meaning of the three gates of emancipation mentioned in the Sutras.

There is no need to do anything to your present wakefulness at that moment; it is already *as it is*. That is the true meaning of naked ordinary mind, *tamal kyi shepa*, a famous term in Tibetan. Ordinary mind means not tampered with. There is no *thing* there that needs to be accepted or rejected; it is simply as it is. The term *ordinary mind* is the closest and most immediate way to describe how the nature of mind is. No matter what terminology is being utilized within the Middle Way, Mahamudra, or Dzogchen, *naked ordinary mind* is the simplest term. It is the most immediate way to describe how our nature really is. It means that nothing needs to be accepted or rejected; it is already perfect as it is.

Do not project outwardly, do not withdraw inwardly, and don't place your wakefulness anywhere in between. Whether the attention is directed outside or inside, it's not necessary to place it in a forced state of calm. We need to be free of the thoughts of the three times. There is nothing easier than this. It is like the previous example of touching space: how much do you need to do before you touch space? It's like that. That is the moment in which no doing is required whatsoever. Mind-essence is originally empty and rootless. To know that is sufficient in itself. Of course you can know your own mind!

To cultivate shamatha and to train in vipashyana is like learning the alphabet. If we do not learn it, we will never be able to read or write. Once meditation has dissolved into the expanse of your basic nature, then it is easier to see and easier to maintain. Easier to see means that recognizing is simple. Easier to maintain means to be proficient in naturalness. Without projecting, without focusing, without thought, get accustomed to the continuity.

To make it extremely short: "Never meditate, yet never lose it." It is not an act of meditating like shamatha. But if you forget and get distracted, you fall back into confusion. Never meditate, and never be distracted. When you forget, apply mindfulness. Without this watchfulness, the old pattern takes over again. The old habit of not seeing mind-essence and being continuously caught up in thought is called *black diffusion*. Without the watchfulness, there is nothing to remind us to recognize mind-essence.

21

THE ACTUAL VIEW OF TREKCHÖ

Tsele Natsok Rangdröl

The actual meaning of self-existing wakefulness has numerous classifications, but here they can be reduced to two: Trekchö and Tögal.

As for Trekchö, in order to recognize the innate condition, the meaning of the view of the natural state, and to cut through misconceptions and doubt, the master should teach, according to the respective meditation manuals, the topics such as first tracing the root of thinking, next searching the innate mode of mind, and finally examining the arrival, dwelling, and departure. These should be taught in combination with the oral instructions and corresponding to the mental capacity of the disciples.

Ordinary worldly people (who have not adopted a philosophical viewpoint) are unable to transcend either solid dualistic fixation or attachment, aversion, and delusion; therefore, they do not realize the actual view.

Among the Buddhist schools, the shravakas hold the view of the four noble truths: suffering, origin, cessation, and path. The pratyekabuddhas hold the view of the progressive and reverse order of dependent origination. The bodhisattvas regard appearance as superficial and emptiness as ultimate. They make (the bodhichitta of) aspiration and application their practice. Thus, the followers of the paramita vehicle only partially realize the view of selflessness.

Kriya practitioners hold the view that the deities of the three families are relative truth, while the ultimate is purity free from the four extremes. The followers of both Upa and Yoga regard what appears—the five families, hundred families, and so forth—to be superficial truth, while their empty nature is ultimate truth.

Adapted from Tsele Natsok Rangdröl, *Circle of the Sun* (Boudhanath: Rangjung Yeshe Publications, 1990), "The Actual View of Trekchö."

The practitioners of Mahayoga consider sights and sounds, the mandala of the peaceful and wrathful ones, and so forth to be superficial truth. Being beyond arising, dwelling, and ceasing is the ultimate truth. The nonduality [of these two aspects] is the *indivisible two truths*. The followers of Anu Yoga regard mind-essence free from constructs as space, its objectless cognizance as wakefulness, and their nonduality as great bliss.

In short, the views of the various vehicles of Mantra are all confined to mind-made limitations and in this context are not considered to be the realization of the actual true view.

What, then, is the actual view in this situation? It is your primordially pure self-cognizance, uncompounded wakefulness, the original state transcending thought, the self-existing single circle, the great primordially free expanse of openness.

Since this view is spontaneously perfect as the nature of emptiness from the very beginning, it transcends arising. Since its cognizant expression is unceasing, it serves as the basis for the manifestation of all the phenomena of samsara and nirvana. Yet, whatever manifests is never beyond being emptiness, since it is utterly untainted in essence.

This view lies beyond the limitations of attributes like shape and color, good or evil, existence or nonexistence, permanence or annihilation. The nature of the view is your original wakefulness itself, beyond thoughts and utterances, unspoiled by the mental fabrications of intellectual fixation like the thought "It is beyond limitations!" and so forth.

To realize the view means to be freed from the fetters of doubt, mental fabrication, and dualistic fixation and to recognize and realize the innate condition exactly as it is. This takes place by the power of your master's various indications and instructions, and especially by the profound and wondrous receiving of his blessings. In actuality there is nothing to be realized that is supposed to arise anew from anywhere separate from the realizer. Rather, it is simply recognizing the natural face of your own wakefulness.

You may then ask, "Is it enough just to realize this view of Trekchö, the nature of the ground?" The answer is that some worthy people of the highest capacity are liberated simultaneously with understanding the meaning of this view. For ordinary people, however, just to recognize it is not enough. It is taught that all their momentary tendencies and obscurations must be exhausted and dissolve back into dharmadhatu. The *Sutra on the Purification of Karma* mentions this:

The Blessed One was asked by bodhisattva Nirvirana-Vishkambin,
"What is the nature of the ripening of karma?"
The Buddha replied, "The nature is the intrinsic nature (*dharmata*)."

He was further asked, "If that is so, it would be logical that all
sentient beings are effortlessly liberated."
The Buddha replied, "No, it would not be logical. As butter does not
appear until the milk has been churned, or as silver does not come
forth before the silver ore has been smelted, sentient beings do not
awaken unless they practice and meditate."

Again he was asked, "If (sentient beings) are primordially the
intrinsic nature, what is the point of practicing?"
The Buddha replied, "They should practice because it is necessary to
clear away the momentary conceptual thinking that is like a cloud
appearing in the sky."

Again he was asked, "If the conceptual thinking is momentary,
it is logical that it could reappear even after one has attained
buddhahood."
The Buddha replied, "With the attainment of buddhahood,
conceptual thinking has been totally annihilated, just like
someone who has fully recovered from smallpox."

22

BUDDHA NOWHERE ELSE

Tulku Urgyen Rinpoche

Everything is included within the seeming and the real. As for the real, remember that mind is primordially empty. It is original wakefulness that is empty in essence, cognizant by nature, and all-pervasive in its capacity. This original wakefulness, *yeshe,* is not a blank void; it is cognizant. It has the ability to know. When we talk about the real, the original, *this* is what it is. Original wakefulness empty in essence is the dharmakaya of all buddhas. Original wakefulness cognizant by nature is the sambhogakaya of all buddhas. Original wakefulness is also all-pervasive in its capacity. The innate capacity in which being empty and cognizant are indivisible is called the nirmanakaya of all buddhas. These three kayas form a single indivisibility, the svabhavikakaya, which is our own mind. This original basic reality present in oneself—as opposed to the seeming—is exactly what we call buddha nature.

Mind is also the unity of experience and emptiness. You could say that the seeming and the real are a unity as well, in that mind is the unity of experience and emptiness. Exactly how this is possible is described like this: "Intrinsic mind-essence is dharmakaya; intrinsic experience is the radiance of dharmakaya." It's like the sun and the sunshine, like the body and limbs, like the sky and clouds. The seeming is the expression of the real in the very same way. Right now, we experience the elements of earth, water, fire, wind, and space as external to ourselves. They appear to us through our five senses, don't they? The seeming presence of that which experiences is mind. Without mind, would there be anything that appears? To what

Adapted from Tulku Urgyen Rinpoche, *As It Is, Vol. 1* (Boudhanath: Rangjung Yeshe Publications, 1999), "Buddha Nowhere Else."

would these appearances manifest? Because mind experiences, you cannot deny that there is appearance. To say there are no appearances is a lie. You cannot deny the seeming reality of appearances, because what experiences is mind. But remember, this mind is empty.

All appearances are empty, in that they can all be destroyed or extinguished in some way. Water dries up, evaporates, disappears. Solid-seeming objects can be destroyed by fire, and the flames themselves eventually burn out and are extinguished. The whole universe vanishes at some point, destroyed by seven fires and one immense deluge. In this way, all appearances are ultimately empty.

Mind is also ultimately empty, but its way of being empty is not the same as that of appearances. Mind can experience anything, but it cannot be destroyed. Its original nature is the dharmakaya of all buddhas. You cannot actually do anything to mind—you can't change it, wash it away, bury it, or burn it. What is truly empty, though, is all the appearances that appear to the mind. Because all these appearances are ultimately empty and will vanish completely, we really don't have to worry about them or analyze them too much. They're really just a magical display, just like when demons conjure up some magic to fool you. All appearances are a magical display, experienced only by mind. In fact, we can say that the experiencing of appearances is the magical display of mind.

The three kayas are primordially present in one moment. They are not something that can temporarily be made or manufactured by anyone. Self-existing wakefulness is the realized state of all buddhas from the very beginning; it is primordial. Self-existing wakefulness is in all beings; it simply needs to be known. Our chance to know it comes when it is introduced to us by a qualified master. Our inherently present wakefulness is not something we'll find in the future, nor something we had in the past. It's present *right now.* And it's something that we don't have to accept or reject. Don't do anything to it: don't adopt it, don't avoid it, don't entertain any hope or fear about it, don't try to change it or alter it or improve it in any way. It is not necessary at all.

Recognizing self-existing wakefulness is not the same as looking at the thinking mind, which means simply noticing what is occurring in one's mind: "Now I am happy, now I am sad." And after noticing, we get involved again in whatever is taking place within our confused thinking. Sentient beings roam about in samsara in exactly this fashion, by chasing after their own thoughts. When they feel happy, they get engrossed in that happiness and laugh and laugh. When they feel sad, they sit and cry.

What I have been explaining here is the theory, the intellectual understanding. But really, it's necessary to gain some personal experience in what I'm talking about here. Explaining the theory of mind-essence is like describing different delicious cuisines—Indian food, Chinese food, or whatever—and explaining what each one tastes like. You get an intellectual idea of what it probably tastes like, but you can hear a hundred lectures and still have only an idea. Once you take a single bite into your mouth and it touches your tongue and palate, you taste the flavor. At that moment, you gain genuine confidence regarding the real taste of that food. That is called experience, when we actually know that this tastes pretty good or that tastes disgusting. Experience is the point at which we know it by ourselves.

To leave the view as mere theory is useless. We hear the statement in Buddhism that everything is empty and devoid of any true existence, from the aggregate of physical form up to and including the state of omniscient enlightenment. This is universally renowned as the main principle of Buddhism. To hear this and to comprehend it is to get the idea as intellectual understanding. Actually, the Buddha taught this not from an intellectual standpoint but out of his own experience that everything from the aggregate of form up to complete enlightenment is empty and devoid of true existence. But the hearer of this might say, "All right, the Buddha said everything is empty and devoid of self-entity." And he might go on to think, "Well, then, good or evil are also empty, so what does it matter how I act?" That is a severely wrong view. If merely believing something was enough, then why not think, "I am a fully enlightened buddha"? Would that be good enough? Are you enlightened by simply believing yourself to be enlightened? It's not enough to merely get the idea of the view as a theory.

To receive the pointing-out instruction is to experience mind-essence. The experience is like putting the food in your mouth. Without doing that, there's no way to taste it. Once you eat the food, you know whether it's delicious or awful; that is the experience. Experience is the adornment of rigpa. When it comes to rigpa, only experience is useful. To leave it as theory is not going to help anything. If it would, we could sit around and say, "The lama says such-and-such about emptiness, so that's probably how it is," but we would never know for sure what emptiness is. That is called theory. Experience of the view is when you recognize the nature of your own mind.

When giving and receiving the pointing-out instruction, one should first chant refuge and bodhichitta. This teaching is not some superficial teaching; it is the real thing. Even though it is the ultimate teaching, one still chants refuge and bodhichitta. It is thanks to the Buddha, Dharma, and Sangha that we can recognize the true object of refuge. The Buddha's words, the Dharma, are written down as texts. And the noble Sangha are the people who have been upholding, maintaining, and propagating this teaching until now.

Next, it is the tradition to imagine your root guru at the crown of your head and make a deeply felt supplication. The original father of all buddhas is Samantabhadra, who represents the dharmakaya. The sambhogakaya is called the five buddhas, while the nirmanakayas are the lords of the three families: Manjushri, Avalokiteshvara, and Vajrapani. The transmission line from these buddhas to you is like water flowing from the top of the mountain down to here. If it is not interrupted anywhere along the line, the water will flow right out of your water tap. Similarly, if the lineage has not been broken anywhere, something called the single uninterrupted transmission of instruction comes out of your present guru and is received by you. In this way, the blessings of the three kayas of the buddhas are unbroken as well. This is the reason to supplicate your root guru.

Simply let mind recognize itself, cut through the thinking. That is called the view of Trekchö, the thorough cut. It's thorough in the same way that a piece of string is cut entirely through into two pieces that are completely unconnected. This emptiness is not something we imagine by meditating; it is naturally and originally so. There is no need to merely think it is empty. Simply remain, without imagining or thinking anything. The moment you think, "Now it is empty," a thought has already snuck in. This is unnecessary. This continual process of forming concepts and being attached is itself the root of samsara. You don't have to think, "This is nice!" or "This is not right!" Be free from even a hair tip of conceptual thought. This is called recognizing present wakefulness.

Trekchö is also called *four parts without three*. The way to be free is free from the three parts that are the conditioned thoughts of past, present, and future. The fourth moment is the timeless great moment. In it, the linking-up of consciousness, sense organ, and sense object is cut through. Once this link is broken, the chain of samsara is broken. Self-existing wakefulness needs to recognize itself.

167

Trekchö, the thorough cut, severs the samsaric connection; there is only the gap of empty air between. Remain without following the past, without planning the future. The Buddha described this moment of recognizing mind nature: "No form, no sound, no smell, no taste, no texture, no mental object." Mental objects are called *dharmas* in Sanskrit, but the word here doesn't mean the sacred Dharma teachings; it means phenomena.

This self-existing wakefulness, in which there is no thing to see, is exactly what is called emptiness, *shunyata*. There are two different kinds of empty: empty and emptiness. Space is empty. Can space, which is completely empty, see itself? Mind, on the other hand, is empt*iness*. What we need to see is emptiness in actuality, not something hidden. We need to see emptiness, and that which sees is our cognizant quality. At the moment of seeing emptiness, isn't it true that there is not even as much as a hair tip to see? This is what Rangjung Dorje, the third Karmapa, meant when he said: "When looking again and again into invisible mind, the fact that there is no thing to see is clearly and vividly seen *as it is*." "Vividly seen as it is" means in actuality, not hidden. Mind-essence in actuality, as it is, is vividly seen the very moment you look. If, on the other hand, we sit and think, "Oh, mind is probably empty like space," that is only imagination. We don't need to do that. We don't have to imagine that mind is empty; it is so in actuality. When you see it as it is, you see it is already empty.

Mind is in essence empty. However, it has a cognizant nature of clearly knowing whatever is at any moment. These two aspects, being empty and being cognizant, are a primordial unity. You don't need to grasp at mind-essence as something like you, the subject, knowing that, an object. Empty and cognizant are a natural unity, just as water is naturally wet and fire is naturally hot. There is no need for an observer and something observed, or for the making of the thought "Now I see it." That would be holding a concept in mind. Recognize the thinker and the thought vanishes by itself, because a thought has no inherent stability. Every thought is empty; when you truly look at it; it can only vanish naturally. Once you truly discover this, there is no need to look here and there; just let be.

In the moment of experiencing mind-essence, isn't it impossible to find any word for how it really is? If you do form words about it—"Now it is empty, now it is cognizant"—aren't those simply words that crowd the mind? When the whole point is to allow our thinking to dissolve, what is the use of forming more thoughts?

You may have heard this quotation: "Transcendent knowledge is beyond thought, word, and description." The moment you recognize mind-essence, it is impossible to find words and descriptions for how it is. Allow your thinking to vanish, to dissolve, to simply disappear naturally. In this world there is nothing else that can make it happen. We can blow up all the nuclear bombs we like, and mind will still churn out thoughts. There is only one way to dissolve thinking, and that is to recognize your nature. The thought at that moment vanishes all by itself, without any trace left. Why is this? It is because the minds of all sentient beings have always been primordially empty. The experience of emptiness is not something that all of a sudden happens out of nowhere. The very moment you recognize the essence of your own mind, there is no thing to see.

Honestly, this doesn't last longer than a couple of seconds. Because of our habit of always being caught up in our thoughts, a habit that has continued through beginningless lifetimes until now, there is no real stability there; our realization gets lost quite quickly. The moment we forget, we start to think of a lot of different things. Then once again we notice, "Oh, I got carried away; now I am thinking of all sorts of other things."

The training in recognizing your essence is simply to let be in naturalness. Naturalness here means without any technique, without artifice. Here is a very simple example of naturalness: does the water in the river require someone to push or pull it downstream, or does it naturally flow? You don't need to do anything to it. The wood that makes up my table here has been crafted into this shape. When it was a tree growing on the mountainside it was natural, unmodified. Then a carpenter took it and worked it into a table. Now it is artificial. We need to avoid shaping our awareness into something artificial. The very moment you recognize, don't worry or judge or speculate about it; don't do anything to it; don't try to improve or alter it. Allow nondistraction to last as long as it lasts, as undistracted naturalness. See clearly that there is no thing to see, without trying to improve or alter that.

People experience different degrees of innate stability in this practice, based on their former training. How long that innate stability lasts is hard to say. It may last a little while, but if there is no former training, it might slip away almost immediately. Don't sit and push very hard and think, "I mustn't be distracted, I mustn't be distracted." Simply allow the instants of nondistraction to naturally take place and unfold. To recognize mind-essence doesn't mean to sit and meditate upon mind-essence. It means simply allowing, simply experiencing, our empty and cognizant nature to be as it already is.

This is what we actually are: empty in essence, cognizant by nature, able to perceive, with no barrier between these two aspects. This empty quality is called dharmakaya. But we are not only empty—unlike space, we possess a knowing quality. This is what is described as cognizant nature, sambhogakaya. The capacity is the unity of these two, suffused with awareness. Capacity here means that being empty and being cognizant cannot be separated; they are an original unity. And "suffused with awareness" refers to rigpa. The minds of all sentient beings are the unity of empty cognizance, but because they are not suffused with awareness, they don't know this. Although their minds are the unity of empty cognizance, they are suffused with unawareness, with unknowing. The very moment we recognize our nature as empty cognizance, it becomes empty cognizance suffused with awareness, with knowing.

The difference between buddhas and sentient beings is the difference between knowing and not knowing. *Knowing* means knowing one's own nature, one's natural face. This present wakefulness that is uncorrected or uncontrived is the true Samantabhadra that has never been apart from you. While recognizing, rest naturally. When this present wakefulness recognizes itself, there is nothing whatsoever to see. *That* is the empty essence—that is dharmakaya. However, along with the realization that there is nothing to see is some knowing or seeing that this is so. That is the cognizant nature, sambhogakaya. This empty essence and cognizant nature are forever indivisible. That is the unity, nirmanakaya.

In the very moment of recognizing, these three kayas are already seen. There is nothing to block this realization, nothing in between the kayas and your awareness. Knowing this is self-knowing wakefulness (*rangrig ye-she*). Unknowing is samsara. To be ignorant is to be a sentient being, but to know is to be a buddha. This teaching is something very precious. To have one's nature pointed out is an incredibly great kindness, and it is only due to the compassion of the Buddha that we have this teaching today.[42]

In short, recognize yourself and be face-to-face with the three kayas of the awakened one. To let your attention stray, to be caught up in the three poisons, is to stray further into samsara. That certainly happens, doesn't it? The moment we see a beautiful form, we love it. The moment we see something ugly, we hate it, don't we? And if it is something in between, we don't care. These are the three poisons, and they go on and on and on. When we see something we like, we become fascinated and we feel attached, while we feel revulsion toward and don't want to look at things we don't like. Toward something in between we feel indifferent, dull, closed-minded. At the moment of involvement in the three poisons, there is no knowing of one's own nature; the three kayas of the awakened state slip away.

There is nothing superior to meeting face-to-face with the three kayas of the awakened state. Isn't that true? Seeing that there is no thought overcomes or expels any previous thought. When the sun shines, there is no darkness. While seeing, it is impossible for any thought to either linger or to be formed. The delusion is completely dissolved. The awakened state is free of thought. But merely thinking, "I want to be free of thought" is not the awakened state. It's just another thought. The same goes for checking: "Is there a thought now, or is it free of thought?" Isn't that just another thought as well? It's necessary to rest totally unmixed with or unpolluted by thought. The awakened state is free of thought, yet vividly awake. If we train in this steadily and gradually, it becomes the fully awakened state, buddhahood.

There is a natural sturdiness or stability in the moment of recognizing mind-essence. To understand natural stability, think of a needle compared to a hair. A hair, no matter how thick it might be, is not stable; it moves in the slightest breeze. But a needle, regardless of how thin it is, cannot be bent by the wind. We need to be naturally stable in emptiness. We don't have to imagine emptiness by meditating. If we do this, it becomes an act of thinking—we are just thinking of emptiness. When we forget mind-essence, we become distracted; confusion arises. Meditating is conceptual, and being distracted is confusion. Instead, be naturally stable in the state of undistracted nonmeditation. This undistracted nonmeditation is not something you have to create. You don't have to hold on to the idea of that. Simply allow present wakefulness to be naturally stable by being free of thought. Be stable not in keeping a thought but in the absence of thought.

To do so is to experience what we call present wakefulness, or thought-free wakefulness. *Thought-free* means free of conceptual thinking, yet the knowing or awake quality is not lost. If you want to find out what it's like to lose this sense of awakeness, have somebody knock you out with an iron bar so you can experience unconsciousness! Right now, in the moment of recognizing, we are not unconscious. The awake quality is not lost, and yet there is no thought. If you spend your life practicing like this, eventually thinking will get weaker and thoughts will decrease. But the continuity of thought-free wakefulness is not lost. It lasts for longer and longer periods naturally, of its own accord, while the moments of conceptual thinking become weaker and take up less and less time. Finally, you become totally free of thought. Conceptual thinking disappears, and there is only present thought-free wakefulness, uninterrupted through both day and night. That is called the buddha mind.

We need to train in this thought-free wakefulness, but not by meditating on it or imagining it. It is primordially present already. Yet this present wakefulness gets caught up in thinking. To get free of thought, simply recognize your present wakefulness. Don't forget; don't get distracted. That doesn't mean to sit and force yourself to be undistracted and unforgetting. Trying like that only fouls it up. Simply allow your basic state to be undistracted nonmeditation. When all the activities of dualistic mind dissolve, when we are utterly stable in the unconfined empty cognizance, there is no longer any basis for remaining in the three realms of samsara.

Even if our recognition of rigpa doesn't become uninterrupted throughout day and night—even if we only manage to sustain it for short moments many times—the value of training in this practice of recognizing mind-essence will become fully evident at the time of death. At some point we are all sure to die; no one escapes that in this world. Anyone who takes birth dies. If we manage to recognize at the moment when the breath ceases and we are separated from this illusory body, we can in three seconds perfect the strength of that recognition and stabilize it. It becomes the dharmakaya state, just like space mingling with space. It's just like what happens to the space within a vase that breaks: the space inside and the space outside, which were up until that point divided by the side of the vase, become one. Similarly, the ground state of unconstructed dharmakaya, which is the buddha nature present in everyone, and the path dharmakaya, which is the empty cognizance we have trained in, combine into an indivisible unity.

The process of our spirit disconnecting from the physical body is accompanied by the dissolution of all gross and subtle thought states or mental patterns. At this point there is nothing covering the basic state of mind at all. This is called the ground luminosity of full attainment, sometimes described as the ground luminosity and path luminosity coming face to face.

At that moment, the power of our training in this life can create the possibility for recognizing the original wakefulness. If we haven't trained at all, the basic state won't last longer than a single glimpse. But if we have trained, then at that moment complete enlightenment is very likely. This is stated in a tantra: "In one moment the difference is made; in one moment complete enlightenment is attained." All that is necessary is to allow the recognition of original wakefulness to be sustained for three seconds. The scriptures describe it as the length of time it takes to wave the long sleeve of a Tibetan robe or a white scarf three times in the air. If we can do this, we can attain complete stability during the post-death state.

The ground luminosity is like the mother, while the path luminosity is like the child. Mother and child always recognize each other, don't they? When the ground and path luminosities recognize each other in that split-second span of time, however small the degree of familiarity might be, it still will be sufficient to take rebirth in a pure buddhafield, in the natural nirmanakaya realms. There you will behold the face of the Buddha, hear his voice, and overcome the remaining obscurations. If there is a strong familiarity, it is like space mingling with space, and you become of one taste with the state of dharmakaya.

The reason training in this lifetime can yield such great benefit after death is that in the bardo state our mind is not connected to a body, so it's free of the continual obscuration we experience in our lifetime. Right now, we might recognize our own mind in a brief glimpse, only to have it immediately covered up again. But after death, the obscurations created by the body are not there.

You need to train in these instructions in order to overcome the cognitive obscuration. Through this training, you will eventually reach the irreversible state, called the state of nonregression, no falling back. This is the real, true outcome, the profit earned from all the effort of practice. We should experience some positive result from our practice. This practice will definitely help at the moment of death. Right now, we may train in recognizing and sustaining the natural state, but we are not immediately enlightened, because body and mind are still connected. Still, practice brings many other benefits that occur in this life. For one, we do not fall under the power of the three poisons. As we recognize, strengthen our recognition, and attain stability, we are always joyful, regardless of who we are with, and wherever we go, the sun of happiness shines. Otherwise, we're like any other ordinary person: depressed when unhappy and overjoyed when happy. In other words, we are totally unstable. Through this practice, good and bad become equalized, without having to adopt one and avoid the other. Even facing death we will be totally at ease.

The real problem is the state of mind of an ordinary person, which is always changing from one thing to another. Sentient beings are totally unstable, but someone who has truly recognized mind-essence and stays in retreat in the mountains is completely free of suffering. Even in this lifetime one can be totally free of pain and progress further and further on the path of happiness. There is great benefit from this practice. It's never pleasant to maintain the state of mind of an ordinary person, which is always changing. When unhappy, one is totally overcome by that feeling. Better to recognize the wide-awake empty cognizance and remain like that.

Basically there is nothing at all to do in this practice besides training in being stable. Simply allowing our mind to be, without having to do anything, is entirely against our usual habits. Our normal tendency is to think, "I want to do this. I want to do that." Then we actually go do it. Finally, we feel happy and satisfied when it's all neat, all completed, accomplished all by ourselves. But that attitude is totally wrong in the context of this type of practice. There is nothing whatsoever to do. We don't have to construct what is unformed. Anything we try to do becomes an imitation, something made up by our thoughts and concepts.

As a matter of fact, it may feel utterly unsatisfying, extremely disappointing, to allow our original nature to be as it naturally is. We might much rather do something, imagine something, create something, and really put ourselves through a lot of hardship. Maybe that is why the Buddha did not teach Dzogchen and Mahamudra openly—because this not-doing is in some ways contrary to human nature.

Buddha nature is free of the three times of past, present, and future, while our mind is under the power of the three times. Wakeful knowing is free of the three times. The three times involve fixating, thinking. Wakeful knowing is free of fixation and thought.

If we really apply ourselves to it sincerely, there will come a time when we discover something called establishing the natural state. When you experience this, suddenly it's not so hard any longer. We realize that this fantastic thing called buddha nature, our mind-essence, is not out of reach at all. Since it is not something very complex, simply allow that to be regularly sustained. When it is totally easy and simple to recognize your natural face, you have established the natural state.

Right now, in the very moment of recognizing mind-essence, there is an immediate absence of disturbing emotions, of ignorance, of deluded thinking. This training is simply to remain undistracted, because it is this nondistraction that brings us all the way to complete enlightenment. Nondistraction doesn't mean deliberately trying to be undistracted, as we do when we replace normal thoughts with the thought "Don't be distracted." It is simply to not forget. The moment we forget—and we do forget—both the practice and all other things get forgotten, because our attention strays. The key point here is not to remain undistracted in a conceptual way. It is simply to allow the state of unconfined empty cognizance, which by itself is undistracted, to continue. That is the training.

Try to imagine what it's like when this moment of empty cognizance suffused with awareness starts to last for a full hour, unbroken. The very first moment of empty cognizance already has the potential for full omniscience, as well as the potential for compassion and loving-kindness—the potential ability to protect and help other beings, as well as to manifest the activity that functions for the welfare of all. All these qualities are present but not fully manifest. The longer this lasts, the more the qualities become visible, actualized. They don't just appear later on, when realization is fully experienced. When the sun rises in the morning, do we have to wait for it to shine before it is warm and brilliant? Although the noon sun may be stronger than the dawn sun, all of its qualities are present from the very first moment, though they may not be fully manifested. It's the same in this training. What is essential is to train in order to attain stability.

Please understand that self-existing wakefulness (*rangjung yeshe*) is primordially endowed with all perfect qualities. The qualities of enlightenment are not a fabrication or a product. They are not something new that we discover or achieve. They are present from the very beginning. It's like the unchanging brilliance of the sun shining in the sky. It can be obscured by clouds, but these clouds are neither primordial nor intrinsic to the sky; they are always temporary, momentary. What prevents full realization of our innate nature of self-existing wakefulness is the momentary occurrence of thoughts and fixation. Because this occurrence is momentary, it can be cleared away. It's very important to understand this.

23

THE MIRROR OF ESSENTIAL POINTS

A letter in praise of emptiness from Jamyang Dorje to his mother

Nyoshul Khen Rinpoche

I pay homage at the lotus feet of Tenpey Nyima,
Who is inseparable from lord Longchen Rabjam
And who perceives the natural state of emptiness
Of the oceanlike infinity of things.

A letter of advice I offer to you, my noble mother Paldzom.
Listen for a while without distraction.
Staying here without discomfort,
I am at ease and free from worries
In a state of joyful mind.
Are you well yourself, dear mother?

Here, in a country in the west,
There are many red- and white-skinned people.
They perform all kinds of magic and displays,
Like flying through the skies
And moving like fish in the water.
Having mastery over the four elements,
They compete in displaying miracles
With thousands of beautiful colors.
There are innumerable spectacles
Like designs of rainbow colors.
But like a mere dream when examined,
They are merely the mistaken perceptions of mind.

From Nyoshul Khen Rinpoche, "The Mirror of Essential Points," in *Crystal Cave: A Compendium of Teachings by Masters of the Practice Lineage* (Boudhanath: Rangjung Yeshe Publications, 1990).

All activities are like the games children play.
If started, they can never be finished.
They are only completed once you let them be,
Like castles made of sand.

But that is not the whole story.
All the phenomena of samsara and nirvana,
Although thought to be permanent, do not last.
When examined, they are but empty forms
That appear without existence.
Although unreal, they are thought to be real.
But, like an illusion, when examined they are found to be unreal.

Look outward at the perceived objects.
Like water in a mirage,
They are more delusive than delusion.
Unreal, like a dream or a magical apparition,
They resemble a rainbow or the reflection of the moon.

Look inward at your own mind!
It seems quite exciting when not examined.
But when examined there is nothing to it.
Appearing without existing, it is nothing but empty.
It cannot be identified; you cannot say, "That's it,"
Because it is evanescent and elusive like mist.

Look at whatever appears
In any of the ten directions.
No matter how it manifests,
The thing in itself, its very nature,
Is the skylike nature of the mind
Beyond the projection and the dissolution of thought and concept.

Everything has the nature of being empty.
When the empty looks at the empty,
Who is there to look at something empty?
As it is illusion looking at illusion
And delusion watching delusion,
What is the use of many classifications
Such as empty and not empty?

Whatever you do is all right.
However you rest, you are at ease
In the effortless and skylike nature of the mind,
The vast expanse of awareness,
The natural state of all things.
This was said by Jetsun Padmasambhava
And the great siddha Saraha.

Leave all conceptual thought constructions
Such as duality or nonduality
To spontaneously dissolve in themselves
Like waves on a river.

The great demon of ignorant and discursive thought
Causes one to sink into the ocean of samsara,
But when freed from this discursive thought
There is the indescribable state beyond conceptual mind.

Other than mere discursive thoughts,
There are not even the words *samsara* and *nirvana*.
The total subsiding of discursive thought
Is the suchness of dharmadhatu itself.

Not made complex by complex statements,
This unfabricated single sphere
Is emptiness, the natural state of mind.
Thus it was said by the Sugata.

When simply left to itself,
The essence of whatever may appear
Is the unfabricated and uncorrupted view,
The dharmakaya mother of emptiness.

All discursive thoughts are emptiness,
And the observer of emptiness is discursive thought.
Emptiness does not destroy discursive thought,
And discursive thought does not obstruct emptiness.
The mind nature of fourfold emptiness
Is the pinnacle of everything.
Profound and quiescent, free from complexity,
An uncompounded, luminous clarity

Beyond the mind of concepts—
This is the depth of the mind of the victorious ones.

In this there is no object to be removed
Nor something that needs to be added.
It is merely the natural
Looking naturally into itself.

In short, when the mind has fully severed
The fetters of clinging to something,
All the points are condensed into one.
This is the tradition of the supreme being, Tilopa,
And of the great pandita Naropa.

Such a profound and natural state as this,
Among all the different kinds of bliss,
Is the one known as the wisdom of great bliss.
Among all kinds of delights
It is the king of supreme delight.
Among all the tantric sections of the Secret Mantra,
It is the supreme fourth empowerment.
This is the ultimate pointing-out instruction.

The view of samsara and nirvana as inseparable,
And that of Mahamudra, Dzogchen, the Middle Way, and so on,
Has many different titles
But only one essential meaning.
This is the view of Jamgön Mipham.

As an aid to this king of views,
One should begin with bodhichitta
And conclude with dedication.

Through skillful means, in order to cut off
The fixation of ego, the root of samsara,
The king of all great methods
Is unsurpassable bodhichitta.

The king of perfect dedication
Is the means of increasing the root of virtue.
This teaching is the specialty of Shakyamuni,
Which is not taught by other teachers.

More than this is unnecessary
To accomplish complete enlightenment,
But less than this will be incomplete.
This swift path of the three excellences
Called the heat, eye, and life force
Is the approach of Longchen Rabjam.

Emptiness, the wish-fulfilling jewel,
Is unattached generosity.
It is uncorrupted discipline.
It is angerless patience.
It is undeluded exertion.
It is undistracted meditation.
This emptiness, the essence of insight,
Is the meaning of the three vehicles.

Emptiness is the natural state of mind.
It is the nonconceptual refuge
And the absolute bodhichitta.
It is Vajrasattva who absolves evils.
It is the mandala of perfecting accumulations.
Emptiness is the guru yoga of dharmakaya.

To abide in the natural state of emptiness
Is calm abiding, shamatha.
To perceive it as vividly clear
Is clear seeing, vipashyana.

The view of the perfect development stage
And the wisdom of bliss and emptiness in the completion stage,
The nondual Great Perfection,
And the single sphere of dharmakaya
Are all included within emptiness.

Emptiness purifies the karmas
And dispels the obstructing forces.
Emptiness tames the demons
And accomplishes the deities.

The profound and natural state of emptiness
Dries up the ocean of passion.

It crumbles the mountain of anger
And illuminates the darkness of stupidity.
It calms down the gale of jealousy,
Defeats the illness of the kleshas,
And is a friend in sorrow.
It destroys conceit in joy
And is victorious in the battle with samsara.
It annihilates the four Maras,
Turns the eight worldly dharmas into same taste,
And subdues the demon of ego-clinging.
It turns negative conditions into allies
And turns bad omens into good fortune.
It results in true and complete enlightenment
And gives birth to the buddhas of the three times.
Emptiness is the dharmakaya mother.

There is no teaching higher than emptiness.
There is no teaching swifter than emptiness.
There is no teaching more excellent than emptiness.
There is no teaching more profound than emptiness.

Emptiness is the knowing of one that frees all.
Emptiness is the supreme king of medicines.
Emptiness is the nectar of immortality.
Emptiness is spontaneous accomplishment beyond effort.
Emptiness is enlightenment without exertion.

By meditating on emptiness,
One feels tremendous compassion
Toward the beings obscured by belief in a self,
And bodhichitta arises without effort.

All the qualities of the path and levels
Will appear naturally without any effort,
And toward the law of the unfailing effect of karma
One will feel a heartfelt conviction.

If one has but one moment of certainty
In this kind of emptiness,
The tight chains of ego-clinging

Will shatter into pieces.
This was said by Aryadeva.

It is more supreme to meditate on emptiness
Than to offer all the infinite buddhafields,
Filled with the wealth of gods and men,
To the sugatas and their spiritual sons.

If the merit of resting evenly,
Just for an instant, in this natural state
Could assume concrete form,
The element of space could not contain it.

Shakyamuni, the peerless lord of the Munis,
Threw his body into pyres of fire,
Gave away his head and limbs,
And performed hundreds of other austerities
For the sake of this profound emptiness.

Although one fills the world with great heaps
Of gold and jewels as offerings,
This profound teaching on emptiness,
Even when searched for, is hard to find.
This is said in the *Hundred Thousand Verses of the Prajñaparamita.*

To meet this supreme teaching
Is the splendid power of merit
Of many eons beyond measure.

In short, by means of emptiness
One is, for one's own benefit,
Liberated into the expanse of the unborn dharmakaya,
The true and complete enlightenment
Of the four kayas and the five wisdoms.
Then the unobstructed display of rupakaya
Will ceaselessly manifest to teach whoever is in need,
Stirring the depth of samsara for the benefit of others
Through constant, all-pervading, and spontaneous activity.
In all the sutras and tantras, this is said
To be the ultimate fruition.

How can someone like me put into words
All the benefits and virtues of this,
When the Victorious One with his vajra tongue
Cannot completely elucidate them all, even if he speaks for an eon?

The glorious lord, the supreme teacher
Who gives the teachings on emptiness,
Appears in the form of a human being,
Though his mind is truly a buddha.

Without deceit and hypocrisy
Supplicate him from your very heart.
Without needing any other method,
You will attain enlightenment in this very life.
This is the manner of the all-embodying jewel
Which is taught in the tantras of the Great Perfection.
When you have this jewel in the palm of your hand,
Do not let it go to waste meaninglessly.

Learning, like the stars in the sky,
Will never come to an end through studies.
What is the use of all the various
Teachings requested and received?
What is the use of any practice
That is not superior to that of emptiness?

Do not seek many special outfits
Such as carrying a staff or wearing braids or animal skin.
The elephant is already in your house.
Do not go searching for its footprints in the mountains.

Mother, meditate on the essence of mind
As it is taught by the master, the vajra holder.

This is the quintessence of the essence
Of all 84,000 teachings.
It is the heart substance of a billion
Learned and accomplished ones.
It is the ultimate practice.

This advice from the core of the heart
Of the fallen monk Jamyang Dorje

Is the purest of the purest essence
From the bindu of my life blood.
Therefore, keep it in your heart, mother.

These few words of heart advice
Were written in a beautiful countryside,
In the palace of the spacious blue sky
That competes with the splendor of divine realms.

To the devoted Chökyi Nödzom,
My dear and loving mother,
And to all my devoted students
I offer this letter of advice.

This letter to my students was composed by one who goes by the name Khenpo, the Tibetan Jamyang Dorje, in the Dordogne herbal valley of great bliss, in the country of France beyond the great ocean in the western direction. May there be virtue and auspiciousness!

24

Three Words

Chökyi Nyima Rinpoche

Garab Dorje's *Three Words Striking the Vital Point* condenses all the teachings of the Buddha into the quintessential meaning: recognize your essence, decide on one point, and gain confidence in liberation.

First, to recognize your essence is the primary root, the starting point. Without having first recognized your essence, you cannot decide on it or resolve it without a doubt. If you are unable to decide upon that as the ultimate, you can never gain confidence in liberation.

The sentence "Recognize the essence of your own mind" simply means recognizing that what you already have, your basic, nonconceptual wakefulness, is a part of yourself and not something new. The word *recognize* literally means to arrive at some understanding that we did not have earlier. Do not mistake it to mean discovering something that you did not previously possess.

Up until now we have studied and learned, and our understanding may have remained an idea, a separate object held in mind. But the natural state of dharmata, the luminous wakefulness as it is, is not a physical object composed of matter nor a shape with a certain color that we can see. It is not like that at all. Moreover, it is not as though we, as one entity, are supposed to look at the essence of our mind as another entity. We do not recognize our essence through the dualistic act of one thing looking at another. Recognizing the basic state is not like that. Basic wakefulness is the very essence of the mind that fixates or thinks of something. Yet our dualistic fixation and thinking is like a veil that covers and obscures this luminosity.

Adapted from Chökyi Nyima Rinpoche, *Bardo Guidebook* (Boudhanath: Rangjung Yeshe Publications, 1991), "The Luminous Bardo of Dharmata."

In short, what is recognized is not a *thing*. What, then, do we recognize? We must experience naked wakefulness directly, and this occurs the instant that our mind is stripped bare of conceptual thinking. That experience, therefore, is not a product of our fabrication. It simply is. The problem is that it is too near to us, just like something held so close to your eyes that it is difficult to see. Moreover, it is too easy. We would prefer something more difficult. Simply remaining free from concepts is extremely easy. The only difficulty is that it goes against our tendencies—we enjoy conceptual activity, we like to have something to take hold of. So, although it is easy to remain freely, our habitual tendencies pull us away from that state.

The Buddhist teachings are structured in levels, one above the other, and people with sharp minds will compare the lower teachings to the higher and find that the lower philosophical schools have some defect, some shortcoming. Yet all philosophical ideas are established intellectually, through concepts. As opposed to intellectual reasoning or conceptual insight, the view of Trekchö is nonfabrication, nonmeditation, and nondistraction. It is beyond theoretical philosophies.

The Buddha said, "I have taught you the path to liberation, but know that liberation depends upon no thing other than yourself." The Buddha described how to realize the ultimate truth, but he could not make us realize it—we have to do this ourselves. We are like a person with cataracts: people may show us an apple and say, "Look at this. See how red it is!" but unless our cataracts are removed, we cannot see clearly. Likewise, in order to directly perceive and sustain the natural state, the ultimate nature of things, the obscurations of dualistic knowledge and habitual tendencies must be removed. The most efficient way of quickly removing these subtle obscurations is, after we have been introduced to basic wakefulness by a qualified master, to simply rest in the continuity of the natural state. However, unless our obscurations have already thinned out to a certain degree and become very shallow, it is impossible to simply cut through them. That is why all the teachings with a conceptual reference have been given: to reduce our obscurations. We must therefore gather the accumulations of merit and do purification practice. That is the whole point of all the teachings: to advance step by step until it is possible to cut through even subtle obscurations.

All things arise due to causes and circumstances coming together. For example, being born with a beautiful appearance is not necessarily due to one's mother and father being beautiful, since beautiful parents can also have ugly children. Additional causes are necessary. Beauty mainly results from having done something by way of one's body, speech, or mind that benefited the physical body of other sentient beings at some point in the past. We can, right now, directly establish how our mental attitude affects things, without getting into long explanations. A calm, gentle, and disciplined person is more capable of doing things in a proper, agreeable way than someone whose mind is disturbed by aggression or a sense of competitiveness. When a disturbed person does physical work, the outcome is somehow distorted. Our actions create habitual tendencies that then reoccur within our mind. Conversely, when we realize the nature as it is, the three poisons and the various negative thought patterns begin to disappear and the obscurations start to diminish. Once the obscurations diminish, realization of the view is easy. Therefore, the whole basis of Dharma practice is very direct and related to our present state of mind. Practice is not based on old stories and romantic narrations from the past.

When an architect, doctor, or artist becomes very agitated by negative emotions due to, say, a problem with his mate or money, he cannot possibly do his job properly. It is difficult for a doctor to even take the pulse of a patient. For an artist, it is difficult to draw a straight line. Why is that? It is because his mind is disturbed. If one is on the verge of a nervous breakdown, deeply depressed or worried, one cannot do anything in the usual way.

When some people get really angry, they cease to see clearly. Even the ordinary perceptions of the five senses are obscured; they are certainly unable to recognize their basic wakefulness. On the other hand, when our mind is relaxed and we feel free and easy, everything is beautiful. This whole world is nice and pleasant. Flowers look pretty, it feels good to be with friends, and food tastes delicious. But when our mind is agitated and disturbed, everything feels wrong. Our best friend is annoying, beautiful things look ugly, and we have no appetite. If we are sitting down, we want to be somewhere else. When going somewhere else, we want to sit down quietly. At night we cannot sleep. At that point, we are actually a little crazy. This is a mild form of insanity. What is making us crazy? It is the manifestations of our own disturbing emotions, karma, and obscurations. Wouldn't it be better to just rest in the natural state in which emptiness and cognizance are a unity?

We must decide on one point. The natural state is totally free from any mental constructs, whether good or bad, special or ordinary; it is perfectly empty. Although empty, it is not blank. It is naturally cognizant, aware. This state of the unity of emptiness and awareness is the natural state of the ground luminosity. It is called "the luminosity of dharmata" in this context (of bardo teachings) and is what is shown by a qualified master during the pointing-out instruction. He says, "That's it!" and we may recognize it. But simply having recognized it is not sufficient. We must also be totally free from any doubt about it. That is what is meant by *deciding on one point*. Having resolved your experience to be the basic wakefulness beyond a shadow of doubt, train in gaining confidence in liberation. Once you possess the confidence of the view, then no matter what scholars or other people say, even if the buddhas and bodhisattvas appear and say, "You are wrong, you are confused, you are still mistaken," there will be no basis for bewilderment because you already experience the natural state of things, the ultimate truth right at that moment. You have gained total confidence.

Based on our confidence in liberation, we progress toward true realization. Passing away is then like a vase breaking: the space within and the space without mingle together without the slightest division. It is like the birth of a baby snow lion, who immediately has the strength to walk and jump, or like a baby garuda bird, which the moment it hatches from the egg is able to fly. Likewise, for the practitioner who has confidence in the view, death and liberation are simultaneous. Our experience of the path luminosity during this life and the experience of ground luminosity that happens at the moment of death mingle and blend into one experience. They are not two different luminosities, but just one that is inseparably mingled with dharmakaya.

We may be the type of person who does not need to depend on elaborate practices in order to stabilize rigpa, nonconceptual wakefulness. On the other hand, we may really need to make use of other practices to stabilize our understanding. If stabilizing rigpa were easy for everybody and they only had to do that and nothing else, then there would not have been much point in Marpa making Milarepa go through all the various trials and tribulations that he underwent. The key point here is that if one can recognize rigpa directly, it is fine. But if it is difficult, then engage in the practices to gather accumulations and purify the obscurations in order to facilitate recognition of your buddha nature.

We may have recognized the nature of mind when it was pointed out, but if we just leave it at that and think, "Last year I received the pointing-out instruction, the transmission of mind nature. That is enough. I've got it now," it is actually not enough. For even though we may have recognized mind-essence, aren't we still completely deluded at night while sleeping? When pleasant and unpleasant events occur in dreams, we either accept or reject, feel happy or afraid and so forth; in other words, we are totally deluded. If that is the case right now, what will happen when we die? As in our present dream state, we will not even remember the teachings, let alone remember to recognize mind-essence. So there is not much chance for an unskilled practitioner to attain liberation during the bardo of dharmata. It is not enough merely to recognize mind-essence once or twice; we need to train in it again and again and become thoroughly acquainted with it so that we do not fall into confusion when meeting different kinds of experiences, even in the dream state.

At present, our days and nights are for the most part spent holding on to a sense of solid reality. We think that things are permanent when they are not; that conditioned existence is happiness when it is not; that impure phenomena are pure when they are not; that there is a true ego when actually there is not. Deluded by fixation on a solid reality, we spend our whole lives in pointless pursuits, thinking that an instant of recognition is sufficient and that later on we will definitely recognize and become liberated in the bardo of dharmata. This is extremely foolish.

Right now, while the mind is in the body, we have the freedom to choose what to do. Wouldn't it be better to spend our time training in the natural state? Stabilizing our experience of basic wakefulness is made possible by the power of our present practice. That is what is really important.

25

SPACE

Tulku Urgyen Rinpoche

Two basic principles in the innermost Dzogchen teachings are space and awareness, in Tibetan *ying* and *rigpa*. *Ying* is defined as unconstructed space devoid of concepts, while *rigpa* means the knowing of that basic space.

In the context of the threefold sky practice, outer *ying* is defined as a clear sky free from the three defects of clouds, mist, and haze. This external sky is an analogy for the actual inner ying and is used as a support for recognizing this state. The inner ying is the nature of mind, a state that is already empty. And the innermost ying, or basic space, is the recognition of buddha nature. The innermost ying is actually rigpa, nondual awareness itself.

We use the cloudless outer space as the example analogy because it is without support—in it, there is nothing for the mind to fixate on or grasp at. It is unbased, unlike all the other elements. A clear, pure sky is ideal for this practice. Because it is vast and open, it is without any support for thoughts. However, it is said that the ocean or a great lake can be used, if its surface is quiet and calm. A huge body of water can also serve as the object without support.

The reason the sky should be clear is that there should be no place or thing upon which to focus. It's a little different when the sky is cloudy, but it does not really make any difference, because it is just an example. The space or sky in front of one, even if it's confined in a tiny room, has no support. Space is essentially open and free. Since both the sky and the lake are examples, their particular form doesn't really matter, as long as the meaning is recognized.

Adapted from Tulku Urgyen Rinpoche, *As It Is*, *Vol. 1* (Boudhanath: Rangjung Yeshe Publications, 1999), "Space."

To reiterate, the outer space is the clear sky. The inner space is the primordial purity of empty mind-essence. The innermost space is the knowing of this, which is the nondual awareness itself. When training with space, do not remain in thoughts: remain in awareness.

Ying likewise implies not arising, not dwelling, and not ceasing. Ultimately, all phenomena, whatever appearances we perceive, are beyond arising, dwelling, and ceasing. The mind that perceives is also called *ying*, in the sense that mind is, by itself, empty. It is beyond arising, dwelling, and ceasing. It does not come from anywhere; it doesn't remain anywhere; it doesn't go anywhere. This describes the inner ying.

Everything that is perceived as an object is ultimately ying, basic space. Needless to say, most things don't appear this way to us. Therefore the other four elements, earth, water, fire, and wind, are not used as an example; only the element of space itself is easily comprehended as being empty. Still, the other four elements are inherently empty. If we investigate where earth, water, fire, and wind come from, we will not find a source. Look very closely: is there a place where earth comes from? Where water comes from? Where wind and fire initially come from? Right at this moment, is there an ultimate place where the four major elements are located? Try to find that. Is there a certain location that the four elements vanish into? Can we say, "They disappeared into such-and-such a place"? They are actually beyond arising, dwelling, and ceasing. That describes the outer ying, the basic space of whatever is perceived. When we discover that all external objects composed of the four elements do not arise from anywhere, do not dwell anywhere, and do not cease into some place—that everything is totally beyond arising, dwelling, and ceasing—that is called discovering the basic space of external phenomena.

Similarly, when we look into mind, the thinker, where does it come from? Where does it dwell? Where does it disappear to? In this way, we will discover the inner space that is totally beyond arising, dwelling, and ceasing. So, if external space is beyond arising, dwelling, and ceasing and inner space is beyond arising, dwelling, and ceasing, how can we make any distinction between the two? Any separation is only a matter of two different names.

Everything we perceive is made out of visual forms, sounds, smells, tastes, and textures. Look into these and investigate: Where do these arise from? Where do they dwell? Where do they go to? When we really examine this, we find there is no such thing as coming into being, dwelling anywhere, or disappearing. On a coarse level, the four major elements of earth, water, fire, and wind and, on a more subtle perceptual level, all perceived objects of form, sound, smell, taste, and texture are all discovered to be by nature beyond arising, dwelling, and ceasing. When both the perceived objects and the perceiving subject are found to be beyond arising, dwelling, and ceasing—utterly empty—everything is then just basic space. This is what is referred to as ying. In Sanskrit, the word is *dhatu*.

Ying and yeshe, basic space and wakefulness, are primordially indivisible, because our basic state is the unity of emptiness and cognizance. This is called the unity of space and wakefulness. The cognizant quality in this unity is called rigpa—awareness.

This basic state, the unity of being empty and cognizant, is at the very heart of all sentient beings. It is inherent within the thinking that takes place in all sentient beings at any moment. All beings possess this nature that is the unity of space and wakefulness, but if they don't know this, it doesn't help them. Instead of being suffused with awareness that knows itself, sentient beings become entangled in conceptualizing subject and object, thereby constantly and endlessly creating further states of samsara. All this occurs because they do not know their own nature.

This unity of space and wakefulness is sometimes called Samantabhadra, the Primordial Protector. Some people think that this basic space is totally vacant and that consciousness is something separate from that. But this is not true. Basic space and wakefulness are primordially an indivisible unity. The basic space is like water and the wakefulness is like the wetness of water. Who can separate wetness from water? If space were a flame, then wakefulness would be its heat. Who can separate heat from a flame? In the same way, basic space is always accompanied by basic wakefulness. Wakefulness is always accompanied by space. You cannot have one without the other; to think so would be a misunderstanding. To hammer it in, if space is sugar, then wakefulness is its sweetness. They are forever inseparable. This dhatu, or basic space, is the unity of being empty and cognizant. In the same way, rigpa is the unity of emptiness and cognizance.

The knowing of this nature that lies beyond complexity or constructs is called rigpa. Buddhas are empty cognizance suffused with awareness, the knowing quality, whereas the state of mind of sentient beings is empty cognizance suffused with ignorance, with unknowing. We cannot say there is any sentient being whose mind is not, at its core, the unity of emptiness and cognizance. But by not knowing this unity, their minds become a state of empty cognizance suffused with ignorance.

Let us return to the threefold sky practice. First of all, the outer empty space is simply the openness right in front of you. The inner space of empty mind is simply the empty quality of your mind. The innermost space of empty rigpa, nondual awareness, is the moment traditionally spoken of as "four parts without three." This last is what is pointed out by the guru. To try to practice this without having received the pointing-out instruction and recognized rigpa is to mingle only two, not three types of space. There are only two spaces because, whether you recognize it or not, the space outside is always empty. The space of mind is always and forever empty. There is no question about that. Is outer space composed of anything? Is your mind composed of some concrete thing? That which is without concreteness is called empty. To train in this without having recognized rigpa is merely a mingling of two, not the threefold space. This is what happens whenever an ordinary person relaxes and looks into the sky.

But here, the practice is called mingling the threefold space, not the twofold space. Once you recognize rigpa, it is possible to mingle the outer, inner, and innermost space. Otherwise, it becomes an intellectual exercise in thinking, "There's the empty sky outside. Now, here's the empty sky within. Now, I need the space of rigpa; then, I'll mingle all three together at once." It's not like this at all. To train in this fashion would be to mingle three concepts. There is one concept of a sky outside, a second concept of mind inside, and a third concept that empty rigpa must somehow appear. But actually, it is like this: you don't need to assume control of space outside. You don't need to take charge of the space within. Simply and totally disown all three—outer, inner, and the innermost space of rigpa. It is not like they need to be deliberately mingled; they are already mingled.

Your eyes need to connect with space, so do not look down at the ground but direct them upward toward space. It's certain that the mind is inherently empty, so just leave this empty mind within rigpa. This is called *already having mingled the threefold space*. In this state, it is possible to be free from fixation, but any deliberate attempt to mingle the three spaces is always fixation—thinking of space outside, thinking of space within, and then thinking, "I should mingle these two and then add rigpa." We should not call this mingling the threefold space but instead mingling the threefold concepts. And if we equate the three concepts with the state of rigpa, it makes concepts seem more important than nonconceptual awareness, rigpa.

Why should we engage in this threefold sky practice? Space, by itself, is totally unconfined. There is no center and no edge in any direction whatsoever. Directing the gaze into the midst of empty space is an aid for allowing oneself to experience the similarly unconfined and all-pervasive state of rigpa.

Outer space transcends arising, dwelling. and ceasing. This is the example for the awareness that is all-pervasive and empty, that, like space, has no end. So mingle means and knowledge. Simply leave the state of mind that you have recognized suspended within unconfined external space. The means is space, the sky; the knowledge is the awareness that has been pointed out by one's master. When suspended like this, you don't need to try to mingle space and awareness—they are already mingled, premixed.

In the ultimate sense, space and awareness are a unity. Placing unfixated awareness in supportless space serves as an enhancement for the view. That is why it is said that one should practice outside. It's best to go to a high mountaintop so that when you look out you can see sky even below where you are sitting. A vast, wide-open vista is of great benefit for understanding the view. The great Drukpa Kagyü master Lorepa spent thirteen years living on an island in one of the four great lakes of Tibet. He said using the surface of water as a support free of focal point brought him great benefit.

To reiterate, perceptions or appearances are empty; the perceiver, the mind, is also empty. Consequently, ying and rigpa are a unity. At present, however, we have split ying and rigpa into two, into *this here* and *that there*, and we do not have this unity. Doesn't it seem to us that appearances and mind are two different things? Everything seems at present to be dualistic—perceived objects and the perceiving mind—and this perception endures as long as we have conceptual thinking. That is why there are so many references in Tibetan Buddhism regarding the unity of space and awareness.

We should understand ying in the sense of both outer and inner space. The four major elements are devoid of arising, dwelling, and ceasing. The mind or consciousness is also devoid of arising, dwelling, and ceasing. Since both are free from arising, dwelling, and ceasing, they are a unity. How can we understand this? Think of the example of the space inside and outside a vase; then imagine what happens when the vase is shattered. There is a very important meaning contained in the prayer "May we realize the unity of space and awareness!"

Everything with concrete substance is called form, and all forms are the unity of appearance and emptiness: that is what is meant by the vajra body. All sounds are resounding and yet empty: this is the vajra speech. When we recognize awareness, we realize that it is free from arising, dwelling, and ceasing. That is the vajra mind. Whatever is devoid of arising, dwelling, and ceasing is empty. This is exactly what is meant by the famous statement in the *Chöying Dzö*: "Everything seen, heard, or thought is the adornment of space and appears as the continuity of Body, Speech, and Mind." In short, everything, without the exception of even a single dust mote, is of the nature of the three vajras.

Take my mala as an example. It seems as though it has physical form; it can be thrown against the table. Similarly, earth, water, fire, and wind appear to possess physical form, but "form is emptiness," as the Buddha said. Even though it seems that forms exist, they do not possess true existence; they are empty of it. The basic fact is that they can all be destroyed. Everything will be destroyed in the end, the whole world and all its different elements. All these were formed at some point, they remain for some time, and eventually they will disintegrate, to be followed by a period of complete voidness. These four periods of formation, remaining, disintegration, and voidness are equal in length.

Even now, when considering whatever seems to us to be form, the proof that it is already an empty form is the fact that it will disintegrate. "Form is emptiness" means that whatever we perceive now, whatever seems to be solid form, is merely empty form, form empty of any inherent being. The next thing the Buddha said was, "Emptiness is also form," meaning that although all things are empty, still they appear as form. This might not seem credible to us. It seems completely contradictory to what we perceive and is not very easy to understand. But all things are already empty. In the ultimate sense, they do not come into being, they do not remain anywhere, and therefore they do not cease—that is to say, all things are beyond arising, dwelling, and ceasing.

Another statement used is: "Sense objects are mere perception and therefore do not have concrete existence." That's a very important statement to remember. All sense objects are *mere perceptions*, and therefore they do not exist. Whatever appears due to causes and conditions is ultimately nothing but a moment of mere perception. Perception never really arises or comes into being, it never remains, and therefore it never ceases to be. Therefore, everything is ying, basic space beyond arising, dwelling, and ceasing. All outer perceived objects are actually space that neither arises, nor remains, nor ceases. At the same time, the perceiving mind is beyond arising, dwelling, and ceasing as well. It is not some *thing* that comes into being, remains, or ceases. So, it is not only the mind that is empty while the objects are real and concrete. If that were true, there could not be any mingling of space and awareness. Both the outside and the inside, both perceived objects and the perceiving subject, are already beyond arising, dwelling, and ceasing. Therefore, it *is* possible to train in mingling space and awareness.

26

FAMILIARIZATION

Chökyi Nyima Rinpoche

No matter what practice you do, before practicing, you should repeatedly form the attitude of renunciation toward attachment, anger, and dullness. Anger, attachment, and dullness create the three realms of samsara. There is not anywhere in these three realms of samsara that is free of the three types of suffering. Understand deeply from your heart that the creators of all suffering are karma and disturbing emotions. If karma and disturbing emotions could not possibly be cleared away, there would be nothing we could do. Karma and disturbing emotions are the nasty roots of suffering and deluded experience, but they can be eliminated. They have one good quality: they are momentary; they can be cleared up.

There are two ways to clear up karma and disturbing emotions: the mundane, regular way and the spiritual way. The mundane way is when we tell one another, "Don't worry, relax, take it easy." Understand those words, because they are in fact very powerful. Often the one who says, "Relax, take it easy, don't worry," may not be aware of what those words hold. Nonetheless, they are extremely beneficial to say to someone. And not only to say them to human beings but to our pets as well. We pat them and say, "There, there, relax, take it easy." It does help. "Don't worry" means don't think so much; don't think so much about whatever you're thinking of. It can also mean don't think so much at all. "Take it easy" means be carefree. "Relax" means don't fixate on anything; release your conceptual attitude. These three phrases actually do have a very powerful meaning. *Relax, don't worry, take it easy.* If you don't particularly know how to be relaxed and not

Adapted from Chökyi Nyima Rinpoche, *Present Fresh Wakefulness* (Boudhanath: Rangjung Yeshe Publications, 2002), "Familiarization Not Meditation."

worry, just to be told may not ultimately help so much. But listen to their opposites: "Be uptight! Worry, please! Be jumpy! Be nervous! Be speedy!"

> Disturbing emotions come because of thinking.
> Thoughts produce emotions,
> Thoughts create karma.
> Therefore, don't follow past thought,
> Don't invite future thought.
> In the present moment, do not correct,
> Do not modify,
> Do not accept or reject.
> Don't try to rearrange your present wakefulness.
> Instead, leave it as it naturally is
> Without any attempt to alter it in any way.
> That is called sustaining your natural face.
> The moment you let be in uncontrived naturalness,
> The essence of your mind is empty
> And at the same time cognizant.
> Cognizing while being empty,
> This is the natural state.

Letting be in naturalness does not mean being absentminded or dull; it is conscious and present. But this clear and cognizant sense of being awake does not necessarily hold on to anything. The Dzogchen teachings call this the primordially pure state of the thorough cut. It is the intent of the fourth empowerment, the nondual great bliss that is present throughout all states, samsaric or nirvanic. When we apply this to ourselves, it is the sense of being empty and uninvolved, utterly naked, wide awake, and vividly clear. When we are involved in thoughts of the three spheres, naked awareness is not seen. When we are not conceptualizing the three spheres, original mind is empty and wide awake, free from fixation. This is also called awareness wisdom, the knowing wakefulness. On a coarse, general level, there are no disturbing emotions present at that moment, and on a more subtle level, the conceptual attitude that fixates is absent.

Just as mercury is never mixed with dust, this empty and cognizant original wakefulness is untainted by karma and disturbing emotions, by the dust of conceptual attitudes. For a short moment, our body may be human, but our mind is a buddha. Because it lasts for such a brief moment, the qualities of abandonment and realization have no chance to become fully manifest. However, there is one special, unique quality already manifest that is unlike any ordinary state of mind. At that moment of recognition, there is no karma or disturbing emotion. The stream of karma and disturbing emotions has been interrupted; it is not present. This is the experience of emptiness, but we have not yet mastered it, we have not trained fully in it. This original, ordinary mind, the primordially pure state of the thorough cut, is real, but because we are not completely used to it, the continuity is not sustained. We may momentarily recognize the empty, aware state of Mahamudra, the natural state, which is the Great Perfection. Unless we grow used to it and have some stability, it will not help that much. Imagine a small child on a battlefield. The child is in a hopeless position, utterly unable to fight, to defend itself. In the same way, the recognition of mind-essence may be genuine, but it has not really "grown up" enough to be able to cope with all situations.

The training in Mahamudra or Dzogchen is not an act of meditating, because any act of meditation is by definition conceptual. Whatever is a training in being conceptual is not a training in the natural state. Mahamudra and Dzogchen training means not fabricating anything, just allowing the continuity of our natural state. This is not our habit. We must train in developing a new habit, but this practice is not *meditation,* but *familiarization.* When we finally arrive at the dharmakaya throne of nonmeditation, there is nothing more to cultivate; there is not even an atom to meditate upon, and yet we are not distracted for even an instant. We need to train in this. It is also phrased as mental nondoing. Nothing is to be done or made in the realm of mind. Mental nondoing is Mahamudra, but do not just sit with the idea "I should not do." To make something in one's mind is conceptual, and to think, "I should do nothing in my mind" is also conceptual.

In the guidance manuals for meditation, it is often phrased like this: Do not alter your present fresh wakefulness. Do not rearrange even as much as a hair tip. Just leave it exactly as it is. This is very profound, and there is a lot to understand here. When people hear about the awakened state, buddha-mind, they think it must be something fantastic, something flabbergasting, totally out of this world. Everything must have disappeared, fallen apart, dissolved. It must be totally unique, unlike anything that they have experienced. With all these enormous preconceptions, one easily ignores the reality of buddha-mind.

> Allow your mind to be composed,
> Empty and awake, alive and vibrant.
> Allow it to be as it naturally is.
>
> Leave it without the need to modify.
> Do not alter this present ordinary mind.
> Be free of accepting and rejecting,
> Correcting, or rearranging
> Your present fresh wakefulness.

That itself is the empty, awake awareness that we call *recognizing*. When this awareness is not focused on something, then it is naturally wide open, undirected. That is exactly what is meant in the statement "the five senses wide open, awareness undirected." Be like that. Rest in the equanimity of that.

There is a sense of awakeness in our present ordinary mind that is not fixated on anything whatsoever. It is unpolluted, pure. When leaving this fresh ordinary mind as it is, without correcting or modifying it, without altering it in any way, without accepting and rejecting, there is no fixating on anything. When one does not direct the mind toward anything, the normal conceptual attitudes that hold things to be permanent, to be real, that "this is me and that is other"—they are all absent. There is total freedom from karma and disturbing emotion.

The key point of the training is this: short moments, many times. Trying to keep awareness too long produces dullness or agitation. Rather than worrying about the length of experience, place the emphasis on that which is genuinely the naturally empty, awake, and unfixated state. Even though it may not last very long, that's okay; it's better to be genuine. Any other state we try to prolong is a made-up "natural state." We may be able to keep that for a long while, but even though it lasts a long time, it is not going to be helpful for true progress.

How do we verify that our natural state is genuine, real, authentic? It must be unmixed with concept. The moment a conceptual attitude is formed, rigpa is polluted, corrupted. *Short moments, many times*—the length of our recognition at this stage probably is only short moments. When we try to stretch it out, what we nurture becomes conceptual; it becomes artificial. But if due to our training the innate nature continues naturally for quite a while, it doesn't mean that we have to cut it short.

That likewise would be conceptual. The point is that we do not have to do anything to it: we do not have to make it short, nor do we have to make it last long.

The Dzogchen teachings tell us to *strip awareness to its naked state*; to separate dualistic mind and rigpa. This means be free of fixation, be free of conceptual attitude. If we hold any conceptual attitude or fix the attention on something, rigpa is not naked; it is covered. The moment no conceptual attitude is formed, the moment attention is not fixed on something, present fresh ordinary mind, present fresh wakefulness, is by itself naked and awake. Just sustain it like that. Ordinary mind or self-existing awareness is characterized as being wide open, while dualistic mind is confined.

Therefore, in our practice, when we notice the state that is wide open, vast, free of reference point, that is ordinary mind, self-existing awareness. When we notice that our state is confined, focused on something, with a reference point, that is dualistic mind. We should know how to make this distinction. Believing that we are sustaining the natural state of mind while we are in fact caught up with ordinary thinking is not much use. We need to identify the genuine, the authentic—this is important. We need to identify that which is utterly empty, utterly naked, not confined to anything, totally clear and cognizant, yet not fixated on anything.

Do you have any doubts, any uncertainty?

STUDENT: Why are only the five senses wide open and not the sixth consciousness?

RINPOCHE: The sixth is connected to the other five. To just have open eyes does not mean there is clear seeing, unless that is connected with mind consciousness; isn't that so?

STUDENT: Is it possible to be in a state of emptiness and still be involved in fixation?

RINPOCHE: When composing ourselves in equanimity, we notice if there is physical discomfort. It catches our attention again and again. It is not like our minds are half empty and at the same time half distracted. It is more a back-and-forth movement between the two states. Our attention is caught by something, then it is released again.

STUDENT: Rinpoche, you were saying there is an awareness without concepts. Is that true?

Rinpoche: Awareness, Dzogchen awareness, is by definition unmixed with concept.

Student: Wow!

Rinpoche: Good reply.

Student: In rigpa, I sometimes recognize the quality of emptiness, clarity and bliss, but I do not get the vastness very often at all. Does that come with more familiarization? Is that a sign that I am somehow fixated, spatially?

Rinpoche: When you totally release every single type of focus and reference point, totally let go, it is impossible not to have that openness and vastness.

Student: I must be sticking somewhere then.

Rinpoche: Yes. A sign of some subtle clinging lingering on.

Student: What is the most skillful way to deal with dullness?

Rinpoche: There are outer ways and inner ways. The outer way is to go up to a higher location with a vast view, a greater vista; you wear less clothing so that you're not too warm; and you raise your gaze upward. You can also expel your breath forcefully, all of a sudden. There is a specific oral instruction in exclaiming the sound *phat,* abruptly and forcefully.

The inner way is to apply mindfulness; either the deliberate or effortless type of reminding, both of which remind you to just be empty, awake, and totally clear again. This means that *the feeling of being dull or drowsy is just another thought.* Abandon that thought.

Student: Practice is one thing, but as soon as I stand up, I solidify my experience again. There is immediately an "I" when I get up. Whenever I try to apply the method while not formally practicing, while walking around or doing anything, it is nothing but fabricating. It drives me crazy because I realize how distracted I am all the time. The method does not seem to work unless I am just sitting down practicing.

Rinpoche: This is where you see the importance of keeping sessions. We have our waking time; we divide that up into sessions and breaks. That is important. During the sessions, there is the meditative state and the postmeditation. When you put your body in a certain balanced posture with the back straight and the breathing natural and unforced, certain factors are aligned. These factors coming together have a certain influence on our state of mind. It is said that when the right coincidence is formed through the body, realization occurs in the mind. Isn't it true that when you put yourself in this posture, your state of mind feels different, more relaxed and open? The posture forms a coincidence for the state of realization.

Now we have begun training in the meditative state, right? As we train, we become more and more used to being this way. When one is really trained, to the extent of being stable, it becomes possible and easier to be that way during the postmeditation. You can then mingle the meditation state with everyday situations of eating, sitting, speaking, and lying down. The most difficult is when lying down, when sleeping, when dreaming. We need to train during all these situations. Lingje Repa, one of the great masters of the Drukpa Kagyü lineage, said:

> The guru said, train in the original nature,
> Which I did, again and again.
> But now my meditation of sessions and breaks has vanished,
> What should I do now?

What you said is true. But some people get more thoughts when they sit. They find that if they move, the situation is a little better, especially if they travel in a bus or taxi, not driving themselves.

STUDENT: I am a little fearful of giving up everything, even though I do experience emptiness and clarity. I have this Western tendency to feel there must be something material there. There cannot be just nothing.

RINPOCHE: That must be the blessing of science.

STUDENT: Will this eventually dissolve through practice?

RINPOCHE: Intellectually you can convince yourself that this empty cognizance is immaterial, in the sense of being inconcrete. And through your own practice, you can prove that experientially. During the authentic meditation state you understand that it is not solid matter. Therefore, when you train repeatedly in letting go of thoughts and preconceived ideas, again and again they will increasingly vanish. It will get better and easier.

STUDENT: How do we prolong the recognition of mind-essence?

RINPOCHE: Meditation in this context is the duration of sustaining the essence. Essence here refers to what we really are, the awake and empty state that is not made out of any material thing whatsoever—utterly open, yet wide awake. We need to sustain this, or, in other words, to keep this as an ongoing presence. For that to happen, a method is necessary. It is indispensable to remind ourselves to recognize our essence, to use the method of *remindfulness*. There is no way around this as long as we are beginners. At first, this remindfulness is an intentional reminding called deliberate mindfulness; later it becomes effortless mindfulness. Mindfulness of whichever type is definitely necessary; otherwise, we never recognize. After forgetting the natural state, apply the reminding repeatedly. Do so not only when sitting down in a session, but at any given moment.

It is as I just said: short moments, many times. When we sit down to meditate, it may seem as if we have to get into a particular state: "Now I am meditating, and it should last for a long while." This is possible for the very rare person, but mostly when one thinks, "I am in the natural state for quite a while," either it is just make-believe, like pretending to oneself, or it is a complete fabrication. We really need to question whether it is the genuine natural state if it lasts for quite a while. It would be better if we were just very honest about this, since we do not really need to pretend to ourselves that we are in a superb, ongoing natural state. It is much better when we just allow it to be as long as it lasts, without trying to create something artificial. First, we remind ourselves to recognize our essence; next, we allow that to last. If lasts only a short time, let it be short; if it lasts a long time, let it be long. We do not have to cut it short, because that would be artificial. We do not have to sit and hold it for a long time, which is also artificial. Be totally without artifice! That is how to train.

As soon as you forget the natural state, use the reminding again, either deliberately or effortlessly. This is how we can progress: through *short moments, many times*, through recognizing repeatedly. To reiterate this point, recognize not only during the meditation session, but at all possible times. Often, when people are lucky to set aside twenty minutes a day, they call that their "meditation practice." But real practitioners do not limit their practice to the meditation session. They practice while walking around, reminding themselves to recognize the essence. By practicing while talking, while eating, while doing any kind of activity, they have all their time to practice, instead of only short periods. If we only practice for short periods and nothing much happens after many years, we may blame the Dharma or the teachings: "Those instructions were supposed to be so high and profound, but look what happened—not much!" Really, though, we only have ourselves to blame.

Instead, train all the time in sustaining the essence. When we do so, real and swift progress is possible. It is like medicine: it only helps if you eat it. Medicine is meant to cure disease. In the same way, our practice is meant to cure the basic disease that causes all of our karmic doing, emotions, and deluded states. That root cause is the very subtle conceptual attitude. And the only thing that can really cut through that, at the very root, is to recognize the nature of mind and simply allow it to be that way, as it naturally is, without any contriving or modifying. Do not try to correct or improve upon it by accepting, rejecting, or placing our mind in a certain state. Rather, train in being totally uncontrived and natural; this is how the root cause of samsara is cut through. At the very moment of recognizing mind-essence, there is no karmic doing, there are no emotions, there is no delusion. All these have been cleared up totally at that moment. We need to train in it. We need to grow used to it. Growing used to it does not mean that it is an act of meditating, like visualizing a deity or concentrating on a sense of quietness, as in shamatha. This training in the vipashyana that is thought-free wakefulness is not an act of meditating, because there is no *thing* being cultivated by meditating. Being totally free of meditating, being totally free of holding something in mind—*that* is the ultimate training.

27

A Comparison Between Mahamudra and Dzogchen

Tsele Natsok Rangdröl

Generally speaking, numerous different types of teaching styles exist in the various traditions of Mahamudra and Dzogchen. In particular, it is unquestionably established that in the ultimate sense there is no difference between Mahamudra and Dzogchen. Nonetheless, according to their presentation, varying approaches have been taught concerning whether or not to regard appearances as being mind, whether or not thought is identical with dharmakaya, and whether or not mindfulness should serve as meditation.

Some Mahamudra followers teach that Dzogchen is the type of sidetrack known as straying into the innate, while the higher stages of Dzogchen teach that Mahamudra is flawed since everything up to and including Mahamudra is considered to be views retaining assumptions. Thus, each has its own specific emphasis.

For worthy practitioners, those who have sat at the feet of a qualified master and have recognized the innate suchness of the natural state exactly as it is, there is nothing to classify—for them, everything is simply the display of dharmata. In Mahamudra it is renowned as ground Mahamudra, or Mahamudra of the natural state. Since everyone agrees that practicing the various types of meditation stages is the method for realizing it, the Dzogchen system is, therefore, not at fault.

Similarly, to call Mahamudra an assumed view is aimed at inferior people who practice that way. Practitioners who realize the nature of Mahamudra as it is, perceive the naked and innate face of mind free from concepts. They are not flawed by this fault since they don't need to depend on assumptions.

Adapted from Tsele Natsok Rangdröl, *Circle of the Sun* (Boudhanath: Rangjung Yeshe Publications, 1990), "A Comparison between Mahamudra and Dzogchen."

Moreover, the two opinions about whether or not thoughts are dharmakaya are in fact the same. The commonplace thought—uninhibited deluded fixation—is not regarded as dharmakaya, even by the Mahamudra system. Similarly, the Dzogchen system does not repress perceptions that have been embraced by the key points. So, in fact, they agree.

As for whether or not appearance is mind: all the key points are identical, in the sense that in the ultimate essence, appearance lies beyond the confines of truth and falsehood. It can manifest in any way possible as a mere relative expression of mind but does not consist of any essence whatsoever. Appearances, furthermore, need not be accepted or rejected and so forth.

Concerning mindfulness serving or not serving as the meditation, some deluded people appear to concentrate with rigid fixation and believe that keeping their mind hostage is the meditation of Mahamudra. That is nothing but their own fault. The authentic great Kagyü masters took self-cognizant mindfulness as their practice, which is identical to the primordially pure self-awareness of the Dzogchen system. Thus, despite different terminology, there is no difference in meaning. Neither system, Mahamudra nor Dzogchen, considers that meditation is the conceptual mind that fixates on mindfulness.

In short, what Dzogchen calls *endowed with the threefold wisdom*—the wisdom of the primordially pure essence, the wisdom of the spontaneously present nature, and the wisdom of the all-pervasive capacity—is described by the followers of Mahamudra as the nonarising essence, the unobstructed nature, and the variously manifesting expression. It is unanimously agreed that they are different aspects of the same identity.

28

CORRELATING
MAHAMUDRA AND DZOGCHEN

Trulshik Adeu Rinpoche

The Mahamudra and Dzogchen systems are identical in essence—you may follow one or the other—yet each has unique instructions. Dzogchen has a particular set of teachings known as Tögal, and the approach of pointing out rigpa directly is found only in the Dzogchen teachings. Mahamudra is exceptional in the instructions known as the nine cycles of mingling.

When embarking on meditation practice in the Mahamudra tradition, the meditator is taught three aspects: *stillness, occurrence,* and *noticing.*

The cultivation of stillness means to train in cutting off involvement in memories; you disengage from entertaining any thought about what has happened in the past. The same regards the future: you are not supposed to construct any plans about the next moment. And in the present, right now, simply and completely let go. Drop everything and settle into nowness. In the Mahamudra tradition, stillness refers to just *being* this way—not following thoughts about the past, the future, or the present, not churning out any new thoughts.

A beginner will notice that totally letting be without any thought involvement does not last that long. Due to the karmic force of the energy currents, new thoughts are formed—thoughts grasping at subject and object, at the pleasant and unpleasant. The activation of such patterns is known as occurrence.

When the attention is quiet and still, there is a knowing that this is so. When one is involved in thinking about this and that, there is a knowing that this is so. In this context of stillness and thought occurrence, this know-

---

From oral teachings given at Rigpa, San Francisco. 1999.

ing is called noticing. These are the three aspects known as stillness, occurrence, and noticing.

Now, the training is this: Each time you notice that you are thinking of something, you disengage from it and pull back—suspending your attention—into being quiet, into being still, and simply remain like that. When after a while you notice that you are thinking about something, again simply return to the stillness. That is the training. By repeating this over and over, you become more familiar, more experienced. That is how to progress.

As you grow more capable, there comes a point when the thought occurrences no longer have such a strong hold on the attention. It becomes easier to arrive back in the quietness. Then later, every time a thought again begins to stir, rather than getting caught up in it, we are able to simply remain, until the force of the thought occurrence weakens and the aware quality grows and strengthens. The dividing line between stillness and occurrence fades away. That is the point at which we can recognize the actual identity of noticing what it really is. In other words, vipashyana can begin.

The great yogi Milarepa said, "In the gap between the past thought and the following thought, thought-free wakefulness continuously dawns." This is the way it is whether you recognize it or not, so the difference is to recognize. The opportunity to recognize is there all the time, and that is the training. In the beginning, a thought vanishes; that is called stillness. Next, a new thought arises; that is called thought occurrence, and one notices that these are happening. These three—stillness, thought occurrence, and noticing—have to do with becoming increasingly aware of the gap between thoughts. This aware quality grows stronger and stronger, which happens only through training; you cannot pull on the gap to make it bigger. You cannot artificially increase the power of training. At some point, once you recognize that which notices and what the awake quality is, that is the difference between shamatha and vipashyana in this context.

If your shamatha practice is simply training in being absentminded, remaining in a neutral, indifferent state without any thought activity whatsoever, this is known in the Dzogchen system as the all-ground. It is simply a way of being free of thought involvement. When attention becomes active within the expanse of the all-ground, according to Dzogchen, that activity is known as dualistic mind. But when the dividing line between stillness and thought occurrence fades away and instead the strength of the aware quality is intensified, that awake quality, according to Dzogchen, is known as rigpa. Depending on whether one is using the Mahamudra system or the Dzogchen approach, there are different terminologies, but the actual training is essentially the same in both cases.

According to the Dzogchen instructions, there are three points in regard to this context. First is tracking down dualistic mind, or the normal attention. Second is discovering the secret identity, dualistic mind's hidden way. And third is revealing its vanishing point. Tracking down means investigating how dualistic mind, the attentive quality, behaves, where it comes from, where it is right now, and where it goes. The second point is actually finding out what it is, namely, a seeming presence—there is actually no *thing* there. It is just some behavior that is mistaken for being a real thing; actually there is no thing there whatsoever. It is only when we investigate that we discover that this attentive quality is no thing whatsoever. Yet it has fooled us. It is what is called a nonexistent or seeming presence. The last point—revealing the vanishing point of dualistic mind—is that the moment you look into where this attentive quality is and what it is made of, you discover that there is no actual thing; it simply vanishes every time you look. This is the approach, according to Dzogchen, to finding out what dualistic mind really is.

This is how to discover and lead into the actuality of rigpa, because first we need to be clear about what dualistic mind is. Try to find out the identity of this awake quality that clings to reality. Where did mind come from? Where is it right now? When it is no more, where did it go? That is called inquiring into the arrival, remaining, and disappearance of dualistic mind.

This is the point when rigpa can be introduced or pointed out in actuality. The procedure, however, begins with shamatha, which is accompanied by certain experiences or meditative moods called bliss, clarity, and nonthought. Once one proceeds into the vipashyana quality in an uninterrupted way, so that one is no longer distractedly flitting here and there but has some ability to sustain that meditative state of mind, this is called one-pointedness, the first stage of Mahamudra. Continuing through that, you reach a level of progress known as simplicity, which leads into another state known as one taste, and finally you achieve a state known as nonmeditation, or, literally, noncultivation. This means that there is no longer anything that needs to be brought forth or cultivated by an agent cultivating it. In other words, the primordial state of enlightenment is discovered. Mind-essence was pre-enlightened; our original ground is already enlightened.

In the Dzogchen approach, this discovery is called being re-enlightened. Mahamudra does not use these terms re-enlightened and pre-enlightened, but at the fourth stage of nonmeditation the meaning is basically the same.

The Dzogchen path begins with being pointed out the actuality of rigpa. This is like being shown the beginning of the road, which does not mean that one should stand there and wait. One must move forward. Sometimes people misunderstand and think that having received the pointing-out instruction and recognized rigpa in one's experience is enough and that they have gone all the way. It is not enough. Recognizing rigpa is only the beginning of the Dzogchen path. We need to follow through, and it requires a lot of perseverance. Of course you could say that the perseverance is effortless, but this definitely does not mean that we should ignore the need for practice. It is said that there are two types of Dzogchen practitioners: the lazy type and the diligent type. For the lazy type there is the practice of Trekchö, the training in primordial purity. For the diligent practitioner there is the Tögal path of training in spontaneous presence. But in both cases one does not stand still and wait. Giving the pointing-out instruction is like pointing to the ground and saying, "This is the road to Lhasa." If you just stand there, you will never get to Lhasa. You need to proceed step by step along the road, putting one foot in front of the other. Similarly, having recognized rigpa, you need to train and progress along the path.

There are four stages of development in Dzogchen. The first stage comes with recognizing rigpa in actuality, which is sometimes called manifest dharmata, or your innate nature—the natural state seen as it actually is. As you progress in this and your experience deepens, it is called increased meditative experience. Third is awareness-rigpa reaching fullness, and the fourth stage is called the exhaustion or depletion of all concepts and dualistic phenomena. This stage is equivalent to the stage of nonmeditation in Mahamudra. The ultimate state of enlightenment is being re-enlightened in the pre-enlightened original ground, as mentioned above. The important Dzogchen master Paltrul Rinpoche often told his disciples, "You should leave room for progress. You should not think that you are already there and that there is nothing more to attain. Even though it is the state of rigpa, leave room for progress. Don't be satisfied yet; it is too early. There is still room for improvement in your practice."

What is pointed out according to the Mahamudra approach is the true state of original wakefulness as your ordinary mind. Once this has been pointed out to you, it is called mind-essence, and the instruction is: "Look into mind-essence. Sustain mind-essence. That is the way." According to the Dzogchen instructions, what is pointed out is called the intrinsic original wakefulness that is present within you. This is called rigpa. You are supposed to recognize rigpa and sustain it. There is no real difference between these two teachings. Of course, there are some extra instructions in the two systems. It is like approaching Bodhgaya from the south or the north: the roads lead to the same destination. The pointing-out instruction is the same as showing the unmistaken way that leads straight to Bodhgaya. If one truly recognizes the way and what one needs to train in to be enlightened and follows this exactly, then there is no doubt that this is the unmistaken path. However, one must still follow the path. How swiftly you reach the goal is entirely up to you and your diligence.

After having given Gampopa all the necessary instructions on meditation, Milarepa told him, "Now it is up to you to go and practice." As Gampopa was leaving, Milarepa accompanied him for a stretch. At one point he stopped and told Gampopa, "I have given you all the teachings, but there is one instruction I have held back." Gampopa thought he should make a mandala offering and made preparations to do so, to which Milarepa said, "There is no need to offer a mandala. I will just give you this teaching." Then he turned around, lifted his skirt, and bared his buttocks. They were so callused that Gampopa could not tell whether they were made of flesh, stone, or wood. After he had given his student a good look, Milarepa said, "If you want to reach perfection in meditation practice, then you should sit as I have. I sat on solid stone continuously for so long that my butt is like a fossil—it's as hard as stone. You should train with this kind of perseverance. That is my last instruction." So, it is not enough to just look at where you are standing and think that you have arrived somewhere else. The recognition of the awakened state of rigpa is not enlightenment but the path to enlightenment. One needs to develop the full strength of this recognition by continually training.

Now let's identify what the real substance of meditation practice is. What is it that we are actually supposed to train in during a meditation session? Generally it is spoken of as being "natural" or "ordinary mind," but what is that? Does it mean our normal state of mind or the specific natural state of mind as described in the Great Perfection? The great tertön of Trengpo district, Sherab Özer, said, "It is not enough to suspend your attention into not distinguishing between anything at all. Simply not meditating or keeping any concept of meditator or meditation object is not enough. This is likely just a vacant state of absentmindedness that is the basis for all of samsaric existence and nirvana as well." What is necessary is to identify the ground of liberation, the natural state of rigpa that is not the same as the ordinary state of mind known in Dzogchen as the all-ground. No matter how many thousands of years one trains in the state of the all-ground, there will be absolutely no progress; one will simply arise again in the state of samsara. Whereas training in the natural state of mind of rigpa is nothing other than the ground of liberation. So it is important to distinguish the normal, ordinary mind of the all-ground and the natural ordinary mind that is the ground of liberation and train accordingly.

That which is pointed out as the essence of the meditation practice according to Mahamudra is within the ordinary natural state of mind; it is pointed out as being the original true wakefulness. According to Dzogchen, it is the self-knowing original wakefulness that is pointed out in our ordinary state of mind. Having recognized this, one can then proceed to train in it, and as the training deepens, according to Mahamudra there are certain stages of progress described as the four yogas of Mahamudra, each of which is further divided into the three categories of lesser, medium, and higher capacity. These are collectively known as the twelve aspects of the four yogas of the path of Mahamudra. Another approach is to apply the structure of the four yogas to each of the yogas, resulting in sixteen aspects. These are equally valid and merely describe the ever-deepening levels of experience and stability in the natural ordinary mind.

The Dzogchen path has a similar explanation. According to Trekchö, there is a growing sense of becoming more and more accustomed to the state of rigpa, which could be described as the stages of the path known as the four visions. These four can also be applied to the practice of Tögal.

But whether you follow Dzogchen or Mahamudra, please understand that ultimately there is no real difference. There is not one awakened state called Mahamudra and a separate one known as the Great Perfection. It is all of one taste within the expanse of dharmakaya. What these two words actually refer to is the basic nature of all things. Since all phenomena, all that appears and exists within samsara and nirvana, have the stamp of great bliss, therefore it is called "the Great Seal," which is the literal meaning of *Mahamudra*. Similarly, since all phenomena, no matter what or how, are perfected in the expanse of self-existing awareness, it is called Dzogchen, or Great Perfection.

The fruition, the final result of the path, is described as awakening to true enlightenment within the expanse of the three kayas, in the sense that the empty essence is realized as dharmakaya, the cognizant nature is realized as sambhogakaya, and the ever-present capacity is realized as nirmanakaya. These three kayas are also realized as being indivisible within the single sphere of original wakefulness, and this holds true whether we call that state of fruition Mahamudra or Dzogchen.

29

MAINTENANCE

Tsoknyi Rinpoche

There is a famous phrase: "Knowing how to meditate but not how to be free—isn't that like the meditation gods?" Certainly we must possess the vital point of practice, but that doesn't mean we grasp at or try to own that experience too seriously. Allow it to be opened up completely. After recognizing, we can emphasize looseness rather than trying to keep a tight grip on rigpa. It is taught that after recognizing rigpa we can from time to time give importance to three qualities: one is *looseness*, another is *brightness*, and the third is *lucidity*. Brightness has to do with having vivid senses—when, for instance, sitting outside in the practice of mingling the threefold sky. The five senses are wide open, not closed in on themselves, simply present. Lucidity is more a quality of being clear that is not dependent upon sensory clarity. Rather it has to do with the clarity of rigpa itself, independent of whether the senses are bright or dull.

It is taught that as soon as rigpa is introduced and recognized, the most important thing to do for a couple of days is just to emphasize a sense of looseness. Do not keep hold of it at all. Be very open, very free, very relaxed about the whole matter. Cultivate an attitude of abandon. One does not really care too much about keeping that which has been recognized; one simply allows it. Focus simply on this for a couple of days. Then, within that state, emphasize a bright presence of mind. After a while, you add the lucid quality. When you train like this, you arrive in a very genuine way at undivided and aware emptiness.

When a beginner recognizes the awakened state of rigpa for the first time, it is, of course, a big deal because it may be something that one has

Adapted from Tsoknyi Rinpoche, *Fearless Simplicity* (Boudhanath: Rangjung Yeshe Publications, 2003), "Maintenance."

waited for and looked forward to for quite a while. It is so important, so precious. Therefore, of course, one tries one's best to maintain it and hold on to it: "This shouldn't slip away. This is so special, I must keep it!" That self-conscious attitude, not wanting to let it slip away, makes us tense, and the looseness disappears. Therefore, especially remember this: be loose and relaxed. When you have this looseness, emphasize a bright or sharp quality. Please understand this point.

The Dzogchen definition of "meditation state" is *while the duration of rigpa lasts*. This state of composure is while you have not strayed from the continuity of rigpa. When straying, it is considered postmeditation, as it's no longer the state of rigpa. Thus, the dividing line between composure and postmeditation consists in distraction or nondistraction. When you are distracted, it is postmeditation; when undistracted, it is composure. When distracted, it is dualistic mind; when undistracted, it is rigpa.

A lot of questions usually come up at this point: Is shamatha training a state of distraction? Is the act of visualizing during development stage a state of distraction? Is recitation of mantras a state of distraction? How about cultivating loving-kindness? When one is explaining the Dzogchen teachings on their own terms, the answer is yes, those are states of distraction. But one must add that these are first-class states of distraction, especially loving-kindness. For most people it is quite difficult to be distracted in those noble ways even when they try. Isn't it true that most people find it quite difficult to be continuously loving and kind? To have very clear visualization in the development stage is also not easy. To have one-pointed concentration in shamatha is easier said than done, isn't it? So from time to time it is perfectly all right to make the wish "May I attain that type of distraction."

In terms of the teachings of the Great Perfection, we have to agree that those states are still dualistic mind, albeit a very fine type of dualistic mind, one that we sometimes need. Nevertheless, the states of distraction *are* distracted states. Occasionally people blunder at exactly this point and lose interest in cultivating any dualistic state such as loving-kindness, one-pointedness of shamatha, or development stage. That is surely a mistake. From time to time we should certainly cultivate those.

The real problem is if one frowns upon dualistic practices because of hearing that the nondual state of rigpa is the real thing. One might incorrectly feel that trying to be compassionate and cultivating noble qualities is an inferior type of practice, so why bother? Unfortunately, the loving-kindness and compassion that should be spontaneously present within the awakened state haven't manifested yet. One is in a vacant and dry blankness where nothing much happens. To fixate one's mind on the unconditioned while rejecting noble qualities is an obstacle. It is a self-created hindrance for practitioners of particularly this type of practice. This obstacle is called "the demonic view of black dissipation," a view that gives credence to neither good nor evil. You could say that it is "Mara's blessing" that causes one to go astray. One feels no interest in cultivating good qualities because such practice is "too conceptual," but one does not naturally have any good qualities either, so nothing happens. That is a big obstacle, and it is one of the reasons the Dzogchen teachings are kept secret. Not because there is anything wrong with the teachings—there is absolutely nothing wrong when they are practiced correctly—but it is possible for an individual to misconstrue the process, and this is where the danger lies. We don't want to do anyone a disservice, do we? The obstacle is definitely not the fault of the Dzogchen teachings, nor is it some kind of built-in flaw in the state of rigpa. It is the individual practitioner's fault for not understanding how to practice correctly.

One can also misunderstand at the outset of the practice how rigpa really is. Yes, it is spacious and open, but it's not simply an extroverted spacious ego. In this distortion, ego is not dissolved, it just makes itself outwardly spacious: "There is so much space there. I am so open. I am *so* open!" And then one stays like that, vacant and frozen. One trains again and again in keeping this open, vacant, frozen state that is definitely not rigpa. If it were truly rigpa, the compassionate qualities and devotion would naturally appear. True practitioners of rigpa sincerely appreciate their guru and the lineage of teachings. True practitioners understand the futility of samsaric aims, and renunciation genuinely arises within their mind. But since it isn't really rigpa, these qualities are not allowed to unfold.

A specific psychological problem accompanies this particular distortion of rigpa, arising as a sort of side effect. It reveals itself whenever one is confronted with doing something noble or meaningful. The misguided Dzogchen yogi tells himself or herself, "I shouldn't do this, because it's dualistic." If compelled to take part in dualistic practices, one feels guilty, as if one had betrayed this vacant, spacious ego. Ego is not self-liberated at this point, not at all, because the knowing of its empty essence is missing.

There is a plastered-over, empty feeling, and cultivating this habit becomes a problem because one becomes stuck there. One simply does not want to create any type of meritorious attitude because one imagines that this would be betraying the Dzogchen teachings. One would rather not develop any further.

This distortion is potentially a huge obstacle. If this arises, one especially needs to supplicate one's guru, receive more instruction, and then dive into the conceptual practices of loving-kindness, training in compassion, and so forth in order to perfect the accumulations. Give up altogether the "state of rigpa" that one was hanging on to so seriously and say, "I don't care for this; let me continue along the path. Obviously I took a wrong turn; let me go on now."

Being caught up in this distortion is actually one huge distraction. It is not the true path. You know the two aspects of means and knowledge? All the different practices that belong to means have very few sidetracks. There is really nothing that can be turned upside down, inverted and distorted. The practice I mainly teach belongs more to the knowledge aspect, especially the view of the Great Perfection. The path of means has few sidetracks, so that one doesn't really go wrong while trying to accumulate merit. Some pitfalls are possible when doing completion stage with attributes, such as *tummo* practice, *tsa-lung,* and the like, but otherwise not much can go wrong.

About this issue Nagarjuna said, "To regard things as concrete is to be as stupid as a cow, but to regard things as inconcrete is to be even more foolish." We may do good actions with the attitude "This is real; this is concrete, solid reality." This attitude is not really so bad, because some good still comes out of it, and the opportunity for realizing the illusory nature of everything remains open. On the other hand, the fixation on the nihilistic view that nothing is real is very hard to cure by means of the Dharma teachings, because one has already decided that nothing is real; one has denied everything. To switch to again acknowledging that there is a certain degree of reality is very difficult. It is much easier to change from believing that everything is real to believing that it is unreal than the opposite.

We may hold these notions in mind: "There is a buddha, and enlightenment is wonderful. There are these offerings, and there is me. I like to give them. I am giving them. I will get something out of it in my future life. It is all good!" This is not such a big mistake. Of course, we are being similar to a cow here, but at least we are no worse than a cow. The other attitude is: "This is all useless! Why should I do that? What is the use of lighting a candle? It's just a candle; it's merely oil in a lamp. How can there be any merit in lighting the wick of a butter lamp? All right, molecules are heated up to a higher temperature so that they emit light, and that light extends into various directions, but where is the merit? I don't see it anywhere. I don't see how lighting something is going to help me. They say there is a buddha named Amitabha in a buddhafield, but I haven't seen one; he's never spoken to me. As far as I'm concerned, he doesn't exist!"

That kind of cynical attitude makes it easy to settle one's mind upon the idea that *there is nothing*—in other words, upon a nihilistic view. There is a certain nihilistic attitude that can be dressed up as spirituality. It goes like this: "I only want the main point. I don't need any of these cultural or religious trappings; they are not for me. When disturbed I want to be calm. Calm is necessary, I understand, and I need it. Whenever I am selfish I should be more kind, because it works, and I feel better, so I need that. But please keep all the other complicated stuff away from me!" Seen from the traditional Buddhist point of view, this is a poor attitude. One does oneself a grave disservice by thinking like this. One is depleting one's own merit and making oneself unfortunate for no reason. I feel it is necessary to be aware of this way of going astray.

Getting back to the heart of the matter: as you get distracted, you stray from rigpa. You are undistracted when you simply allow the continuity of rigpa to carry on, to endure. While you remain composed, undistracted from the continuity of rigpa, two types of distraction can happen. One is not even noticing when after only a few minutes you find yourself already out of rigpa. How you came out of it you don't know, but suddenly you realize it. The other is that during the continuity of composure, something begins to move about in the periphery. It catches your attention and carries you off, even though you are aware of it. That is mainly the way a beginner gets distracted. The first type happens more to practitioners who have the confidence of being "advanced meditators." The looseness is perhaps too loose, so that one does not care too much to apply a remedy against whatever happens. That is why it is possible to slide away.

What is necessary? When one is distracted, what is it that gets distracted? It is the cognizant quality that gets distracted. How does the cognizant quality wander off? Because of forgetting its empty essence. What is the job of this cognizant nature? To *re-recognize* its empty essence. Having recognized its empty essence, this cognizant or awake quality is already complete. Its job is done. The problem here could be that the cognizant quality tries to make empty essence into a concrete meditation object, and then, because of holding it strongly in mind, distraction occurs. In fact, empty essence means there is no object. Making it into a concrete meditation object would mean attempting to render it almost tangible, like when I try to touch this gong. Recognizing empty essence means *recognizing that there is no object*. If emptiness were an object, then it could be touched, but it is not an object. It is like touching nothing, then simply leaving that nothing open. But because of coemergent ignorance, because of our innate habit of not knowing, cognizant nature gets kind of fidgety. It is not happy with no thing to touch and begins to look around for something to grab. This is the root cause of getting distracted from the state of rigpa.

There is possibly an instance when cognizant nature begins to look for an object, a very particular object; it won't settle for anger, attachment, or belief. Rather, it turns space into an object. This is when spaced-out meditation happens. At this point rigpa is definitely lost—or maybe it was not correctly recognized to begin with. One begins to solidify the spaciousness as an object of meditation. Does this make sense to you?

STUDENT: That spaciousness becomes the object?

RINPOCHE: Yes, the cognizant quality begins to objectify space. It takes itself as subject and space as object. This obviously becomes a dualistic state of mind. It is possible that you all are very intelligent and that you get this point immediately, but somehow I'm not sure that you've gotten it, so I keep repeating myself. You are welcome to say, "That's enough! I've got it."

There are several ways of being distracted, a so-called similar type and a dissimilar type. It is much easier to notice when distracted by a dissimilar type, meaning entirely different from rigpa. If it is a similar type, something that feels like rigpa, then it's not so easy to notice. Making spaciousness into an object held in mind is a state of distraction that resembles rigpa. It is not entirely different, because rigpa *is* empty and spacious. The difference is that rigpa's spaciousness is not an object held in mind. The spaciousness of rigpa is very natural, open, and free, whereas making space into an object means we form the *notion of spaciousness* and then try to maintain this notion. It might feel as if it is rigpa, but it definitely is not; it is a state of distraction. Because it is similar, though, it's hard to notice.

220

As a general rule, the similar type is much more difficult to get out of than the dissimilar type. An example of the dissimilar type would be anger, which is completely different from the state of rigpa. Its very presence alerts you and makes you feel, "Of course, now I am distracted." It's the same with strong drowsiness, for example; you can easily feel that you got distracted there.

I just explained how distraction occurs. The next subject is how to deal with it. Distraction slowly begins when the cognizant quality seemingly dims. This awake quality, the cognizant nature, seemingly begins to dim, and together with that is a freezing of the attention toward something. When this occurs to such an extent that the cognizance loses track of being empty, then distraction has begun. But if you are aware of this just as it is about to happen—if you are aware that your attention is about to move into a thought, about to become distracted, and at that moment you re-recognize the empty quality of this awake state—then there is no distraction. The quality of freedom is reestablished.

There are three styles of freedom: freed upon arising, naturally freed, and freed beyond benefit and harm. The situation I am currently discussing is freed upon arising, which has two manifestations. Re-recognizing is one type of freed upon arising. As the thought is about to be formed, it dissolves again. The analogy for that is drawing on water. This whole process takes place during the state of composure. Another aspect of freed upon arising occurs during the postmeditation. Together with knowing you're being distracted, you remember and immediately arrive in rigpa. For example, you are just about to get angry. You notice, "I am getting angry," and you immediately recognize rigpa. Based on the anger, you recognize rigpa: "I am getting carried off here. I am not in rigpa." Simply because of noticing this, you are immediately back in nondual awareness: "Oh, now I am out. Wait. Look. See." You do not need to go through this whole process step by step. You arrive directly. Certainly it's not easy to notice every time you get carried away, and this does not come readily for most people. During a two-hour stretch it rarely occurs even once. Mostly it comes in the evening when one is really tired and says, "Hey, I am really distracted here. I really got carried off." Then one notices, but otherwise it is a rare thought.

The second type of freeing is naturally freed. Natural freeing means "not dependent upon a remedy." When the wakefulness of knowing is recognized, no matter what type of object distracts you, the distraction dissolves without the use of any other remedy. The adept meditator does not have to take the support of a specific remedy against each particular object of distraction. Whatever might arise, if you can recognize rigpa during it, it is freed. It's the same for thoughts and emotions: there is the ability for these knots to be untied by themselves, without any other remedy, if you simply recognize rigpa. Rigpa is truly the single sufficient king.

The third way of freeing is freed beyond benefit and harm, and it is compared to a thief entering an empty house. Here, at this rather advanced level, you have recognized in actuality that all phenomena, whether belonging to samsara or to nirvana, are nothing other than the play of rigpa. When you have become familiar with that, then even though thoughts still move as the flow of karmic patterns, they don't have anything to hook into. Not only are all phenomena seen as empty, but the thought flow itself, all the various patterns, are seen as empty as well. At this point, there is no real danger of losing anything to any thought or emotion that arises. The thoughts "know" by now there is no longer anything to get, since they lost so many times before, but they still have to come because it is their job. There is still some karma left that is not yet purified. The thoughts are still being spewed forth to a certain extent, but that is not such a big deal, because there is no real danger of getting anything or losing anything.

Once we have recognized rigpa, how is it maintained afterward? This is the next key point. Is it by trying so hard to be one-pointedly mindful, trying not to be distracted? Or just looking into rigpa once and then going to sleep? Other, more tangible kinds of teachings are easier to maintain. If the view is tangible, then the meditation training to maintain it will also be tangible. But here the view is beyond the tangible, so your maintaining must also be intangible.

Let's say that the view is comprehensible, that it is something graspable to keep in mind. Doing that, of course, would be called maintaining. But what if the view is no *thing* to hold in mind—an intangible view? How do we maintain that? That is why we have the sequence of first looking, then seeing, and then letting be. There is another term for letting be: not fabricating. How do we *do* "not fabricating" or "not contriving"? If we do it, it is by definition fabricated. If we don't maintain it, we lose rigpa. So, how to maintain the view? Do you understand this dilemma?

We have to use words to communicate, and here are some important words: First, see the view of the Great Perfection; next, maintain it. The

Dzogchen teachings have a name for this maintenance: *training in the threefold motionlessness*. Remember this phrase. There is a relationship between not fabricating and motionlessness, because the moment we try to create something artificial there is immediately a moving away from the natural state. The finest way of motionlessness is to not fabricate anything artificial.

The first aspect of the threefold motionlessness is the *unmoving body like the king of mountains*, like Mount Everest. This is how to place your body at the beginning. *(Rinpoche demonstrates the sitting posture.)* After mastering it, you can place your body however you want. Putting your butt up in the air and your head down is fine. Having closed eyes is okay; open eyes are fine too. You can sit on a chair or in your car, or you can lie face down on your bed; it does not matter.

Once we attain stability in the correct body position, it does not matter how we sit. In fact, we should try to seek out what is difficult. Go to a scary place or an uncomfortable place, a situation where we are not at home or comfy, maybe somewhere crowded with many people, a place with all sorts of turmoil, a place where we get flattered, criticized, have pleasant or unpleasant experiences—all different types of places. In doing this, we should take support of *the symbolic master of experiences* who is teaching us at that very moment, because in those situations we can recognize mind-essence and still be free. The liberated quality of the experience at that time is *the true master of natural knowing*.

There are four types of teachers. The first of these is our ability to learn and progress during difficulties. This is the symbolic master of experiences. Another is when we are able to recognize the natural knowing during an unpleasant experience and are capable of overcoming the unpleasantness. The sense of freedom here is the true master of natural knowing. The quality of being free in the emptiness during difficulties is also a teacher.

The point is, when we are able to recognize the liberated state within any difficult situation or any body posture, then it doesn't matter how we sit. But right now, while we are training, our mind is in some way dependent upon the channels, energies, and essences. Mind is supported by the essences, the *bindu*s. The essences in turn are supported by the energies, while the energies are supported by the channels. The channels themselves are supported by or dependent upon the physical, material body. Therefore, the 72,000 channels in the body are in their naturally aligned mode when this material body is placed in an upright, straight position. With the 72,000 channels in their natural mode, the energies that move within them—the upward-moving, the downward-clearing, and so on—all flow freely and can dissolve within the central channel. When the energy currents are in their natural mode, when they are purified in this way, then unnecessary thought movements diminish. Why? Because the pathways through which the thought currents move have been eliminated, cut off. When the energy currents move nicely, the pure forms of the essences, which are interconnected with mind, are in their natural mode as well. We experience this as a state of mind that is at ease and feels more natural, relaxed. When mind is at peace, it has a greater opportunity to recognize its own nature. A kind of natural intelligence is revealed. On the other hand, if there is a lot of disturbance, turmoil, and constriction, then our sense of intelligence is preoccupied. Therefore, sit with a straight back for this practice.

For Dzogchen practice, there is the posture of mental ease. Place your hands on your knees, like Longchen Rabjam. Another way of placing the hands, which is used in Zen and other practice traditions, is in your lap, one on top of the other. I personally prefer placing my palms on my knees. The shoulders are drawn slightly back and down. There could be a bubbling energy, a difficult-to-explain feeling of a rush—just let it settle. Let the belly area relax a bit. This is known as the soft breath. Many people experience a constriction in the belly area. The shoulders go up a bit, the neck goes down, and there develops a traffic jam in the energy currents, a sort of congestion. The remedy for this is to let it settle, relaxing the shoulders down. Then you just sit there, not moving, not fidgeting. You sit and just drop every concern about having or not having a body. Sit loose, happy, and relaxed, but still keeping your shape. This is all about the first motionlessness, the unmoving body that is like the king of mountains.

Next are the *unmoving senses like planets and stars reflected in a lake*. It's a serene lake here, not a turbulent one. All your senses are open. Your ears are not blocked, nor are your eyes closed; you have feeling in all the pores of your body, and the thoughts in your mind are not blocked either. Nothing is obstructed. You are not looking right and left, fidgeting about trying to listen to this and that. "While keeping my ears open like Tsoknyi Rinpoche told me, should I now listen carefully to every single sound that comes along?" No, that is not what's meant. You do not have to listen deliberately or intently, and yet all senses are simply wide open.

At this point, breathe through the mouth, between the teeth. The lips and teeth are just slightly parted so that the breathing flows naturally, unforced—not like this. *(Rinpoche opens his mouth and gasps.)* You can keep the teeth just touching if you want; that is fine. The mouth is slightly open so that the breath can flow as it pleases. The mouth is neither gaping wide open nor closed so that you're breathing through the nose. Leave the mouth slightly open and let the breathing be totally unforced. It is better to grow accustomed to this slowly so that the inhalations and exhalations become long and relaxed, so that we are not so nervous, palpitating and panting. Long, easy breaths. The eyes look straight ahead. The gaze is simply left there to itself.

Wide-open senses may be a bit uncomfortable for someone who has been used to meditating with closed eyes, but you can adjust slowly. In fact, it is best to train with open eyes, because when we get up and walk around, we need to do that with open eyes. If you were to continue training with closed eyes when you walk around, wouldn't you bump into things and hurt your head?

In other words, leave all the senses very open and alive, not necessarily reaching out toward objects, but simply aware. Our lineage masters all agreed that you do not have to be *deliberately aware* of things. Rather, just allow them to be reflected, to appear by themselves. When you look at the placid surface of a clear, quiet lake at night, the planets and stars just appear there. They present themselves, and when the surface is very serene and quiet, you can see them very clearly. It's the same way with our senses when they are left wide open.

This second motionlessness, the unmoving senses like planets and stars reflected in a lake, is a very important point. Placing your sense faculties in the correct way facilitates a particular type of intelligence—the intelligence that discerns all phenomena thoroughly and fully—unfolding as you progress. You now see very clearly what is correct and incorrect. One could say that the circumstance of the senses being left wide open facilitates that intelligence or allows for it to happen.

The third motionlessness is *unmoving mind-essence like a cloudless sky*. The mind itself resembles a clear sky, totally lucid and bright, not forming any clouds at all. When we leave ourselves in this threefold way of motionlessness, that is called maintaining rigpa. But it is possible to maintain rigpa only after having recognized it. If we are unaware of what rigpa is, then there is no maintaining it either.

Another point is that there are two aspects of getting rid of what needs to be eliminated: through understanding and through training. Through the process of training, getting more and more accustomed to this way of being, certain factors are discarded. The way of training here, the key point of maintenance according to the specific terminology of Dzogchen, is to be *undistracted while not meditating.*

What happens if one is meditating? You can say whatever you want, but do say something.

STUDENT: There is some fixing or clinging.

STUDENT 2: Conceptualizing.

RINPOCHE: That is why the key point is *while not meditating*, right? But undistracted. What happens if one is distracted?

STUDENT: One is taken away by the thoughts.

RINPOCHE: Right! Therefore, undistracted. So why combine these two terms, "undistracted" and "not meditating"? How about "undistracted" but not training in that? Will one get good at that without training? Unless we train, isn't it true that we will just remain distracted? To be undistracted, don't we need to train and grow accustomed to it? Yet the instruction says "while *not* meditating." Doesn't that sound like "don't train"? No? What does it sound like then?

STUDENT: Train, but don't get distracted and don't meditate. (*Laughter*)

STUDENT 2: "Undistracted" means maintaining clarity or lucidity. "While not meditating" means maintaining the emptiness. There is no subject or object; you are not *doing* anything.

RINPOCHE: Yes, it is like that. The cognizant nature needs to be allowed to be cognizant naturally, by itself, not by our trying to make it so by meditating.

So how do we do rigpa? Is it by meditating? The question arises, "Then what is there for me to do? Rigpa is just automatic and natural. There is nothing I have to do about it. I'm told that anything I try to do is just conceptual—so what do I need to do? Won't I go crazy?" No, you won't go crazy.

Our task here is first to recognize the essence, rigpa itself. We don't need to *do* anything about rigpa after that. Rigpa does not require our assistance.

All we need to do is simply refrain from accepting the invitations that come along to be distracted, to disturb rigpa. The distractions come and say, "Let's disturb rigpa now! Let's cover it up!" But we simply refrain from accepting that request, again and again. That is our task. We do not need to improve rigpa. Let's say there is a glimpse of recognizing the awakened state that is rigpa. There is no way we can expand it, even if we try to. Trying to do anything to it just covers it up more. Some people misunderstand this point. They think, "I should *get* rigpa, *hold* rigpa." If they try to do that, though, the nondual state will never last. That is how it is.

The phrase is *undistracted while not meditating* because if our meditation is conceptual, we are by definition distracted, in the sense of ordinary people who are always distracted. Usually, in order not to be distracted, we try to keep mindful, right? What is it that maintains shamatha, the state of mental stability? The best way is mindfulness, right? To keep undistracted in shamatha, we remain mindful. The main purpose of mindfulness is to be undistracted. The Dzogchen perspective is different, and in fact this is one of the main distinctions between shamatha and rigpa. Rigpa, of course, needs to be undistracted as well, but the rigpa that needs to be *kept* undistracted by means of mindfulness will only turn into a conceptual state. Here there seem to be two possibilities: being undistracted by keeping mindful and being undistracted *without* trying to keep mindful. Rigpa's type of undistractedness is the latter; it is not kept by being deliberately mindful.

The Dzogchen teachings actually mention four types of mindfulness: deliberate mindfulness, effortless mindfulness, true mindfulness, and supreme mindfulness. Briefly, however, we can operate with just two types: deliberate and effortless, one for shamatha, the other for Dzogchen. Deliberate mindfulness is used in shamatha training, while effortless mindfulness is during vipashyana, in the Dzogchen sense. From a Mahamudra perspective, the true mindfulness is during one taste, while kinglike supreme mindfulness is during nonmeditation.

One might sit and think, "I should *not* be distracted. I should remain quiet and still … quiet, still … just knowing this … quiet … undistracted." Of course this is very nice and is necessary—I am not criticizing it. Please don't misunderstand this point. Explaining the distinctive features of Dzogchen may sometimes sound like criticizing shamatha. Some of Milarepa's poetry even sounds like a critique of the Buddha, but it surely wasn't. It is just that in one specific context special qualities need to be brought forth in order to be seen more clearly. The issue is this: the view is supposed to be nonconceptual, but what happens if the training in the nonconceptual view turns conceptual? When view and training are in conflict, we hamper progress.

30

SPACE WITHOUT CENTER OR EDGE

A song by Longchen Rabjam

Glorious protector, lord of Dharma, your purity is like the sky.
Realizing dharmata, you freed samsara and nirvana in the ground.
Now no longer are you separate from Samantabhadra's mind.
O guru, matchless lord of beings, at your feet I bow!

Samsara and nirvana, undivided, as a stream of knowing,
Basic unborn state, phenomena exhausted beyond concepts,
Innate mode of knowing, free from perceiver and perceived,
Naked and unending, all-pervasive—such an open vastness!

All appearances are baseless empty forms,
Nonexistent, vivid presence, magical illusions, moons in water.
Visible and unreal, they have never existed in the ground,
Unreified, empty, naked—such an open vastness!

Every moment is an unbound flow of empty, natural knowing.
Memories and thoughts all vanish, empty, traceless, like the sky.
Mind and mental states are baseless, rootless, inconcrete,
Empty and devoid of entities to grasp—such an open vastness!

Samsara and nirvana, appearing worlds and living beings, whatever
    is experienced,
Are all an empty, fresh, original, unfabricated state.
Without support or ground, this stream of self-existing knowing
Unobstructed, free in its unfolding—such an open vastness!

From a collection of songs by Drimey Özer (Longchen Rabjam) (Boudhanath:
Rangjung Yeshe Publications, 1993).

Within this natural, lucid, unbound ground of dharmadhatu knowing,
Insight of the conquerors, infinite, completely free,
Where myriad phenomena are primordially pure,
A thought-free, innate nakedness—such an open vastness!

Without conceptualizing any moment you experience,
Not fixating on a thing, no matter how it may appear,
Neither focused nor projecting, free and artless flow of knowing,
All-pervasive, naked, natural state—such an open vastness!

Not projecting outwardly and not focused within;
Not creating thought constructs, it transcends all reference points.
This flow beyond the thoughts of meditating and not meditating,
Naked self-existing wisdom—such an open vastness!

Unconfined basic knowing, seamless in both sessions and breaks,
Is a naked, natural cognizance, free from reference point.
Dharmadhatu's primal continuity, beyond all entities within or without,
And dharmakaya's ceaseless knowing—such an open vastness!

Primal insight of the conquerors, spontaneously perfected,
A basic stream, unfabricated, that is by nature present,
Beyond dualities of causes and effects, rejecting a samsara or
     preferring a nirvana,
Sambhogakaya's luminous awareness—such an open vastness!

Within this flawless state of knowing, undistracted and nondwelling,
Not composed of any thing, completely unobstructed,
A flow transcending all limits, partiality, a presence, and an absence,
Nirmanakaya's ceaseless venues of displays—such an open vastness!

Samsara's guises are but baseless, empty forms,
Basically deluded states that never have existed.
These magical illusions, a vivid presence not to be discarded;
This insight churns samsara's depths—such an open vastness!

Personal experience unfolds in countless ways,
Kayas and wisdoms, pure realms, and so forth,
However all these groundless, empty forms appear,
Still an emptiness, beyond the name samsara or nirvana—such an
     open vastness!

Everything that is perceived while in this state of knowing
Is personal experience, a mere display of empty cognizance,
	unbound.
Not straying elsewhere and from no thing is it formed;
Nondual, individual experience of knowing—such an open vastness!

Phenomena of labeled forms, imputed by mistaken mind,
Besides that they do not exist, a stream defying an outside and an
	inside.
Such self-existing wakefulness, transcending limits of all mental
	constructs,
Qualities perfected, every concept dissipated—such an open vastness!

Samsara and nirvana both, living beings and appearing worlds,
Perceiver and objects perceived, all is groundless, rootless.
Within the Great Perfection, final summit of the vehicles,
Primeval buddhahood of dharmakaya—such an open vastness!

Space of great awakening, beyond accepting and rejecting,
Expanse of self-existing and unchanging knowing,
This flow of Great Perfection that transcends the intellect,
Omnipotent knowing that embraces all phenomena—such an open
	vastness!

Ground of great pervasiveness, no thought, no pondering,
Dharmakaya path, the natural state, which never strayed from
	dharmadhatu,
And the fruition's continuity; the realized, immaculate and natural
	knowing,
An awareness, self-existing and unchanging—such an open vastness!

Within the space of dharmakaya that transcends all effort,
A self-existing knowing, realized, in full-fledged force,
Flies high above the abyss of the yanas of causation;
The great garuda of awareness, the primordial—such an open vastness!

Innate body, indestructible, perfection of great strength,
Nature of the Great Perfection, final summit of the yanas,
I, Longchen Rabjam, who has realized it as it is,
Now hoists the never-ending banner, the victory of freedom for the
	triple realms.

When every being, no exception, reaches liberation, free from effort,
May they be spontaneously perfected as Samantabhadra's
dharmakaya!

*This completes the song of the Vajra Garuda, the ultimate space of the Great
Perfection, written at the hermitage of Lhündrub Ling for the sake of Lobpön
Rinchen Sherab. This song entitled Space without Center or Edge was composed
by Longchen Rabjam, a yogi of the supreme vehicle.*

31

CONDUCT

Tulku Urgyen Rinpoche

First we need to recognize self-existing wakefulness. Slowly, slowly, we need to repeat the instants of uncontrived naturalness, developing the strength of the recognition. Once we reach stability, there is nondistraction day and night; space and awareness have mingled. Our minds have been under the power of dualistic grasping and fixation for so long that we have taken the nondual for a duality. Thus, it's difficult to immediately be used to the awakened state. We have trained for so long in the opposite of recognizing mind-essence, which is exactly what samsara has been in all our past lives, up until the present moment. We have this unwholesome and deeply ingrained habit. Now we must change this habit into the habit of recognizing mind-essence. Since for a beginner the moment of recognition lasts only a very short time, we have to repeat it many times. To repeat the recognition of mind-essence, you don't necessarily have to sit down. Do not make any distinction between the training when sitting and the training when moving around in daily life situations—walking, talking, eating, and lying down. Do not limit the practice to sessions. The view is rigpa, the meditation training is rigpa, and the conduct is rigpa. This is the way to get used to the awakened state.

The moment you recognize rigpa as the view, *this* is the meditation training, *this* is the conduct, and *this* is the fruition. At that moment, all of samsara and nirvana are subsumed within the state of rigpa, in one sweep. When you are fully stable in the recognition of rigpa, samsara has totally vanished into nirvana and there is neither distraction during the day nor confusion during the night. There is only one—the oneness of rigpa.

Adapted from Tulku Urgyen Rinpoche, *As It Is*, *Vol. 2* (Boudhanath: Rangjung Yeshe Publications, 2000), "The Heart of the Practice."

The actual meaning of meditation state in Buddhism, when using the term *nyamshak*, is equality, composure, equanimity. In the moment of recognizing rigpa, there is no need to accept or reject, adopt or avoid, hope or fear. There is an evenness, regardless of the situation. The very basis for such equanimity is this present wakefulness, without which we would be corpses, only physical bodies, material forms. Yet now we are alive because of this present wakefulness. Once you recognize this present wakefulness that does not accept or reject, affirm or deny, hope or fear, that in itself is sufficient. It is not your mind from yesterday or from last night, tomorrow, or next month. It is this very moment, right now. Where is it? Can you find it? Can you find this instant? Recognize this instantaneous wakefulness. Let your mind recognize itself, and immediately you know that there is no thing to be seen. This is just as Rangjung Dorje, the third Karmapa, sang:

> When observing objects, they are seen to be the mind, devoid of objects.
> When observing the mind, there is no mind, as it is empty of an entity.
> When observing both, dualistic fixation is spontaneously freed.
> May we realize the luminous nature of mind.

When examining outer objects, you understand that there are no *real* objects—there is only the perceiving mind. Recognizing the nature of this mind, you find no entity. When you look into both subject and object, the fixation on duality dissolves; the existence of a concrete object and a separate concrete subject simply falls away. The duality of perceiver and perceived collapses.

"May we realize the luminous nature of mind." Here, *luminous* refers to the fact that rigpa is empty and yet cognizant. Physical space cannot be lucid; it has no capacity to know either itself or something else. This is why rigpa is defined as unconfined empty cognizance suffused with knowing. It is the unerring original, natural state. If you do not contrive it in any way but simply let it be what it is, then right now the awakened state is spontaneously present. Your immediate, natural, present wakefulness is itself the true Samantabhadra.

In short, giving up doer and deed, rest in nondoing. When you train in giving up doer and deed, you will approach nonaction. Doer and deed refers to the subject-object structure. When you recognize mind-essence, do you find any place from which your thinking arises, any place where it dwells, any location into which it vanishes? Right then and there you have reached nonaction. Consider this: have you ever been able to find a place where space came out of? A place where it began? A place where it abides and into which it will disappear? This is described as devoid of mental constructs, beyond arising, dwelling, and ceasing. It is also called nonaction. When something does not arise, dwell, or cease, it is 100 percent certain that it is empty.

So, mind is empty, but if it were *only* empty, it would be impossible to have pleasure and pain or the experiences of buddhafields and hells. Since they are definitely possible, it proves that mind is both empty and cognizant. Because of this there is samsara and nirvana, pleasure and pain, joy and sorrow—the results of virtuous actions, the higher realms and buddhafields, and the results of negative deeds, which are the three lower realms and the suffering that comes with these. There is samsara below, nirvana above and in between, the path that is the karmic actions of good and evil. All this cannot be denied.

It is all like a dream. We have not yet woken up from the deep sleep of ignorance. Usually we dream while we sleep. The moment we wake up, we do not dream anymore. Buddhas and bodhisattvas are like somebody who has already awakened from sleep. There are all these different dreams—pleasant, unpleasant, fascinating, horrifying—but at the moment we wake up, where are they? Where do they go? Since they are just habitual tendencies, how can they come from anywhere or go anywhere? Similarly, all the different experiences that arise during the day take place within the framework of dualistic mind. The moment dualistic mind is suspended in rigpa—the moment thinking dissolves—the outcome is the wakefulness of knowing (*rigpey yeshe*), which is essence without thought.

I have told you the "story of mind." Now you need to train in the unfabricated present wakefulness that is possible only through recognition. Knowing how to recognize mind-essence is similar to turning on the light. The light doesn't come on unless you press the switch. When you have pressed the switch, when the light is on, you naturally meet empty cognizance suffused with knowing. This is exactly what sentient beings never do. They don't know how to recognize. They don't switch on their light. If they did, this one taste of empty cognizance suffused with knowing would automatically be present, because our own nature is dharmata; our essence is rigpa. But even if sentient beings do happen to glimpse the natural state, they do not know what it is—they fail to acknowledge it—and it turns into the indifferent state of the all-ground.

When you are face to face with your nature, if you do not begin any striving in terms of shamatha and vipashyana or ordinary confusion, you have already seen the essence of mind. It looks like no thing whatsoever. Because it is no thing whatsoever, there is no thing that you can label or describe, no thing about which you can form concepts. It is beyond thought, word, or description. This is prajñaparamita, transcendent knowledge, since it transcends any subject and any object to be known. Let me repeat a famous quote:

> Transcendent knowledge is beyond thought, word, and description.
> It neither arises nor ceases, like the identity of space.
> It is the domain of individual self-knowing wakefulness.
> To this mother of the buddhas of the three times, I pay homage.

Since it is within the individual domain of cognizant wakefulness, anyone can know it. Domain here means that it is possible to recognize. What is recognized is not something that can be thought of, described, or illustrated through example. This knowing is the mother of the buddhas of the three times, named Prajñaparamita, the Great Mother. The experience quality of this is called the male buddha, and the empty quality is the female buddha. Their unity is the primordial Buddha Samantabhadra with consort, also known as Changeless Light.

There is one single essential point that encompasses view, meditation, conduct, and fruition—one phrase I have now mentioned quite a few times: undivided empty cognizance suffused with knowing. This is of unparalleled importance. This undivided empty cognizance is our basic nature, which is exactly the same whether we are a buddha or a sentient being. What makes the difference is whether it is suffused with knowing or unknowing. The difference lies simply in recognizing or not recognizing. An ordinary sentient being is unaware of his or her nature. Ordinary sentient beings are undivided empty cognizance suffused with unknowing, caught up in the three poisons. A yogi, a true practitioner, is someone who has been introduced to this natural state and is undivided empty cognizance suffused with knowing, the three kayas. A yogi does not take it as enough to merely have recognized. Without training, the strength of that recognition will never be perfected, and there is no stability. A yogi trains in this until perfection, the fruition of the three kayas.

Do not be content with just recognizing the nature of mind—it is essential to train in it also. The way to do so is as Padmasambhava said in these four lines from the *Lamrim Yeshe Nyingpo*:

Empty cognizance of one taste, suffused with knowing, ༔
Is your unmistaken nature, the uncontrived original state. ༔
When not altering what is, allow it to be as it is, ༔
And the awakened state is right now spontaneously present. ༔

As it is here means in actuality. *Actuality* means seeing directly how it is, not as an idea or a concept. By recognizing the nature of the thinker, one realizes the fact that emptiness and cognizance are an indivisible unity. This fact is no longer hidden; it is experienced. When this actuality is allowed to be as it is, it is not contrived in any way whatsoever. Then the state of a buddha, the awakened state, is, right now, spontaneously perfected. All obscuration has dissolved. These are quite impressive words, these four lines spoken by Padmasambhava himself. They encapsulate the whole meaning of training in the view, meditation, conduct, and fruition.

Once more, it is not enough to recognize the nature of mind as being empty and cognizant. We have to train in perfecting its strength. The training is to recognize again and again. The moment we recognize undivided empty cognizance, that is rigpa itself. But it is not fully grown—it is not an adult state of rigpa. The level of recognition we are at now is called baby rigpa. It needs to grow up, because at present it is not capable of conducting itself or functioning fully. We need to grow to the level of a human who has "developed the strength," who has reached the age of seventeen, eighteen, or nineteen, and has become independent and can take care of himself or herself. That is stability. For that to happen, we need to train repeatedly. That is essential!

The word *simplicity* is extremely important in Dzogchen. Simplicity means free from mental constructs, free from extraneous concepts. A famous statement says:

See the view of no viewing.
Train in the meditation with nothing meditated upon.
Carry out the conduct of nondoing.
Achieve the fruition in which there is no thing attained.

This statement is incredibly profound, and it is very important to understand exactly what is meant here. It is pointing at simplicity, at nondoing, at nonaction, at the very fact that our innate nature is not a view to be seen as a new orientation that we somehow gain comprehension of. The true view is not like that at all.

Complexity obscures simplicity. In all the other vehicles, starting with the vehicle for shravakas and up to and including Anu Yoga, there are principles to grasp and objects to hold in mind. There are actions to carry out and results to achieve. But the view, meditation, conduct, and fruition of Ati Yoga transcend everything other than acknowledging what is originally present as our own nature. This vehicle is simply a matter of acknowledging that our essence is already an undivided empty cognizance. Why imagine what is already empty as being empty? There is no need to grasp an emptiness that is anything other than what already is. This is the meaning of "see the view of no viewing."

Next, "train in the meditation with nothing meditated upon." To meditate means to keep something in mind. Do we have to keep in mind the empty cognizance, or do we rather simply acknowledge what is already present? How can you imagine empty cognizance, anyway? It is not necessary to do anything fancy; simply see how it already is.

About "carrying out the conduct of nondoing": in all the other vehicles there is something to do to keep oneself busy with, but here the ultimate conduct is to abandon the ninefold activities. It is said, "Don't busy yourself with deeds and doings." Deeds and doings means activity involving subject and object that obscures the state of nonaction. It is also said, "Being free from deeds and doings, you have arrived at nondoing." That is the very key point. In this teaching, we simply need to recognize the original state of empty cognizance. At that point there is no "thing" to concentrate upon, no struggle to achieve.

All teachings are completed in the Great Perfection. The sutras all start out with, "In the Indian language, the title is such-and-such," and end with, "Hereby the sutra called such-and-such is completed." The word *completed* means finished, perfected. In other words, in the moment of recognizing the nature of mind, all the vehicles are perfected. Great Perfection means that our nature itself is already fully perfect. We don't have to make our empty essence pure; it is primordially pure. We don't have to make our basic nature cognizant; it is already spontaneously perfected as cognizance. Nor does the all-pervasive capacity need to be fabricated. Honestly, how could you possibly create the empty essence or cognizant nature? They are spontaneously present, effortlessly. Train in this effortlessness!

32

Enhancement

Tsele Natsok Rangdröl

For Mahamudra

Having briefly described the view and meditation, I shall also briefly explain how to practice the conduct, the application of enhancement.

According to most paths of Secret Mantra, the different types of conduct mentioned are the three of elaborate, unelaborate, and very unelaborate. There are also secret conduct, group conduct, awareness discipline, completely victorious conduct, and so forth. Many such categories exist, but they are for the most part general enhancements for the stages of development and completion. In this context, the ever-excellent conduct—sustaining the natural mode of the innate, free from conceptual mind—is alone important.

First of all, even during the preliminary stages of gathering the accumulations and purifying the obscurations and as the means for receiving the blessings, you should exert yourself in practicing the ever-excellent conduct of being untainted by the defilement of any of the eight worldly concerns and of not feeling ashamed of yourself.

Next, when gaining certainty about the view and meditation of the main part of practice and becoming clear about self-cognizance, you should exert yourself in the ever-excellent conduct of being "skilled in all by knowing one" and "knowing all that liberates one." That is the means of "hammering down the nails" of many plans from within yourself and cutting through the arrogance of doubt in your own mind.

Adapted from Tsele Natsok Rangdröl, *Lamp of Mahamudra* (Boudhanath: Rangjung Yeshe Publications, 1988), "Enhancement"; and *Circle of the Sun* (Boudhanath: Rangjung Yeshe Publications, 1990), "Enhancement."

Finally, although various authoritative scriptures and oral instructions have taught different types of conduct as means to enhance one's practice, the essential key points are as follows: Cut your worldly attachments completely and live companionless in secluded mountain retreats; that is the conduct of a wounded deer. Be free from fear or anxiety in the face of difficulties; that is the conduct of a lion sporting in the mountains. Be free from attachment or clinging to sense pleasures; that is the conduct of the wind in the sky. Do not become involved in the fetters of accepting or rejecting the eight worldly concerns; that is the conduct of a madman. Sustain, simply and unrestrictedly, the natural flow of your mind while unbound by the ties of dualistic fixation; that is the conduct of a spear stabbing in space.

While engaging in these types of conduct, cut the fetters of deluded wandering, distraction, hope, and fear. Becoming involved in even as much as a hair tip of the inner fault of desiring to have signs and indications, experience and realization, or siddhis and so forth, will gain you nothing but obscuring your real condition, your innate state, the natural face of dharmakaya. Focus exclusively on sustaining the unconstructed innate nature; that is the most eminent ever-excellent conduct of bringing things into the path.

Regardless of any difficulties such as conceptual thinking, disturbing emotions, suffering, fear, sickness, or death that may temporarily occur, be able to bring these into the path as the main part of the natural Mahamudra practice, neither hoping for nor relying on some other means of benefit through an antidote. That is the king of all types of enhancement.

The person able to practice like this will gain mastery over all of samsara and nirvana, appearance and existence. So, the nature of things is that you will be free from any basis of obstacles, the great ocean of siddhis will overflow, the darkness of the two obscurations will be cleared, the sun of signs of accomplishment will shine forth, the buddha will be discovered within your own mind, and the treasury of benefiting others will be opened wide.

It is, on the contrary, indeed cause for despair to see the meditators who seem to be exclusively throwing away the *single sufficient jewel* that has been placed in their hands and, like a child picking flowers, spending a lifetime wishing for one better thing to do after another.

For Dzogchen
The Seven Types of Conduct:

So far, I have briefly explained the view and meditation; now, in conformity with the general Dharma system, it would seem sensible to explain the different kinds of conduct—how to behave, the means of enhancement, goals, and so forth—as an aid to your practice. If one has not attained some realization of the effortless Great Perfection, it is difficult to find any need for this. Nonetheless, like planting a mere seed, here I shall condense the twenty-one types of conduct taught in the *Union of Sun and Moon Tantra* and elsewhere into seven vital points. What are they?

1. As a beginner, using the beelike conduct of integrating numerous Dharma teachings, you should attain certainty as to learning, reflection, and meditation.

2. With the conduct of a swallow entering its nest, you should cut through misconceptions about the oral instructions and ensure that the deviations of doubt, obstacles, and faults do not occur.

3. Following this, during the actual practice, you should have the conduct of a wounded deer and keep to unpeopled mountain dwellings, free from the ties of worldly distractions.

4. As an aid to this, you should keep silence, having the conduct of a mute. For your entire life refrain from engaging in flattery or slander.

5. Keeping the conduct of a madman, cast away prejudice, attachment, like, dislike, and indifference toward friends and enemies.

6. Adopting the conduct of pigs and dogs, you should be content with whatever happens and take whatever is experienced as your companion, without concepts of purity and impurity concerning your food, clothing, dwelling, and sitting place.

7. Through the lionlike conduct of the king of beasts, you should be free from anxiety about events and completely cast away all fetters of hope and fear. Until you have realized the fruition, practice so that you can endure heat and cold and good and bad equally, without falling under the power of circumstances.

Advice

Condensing these seven types of conduct to their essence, from the moment you first enter the door of these teachings until you finally reach the exhaustion of concepts, lay your foundation with love, compassion, and bodhichitta. Keep it stable with devotion and pure perception, and observe your samayas. Remain firm, with renunciation, contentment, and perseverance.

Any practitioner, whether male or female, able to put one-pointed effort into the essence of practice, the union of Trekchö and Tögal, will permanently depart from samsara, establish the basis for the Practice Lineage, obtain the eye of the oral instructions, and make the differentiation of the practice.[43] Thus, for those worthy people who attain the result of buddhahood by dissolving all the phenomena of samsara and nirvana into the primordially pure expanse of self-cognizance—the original Great Perfection—appearance and existence will manifest as the guru, causing the sea of blessings to overflow. Apparent objects will manifest as a buddhafield, emptying out the basis for misfortune and obstacles. Their physical forms will be liberated into the body of light, exhausting the basis for sickness and causes of death. Their minds will dissolve into primordial purity, causing the falsehood of view, meditation, conduct, and fruition to vanish. They will discover the three kayas within themselves, exhausting the basis of dependence upon a subject and object for attaining buddhahood. They will have no difficulty in swiftly arriving at such a stage.

The superficial Dharma practitioners of the degenerate Age of Strife are fermenting with samsaric attachment and clinging, afflicted by the tumor of selfishness and conceit, and possessed by the spirit of perverted ambition and the eight worldly concerns. Unable to persevere in their practice for even one day, they dissipate into sleep and the business of obtaining food and clothing. When observing the abundance of such "meditators" who expect the signs of realization to appear spontaneously like mushrooms, the experiences, realization, and qualities of the paths and bhumis, though hoped for, will be scarce like rain in the autumn. Intelligent people, do you understand this?

The *Gandhavyuha Sutra* says:

Failing to practice the Dharma is like dying of starvation
Although one may have given food and drink to numerous beings.

The sutra continues:

By not fully practicing,
One will not perceive the nature of things.
Although one may see or hear about water,
How can it quench one's thirst if one doesn't drink?

Therefore, it is essential to practice.

Other teaching systems consider that the details of how to clear away hindrances and the different types of errors and sidetracks are important. You can understand the mistakes, errors, and sidetracks concerning the natural state of Trekchö from what I have explained in my *Notes on Mahamudra*.

Entering Tögal practice without correctly understanding the vital points of Trekchö is inappropriate. Even if one did practice, it would be pointless. However, having assimilated the key points of Trekchö, you will transcend the domain of hindrances, flaws, errors, and sidetracks in Tögal practice. So they need not be mentioned here.

33

TÖGAL

Tsele Natsok Rangdröl

The supreme method for recognizing the ground luminosity of the first bardo and attaining liberation is to become fully resolved about the mind right now in the bardo of the present life, and then to exclusively concentrate, beyond meditation and distraction, on the continuous practice of the ultimate nature of ordinary mind, the unfabricated and natural state of dharmakaya. Knowing how to maintain it, unspoiled by the obstacles of defects or defilements, mental constructs, and fabrications, is crucial not only in the first bardo but at all times. It is the ultimate essence and supreme extract of all the sutras, tantras, and oral instructions. Since all the 84,000 teachings are contained and complete within this, it is the Great Perfection. Since nothing departs from the three kayas, it is the Great Seal. Since it transcends intellectual constructs, it is Transcendent Knowledge. Free from all extremes, it is the Middle Way. Actualizing the result of the supreme path, it is Path and Fruition (*Lamdre*). Since it naturally pacifies disturbing emotions, it is the Pacifier (*Shije*). Since it cuts clinging and fixation to dualistic experience at their root, it is the Cutting (*Chöyul*). Since it in actuality unites one with the state of enlightenment, it is the Six Unions (*Jordruk*). Since it purifies ignorance and confused thinking, it is Mind Training (*Lojong*). In short, all the innumerable kinds of profound teachings converge here at exactly this vital point. So, if one does not vigorously concentrate on this true meaning, one's intellectual pursuit of numerous plans will prove ineffective at the time of need. This is described in the *Tantra of the All-Creating King*:

Adapted from Tsele Natsok Rangdröl, *Mirror of Mindfulness* (Boudhanath: Rangjung Yeshe Publications, 1987), "The Luminous Bardo of Dharmata."

244

When you realize the suchness of your mind,
The Buddha will not linger among mere words,
So the highest yoga is attained right now.

For the unworthy ones of inferior fortune,
Even were the hidden revealed, they would not understand,
Just as someone wishing for a precious jewel
Will not gain it from polishing a piece of wood.

Thus, it is essential to exert oneself in the unmistaken nature right now.

In particular, one should also apply oneself assiduously to the steps of training in luminosity as they occur in texts such as the *Six Doctrines*, *The Liberation through Hearing*, and so forth. When one attains stability in the luminosity of realization during the state of deep sleep, recognizing the ground luminosity at this point in the bardo of dharmata will not be difficult.

Know, then, that if one can practice virtue while sleeping, one can recognize the first luminosity. This differentiates between actually remaining in meditation and just remaining in the body due to attachment. When someone appears to be genuinely remaining in meditation, one who knows how can give the reminding instruction. Complex practices such as *phowa* cannot be performed with concepts. In short, it is evident that for such realized people there is no need to depend upon deliberate ceremonies such as purification rituals or name-burning.[44]

As for the pointing-out of the apparent luminosity, the person who is acquainted with such practices as the five-fold Path of Means, Jordruk, and so forth should recognize that whatever appears—such as the mirage, whiteness, and other signs—is all simply a manifestation of dharmakaya, one's self-cognizance. For practitioners of Tögal according to Dzogchen, it is essential to trust that whatever appears, such as the sounds, colors, and lights, the peaceful and wrathful deities, the bindus, light rays, light paths, and pure realms, are nothing other than one's natural manifestation, and then rest evenly in the state of having resolved that. To be able to do this, one should without a doubt practice right now in becoming certain about the ground nature of Trekchö and in concentrating on the pointing-out instructions of the path of Tögal.

According to Dzogchen root texts, Trekchö has these three points: recognizing one's essence, deciding on one thing, and gaining confidence in liberation. Tögal has the various points, after resolving the nature of the six lamps, of laying the basis on the threefold motionlessness, keeping the measure of the threefold remaining, planting the stake of the threefold attainment, and showing the degree of liberation through the fourfold confidence.

When one does not let these and other points remain as mere rhetoric but applies their meaning to one's being, one will perfect the four visions, and, at best, liberate the physical body into the unconditioned body of light. As the next best, one will attain stability in the ground luminosity just like the space within and outside a vase mingle together when the vase breaks, and thus, just like a lion emerging from the enclosure of the womb or a garuda leaving the enclosure of the eggshell, one's mind attains dharmakaya simultaneously with being freed from the enclosure of the physical body of karmic ripening. As the third best, when the spontaneously present luminosity of the rupakayas manifests in the bardo of dharmata, it is of utmost importance to possess the key point of knowing how to enter at the time of luminosity dissolving into union, the key point of liberated body at the time of union dissolving into wisdom, and the key point of recognizing the perfection at the time of wisdom dissolving into the vidyadhara level of spontaneous presence.

Concerning this time of spontaneous presence, a tantra states:

> As for how the spontaneously present awareness manifests,
> It manifests as eight kinds of gates.

According to this statement, the expression of awareness itself is manifest as capacity, manifest as light, manifest as bodies, manifest as wisdom, manifest as nonduality, manifest as freedom from extremes, manifest as the impure gate of samsara, and manifest as the pure gate of wisdom. When these gates are embraced by the oral instructions, there will also be eight modes of dissolution.

By capacity dissolving, samsaric sentient beings are liberated as personal experience and thus there is not even a hint of confusion. Likewise, by the light of dissolving, there is one taste as dharmadhatu, which is not made of conceptual colors and not divided into families. By the bodies dissolving, there is purity as complete as the essence that transcends the elaborations of heads and arms. By the wisdom dissolving, the mother and child of dharmata mingle together. By nonduality dissolving, the three-thousandfold world system is liberated into the essence itself. By the freedom from extremes dissolving, the referential objects are exhausted. By the gate of samsara dissolving, one is free from the deluded object of a birth place. By the pure gate of wisdom dissolving into the essence body, one is enlightened in the great primordial purity, the exhaustion of phenomena beyond concepts. As the *Tantra of the Great Vastness of Space*[45] states:

> As long as this material body has not been abandoned,
> The enlightened qualities will not manifest,
> As, for instance, a garuda chick within its egg
> May have fully developed wing feathers,
> But it can not fly before hatching.
> The egg breaking open and the ability to fly then occur simultaneously.
> Similarly, the qualities of buddhahood
> Are not manifested at present but are veiled by the body.
> As soon as the body of karmic ripening is discarded,
> The enlightened qualities will be manifest.

The *Gongpa Tigdeb* also states:

> If one possesses the great confidence of realization,
> Just like a lion covers a great distance in a single leap,
> Through the great openness of wisdom
> There will be no bardo and, in one instant,
> One will attain enlightenment in the precious sphere.

As for the measure of liberation, the *Union of Sun and Moon Tanta* says:

> There are three levels of capacity: Those of foremost capacity will be liberated in three instants. The mediocre can be liberated in five meditation days or will definitely attain stability in twenty-one instants. Those of the lowest capacity will be assured of going to a natural nirmanakaya realm and will attain enlightenment without further bardo.

But all this chiefly depends upon one's present practice.

PART FOUR

THE FRUITION

34

THE FINAL FRUITION

Padmasambhava and Jamgön Kongtrül

In the third section, the explanation of the fruition, the final destination, has two aspects: a brief statement and the detailed explanation.

1. Brief statement

The *Lamrim Yeshe Nyingpo* root text says:

> To have realized the result of purification is as follows. ⸸

In this way, when the objects to be purified—the temporary defilements that are based on the ground of purification, the all-pervasive sugata-essence—have been thoroughly purified by means of the two stages of the path—the means to purify—you have realized the result of purification. Through that, the way this result naturally manifests as the great mandala of kayas and wisdoms, beyond rejection and attainment, is as follows.

The *Magical Illusion* specifically describes the identity of the fruition just mentioned:

> The accomplished yoga, the great yoga,
> Fully realized, as it is spontaneously present,
> Is merely a label; they are not two,
> And therefore it is described like that.

The definition is mentioned in the *Framework*:

> To reach the end of accomplishment is called fruition.

From Padmasambhava and Jamgön Kongtrül, *The Light of Wisdom*, Vol. V (Boudhanath: Rangjung Yeshe Publications, 2006), "Fruition."

Accordingly, the word *fruition* describes when a yogi has reached perfection in the supreme accomplishment of the pursued object of achievement. Its different aspects are described in the previous source:

> The identity of fruition is the five aspects
> Of body, speech, mind, qualities, and activities.
> According to context, each of these is five.

These correspond to the identity of the twenty-five qualities of fruition, to be explained, five aspects for each of the five comprising body, speech, mind, qualities, and activities.

2. Detailed explanation

The *Lamrim Yeshe Nyingpo* root text says:

> The perfection of the benefit of oneself is the peaceful dharmakaya. §
> The spontaneously present benefit for others is the unified
> sambhogakaya. §
> The manifold skill in means to tame beings is the way of nirmanakaya. §
> The distinct and unmixed appearance aspect is the abhisambodhikaya. §
> Their one taste as dharmadhatu of the emptiness aspect is the vajrakaya. §

> Having attained the five kayas, these are the five kinds of speech
> expressing their meaning: §
> Pure and ineffable is the ultimate speech of dharmakaya. §
> Illustrating through bodily form is the symbolic speech of
> sambhogakaya. §
> Possessing the voice of Brahma is the verbal speech of nirmanakaya. §
> Distinctively manifest is the knowledge speech of abhisambodhikaya. §
> The nonduality of audible emptiness is the wisdom speech of vajrakaya. §

> The essence of the kayas that is mind, the five wisdoms, §
> Manifests from dharmadhatu as being mirrorlike, §
> All-accomplishing, discriminating, and equality. §

> As sub-aspects of the kayas are the five perfect qualities §
> Of realm, palace, light rays, throne, and ornaments. §

> Through the pacifying, increasing, magnetizing, wrathful, and
> spontaneously accomplished activities, §

For as long as the sky exists, without knowing interruption, ৪
For that long, the benefit of all beings filling space ৪
Will occur spontaneously and free from effort. ৪

To explain this, there are five parts: the kayas in terms of that which serves as support for the superior qualities of all buddhas; the speech, being that which communicates the meaning of the Dharma to those to be tamed; the mind, being the supported which is the unmoving essence; the qualities, being the source of all needs and wishes; the activities, since they accomplish the benefit of others.

I.   The five kayas

Dharmakaya is the *essence*, having perfected the benefit for oneself through great abandonment and realization, in which every type of construct has completely subsided due to the wakefulness of knowing being liberated into basic space.

Sambhogakaya is the *nature* that spontaneously accomplishes the benefit of others, through the great compassionate frame of mind, which, while not departing from dharmakaya, appears as the unity of appearance and emptiness endowed with the major and minor marks of extraordinary causation in the perception of the offspring of the conquerors, the pure disciples on the ten bhumis.

Nirmanakaya is the *capacity* with the skillful means to tame whoever needs to be tamed—in accordance with the inclinations of impure disciples, the six classes of beings—through a display, in the manner of emanating indefinite myriad of apparitions, which appear as the crafted, the incarnated, the supreme, and so forth.

Abhisambodhikaya describes the manifest aspect of the individual and distinct virtues these three display in accordance with the individual karmic fortunes of disciples, while endowed with inconceivable qualities of wisdom, compassion, and capability such as the tenfold strength, the fourfold fearlessness, the eighteen unique qualities, the thirty-seven aspects of enlightenment, and so forth.

The unchanging vajrakaya is the empty quality endowed with the twofold purity and the fact that even the two rupakayas do not possess any separate solid existence, which is the indivisible one taste of the three kayas within the unchanging space of luminous dharmata.

II. The five types of speech

Having attained these five kayas, the respective five types of speech communicate and reveal meaning to the retinue.

To explain, the dharmakaya speech of ultimate nonarising is the aspect of utterly pure wisdom of dharmata beyond word and description that serves as the basis for all kinds of thought and expression.

The sambhogakaya speech of symbolic intent shows the wisdom that communicates meaning to the minds of the retinue through simply seeing the bodily form, just like a mirror that helps to identify flaws on the face so that they can be eliminated.

The nirmanakaya speech of verbal expression, endowed with the sixty aspects of Brahma's melodious voice, brings understanding with each word simultaneously in their own language as perceived by whoever needs to be influenced.

The abhisambodhi speech of knowledge manifests, while in fact not uttering even a single word, in whichever way the individual language or inclination of the six classes of beings may be, and is a completely unobstructed wakefulness that is lucid self-knowing.

The vajra speech is the wakefulness that communicates meaning free of the two extremes because every sound or voice is the nonduality of audible emptiness.

These five aspects of speech are identical in communicating, while their manners of expression and understanding are different.

III. The five wisdoms

As the essence of the five kayas, the five aspects of mind are the five wisdoms, the supported.

That is to say, the dharmadhatu wisdom, totally beyond focus, refers to the actualization of the ultimate alaya of the ground, having realized its nature, which without the act of abandoning is free from all temporary obscurations.

The mirrorlike wisdom manifests at that time from the transformation of the ultimate alaya of joining as being lucid and nonconceptual that serves as the basis for the remaining three to appear.

The all-accomplishing wisdom is the transformation of the five sense doors that is unobstructed and acts for the benefit of beings.

Discriminating wisdom, the transformation of the mental faculty, perceives all knowable objects and phenomena of the three times, as clearly and distinctly as the petals of a lotus flower.

Both of these are subsumed as the wisdom of equality, the transformation of the klesha-mind, which transcends accepting good and rejecting bad.

Among these, the dharmadhatu wisdom of emptiness is the nonconceptual mind of dharmakaya. The wisdom of equality is the sambhogakaya mind of great sameness. The all-accomplishing wisdom is the nirmanakaya mind that liberates beings. The mirrorlike wisdom is the abhisambodhi mind that clearly perceives everything. The discriminating wisdom is the indivisible vajra mind.

IV. The five qualities

The subsidiary attributes of these kayas are complete as the qualities that include the realm of total purity, the celestial palace beyond dimensions, the clear and pure rays of light, the especially exalted throne, and the ornaments of enjoyment.

To explain these in slightly more detail, the dharmakaya realm is basic space that by nature is utterly pure. The sambhogakaya realm is the self-manifest circle of spontaneously present radiance. The nirmanakaya realm consists of the one hundred billion threefold world systems.

The celestial palace is, in the case of dharmakaya, dharmadhatu, transcending constructs. In the case of sambhogakaya it is the spontaneously present dhatu displays, and for nirmanakaya it is of the nature of precious wisdom.

The rays of light are, for dharmakaya, the light rays of the five wisdoms. For sambhogakaya they blaze as the five colors that are the natural radiance of the wisdoms. And for nirmanakaya they are the sixty trillion light rays shining from each pore of the body.

The throne is, for dharmakaya, the unified view, for sambhogakaya the unified knowledge, and for nirmanakaya unified compassion.

The ornaments are, for dharmakaya, pure nonarising labeled as being ornaments. For sambhogakaya they are the extraordinary major and minor marks that are ornaments of natural radiance, and can be divided into outer, inner, and innermost aspects. Moreover, there are the famous ten sambhogakaya ornaments: the crown, earrings, choker, necklace, upper-arm ornaments, the two bracelets, the two anklets, and the long necklace.

The nirmanakaya ornaments are the common thirty-two major marks of excellence and the eighty minor marks. They are called common because the universal monarch also is endowed with a corresponding version of them.

V. The five activities

The activities are those of pacifying karma, emotional thought states, illness, and evil influences; of increasing life span and merit, splendor and wealth, and the realization of self-knowing wakefulness; of magnetizing and bringing under one's control all the phenomena of samsara and nirvana comprising the prana-mind displays; and of subjugating through wrathful compassion the enemies, obstructers, and misguiders who are not tamed by peaceful means. The spontaneously accomplished activity—while completely free of focus on doer and deed—is beyond partiality and bias, because of having realized the natural state exactly as it is.

These activities that influence those to be tamed have the nature of being everlasting, all-pervasive, and spontaneous. That is to say, they are everlasting, since as far as space reaches, samsara also does not end, and as long as samsara has yet to be emptied, the activities of the buddhas never cease. Just as the *Ornament of Realization* declares:

> For as long as samsara lasts, it is held,
> This activity will also not cease.

Though the activities may be everlasting, they are also not employed in separate directions but impartially pervade the realms of sentient beings to be tamed as far as space reaches. Just as the *Uttaratantra* states:

> Thus as far as endless space,
> Spontaneously and constantly,
> With unimpeded wisdom, they
> Engage in the true benefit of beings.

When the time for influencing those to be tamed has arrived, the activity is spontaneous in the sense of taking place effortlessly and naturally, exactly and unmistakenly in accordance with their abilities. The *Three Stages* mentions this:

> As the qualities of the fruition are spontaneous,
> They appear like the wish-fulfilling gem.

35

Signs and Levels of Progress

Padmasambhava

Homage to the blessed wisdom deity of awareness.

Without these signs and levels of progress on the path
That surely show when results have been obtained
In Dzogchen's innermost and total freedom,
You are no different from an ordinary person, and your practice is wasted.
Since your diligence wanes when signs of practice fail to appear,
This text describing them is of utmost importance.
My child, here are the signs of the path
For the person who trains in dharmata.

When a person practices with perseverance, there are two types of signs of the path, indefinite and definite, which indicate that the result will be swiftly attained.

The indefinite are known as basic signs, which appear due to one's previous connection even without having practiced. As they are unreliable, I will not describe them here.

The definite signs appear due to practicing, and they are of two types: changing and unchanging.

The changing signs can appear in actuality or as moods. The first kind is, when doing the ngöndro or rushen practices, your body feels at the brink of collapse, like the walls of a house in shambles; your voice feels worn out like when exhausted; or you convulse like someone possessed. These indicate that you have separated samsara and nirvana.

From Padmasambhava's *Single Cut of the Great Self-Liberation* (Boudhanath: Rangjung Yeshe Publications, 2006).

The moods are disenchantment with the samsaric body, speech, and mind. They indicate having purified the obscurations of the three realms and separated from samsara. Their absence indicates not having gained experience, so repeat the practice.

Based on the tiredness of body, speech, and mind, as the actual signs your body is blissful, your voice wants to speak out, and your mind experiences everything as space. You feel, "Now nothing exists!" As well as compassion for beings who fail to realize this, enthusiasm for the Dharma will also arise. As moods, you forget that you have a body, don't notice your breathing, and mentally don't want to part from the state of nonthought, thinking, "This is it!" These are the signs of having taken hold of the nirvanic type of mental stability. Their absence indicates not being well trained, so exert yourself and continue.

All these are only temporary signs; they change and are not reliable.

Next are the signs of the main practice, signs of having established rigpa in actuality through the view. The actual signs are feeling disenchantment with body, speech, and mind in a way that is visible to both yourself and others, and also having no interest in the activities of this life. Your voice is like that of a mute. In mind, you are tired of samsaric things, you feel a profound devotion for your guru, and a compassion for all beings wells up so that tears flow. There is trust in the consequence of actions, and you exert yourself in giving up misdeeds and practicing virtue.

The mood signs include lightness of body, even at times forgetting that you have a body, not noticing your breath's movement, and mentally feeling that everything is insubstantial and evanescent.

All these signs change and don't last. The signs of lasting value are the following.

Within the expansive space of the view, when awareness is utterly laid bare, without fluctuations, and doesn't project experience as being "other," that is the sign of having anchored awareness within dharmata.

The mood signs of having understood this are: no matter where your attention moves, understanding and realizing that it is your own mind, seeing that thoughts are projected and return as self-display, and understanding that they are like space, completely insubstantial. These are the signs of having established, through the view, that appearances are mind.

To recognize this even while dreaming is the sign of having reached the fullest degree of steadiness. If you sustain this, in seven years you will awaken to the state of nirmanakaya with the vanishing of the material body. If you don't recognize while dreaming, you will awaken at death. Therefore, to persevere in the practice is the conduct of the foremost person.

Now come the signs of experiencing the state of realization in actuality. In your body, speech, and mind, the actual signs are that your body is light and energetic, your voice is clear and able to express teachings you have never even heard, and your mind at times has some degree of clairvoyance. You see everything lucidly as rainbows, sometimes full of bodily forms and circles, sometimes becoming void and without reference points. As devotion to your guru grows even deeper and your concern for karmic consequences becomes more relaxed, you feel that your body emits light, at times your body is absent, your voice speaks unintentionally like an echo, and your mind is clear and blissful and does not project anything; now and then it turns void and forms no thoughts. All these occurrences change and cannot be relied on. The unchanging signs are the following.

There is no longer any experience in which you cling to a solid reality; instead, everything is sheer luminous display. Everything appears, but there is no solid reference point or clinging. To realize this is the sign of having established, through experience in training, that mind itself is empty.

To experience this even while dreaming is to have reached the fullest degree of steadiness. If you sustain this, in three years the material body will vanish and you awaken to the state of sambhogakaya's intangible wisdom body.

Next, the sign that this emptiness is spontaneously and effortlessly liberated in itself: regarding body, speech, and mind, the signs in actuality are that there is no attachment to a body, such as no fear of water. Moreover, previously unseen marks of excellence can be witnessed by both you and others. Your voice can express beneficial Dharma teachings simply from you directing your will toward others. In your mind, untainted clairvoyance arises.

The signs as meditation moods are that you neither remember nor even think of clinging to your body, speech, and mind; that whatever you experience is spacious and not taken as real; and that you feel as if you can move freely through rock, mountains, and the like. The unchanging signs are the following.

No matter what you experience, there is neither any conceptual focus nor any attempt to accept or reject. Rather, it is liberated without being assumed to be real, so whether day or night, without needing to remember it, appearance and emptiness are naturally liberated into nonduality. That is the sign of having established self-liberation through spontaneous conduct.

When the delusion of dreaming ends, you have reached the fullest degree of steadiness. If you sustain this, in one year the material body will vanish and you awaken to the state of dharmakaya without remainder.

Then, the sign that this self-liberation is brought to consummation, the fruition of spontaneous presence, appears only in others' perception, whereas in your personal perception, all kinds of signs and indications of progress on the path have ceased. This state, known as the vision of exhaustion in dharmata, means that the moving force of appearances has ceased, while the still quality of emptiness is no longer. Thus, the nondual nature of appearance and emptiness neither fluctuates nor changes in any way whatsoever. Instead there is a naturally awake quality that transcends meeting and separation—an unfabricated presence, an absence without any dismantling—which is an utterly naked state of aware emptiness free of clinging. In others' perceptions, since an unobstructed knowledge—original wakefulness as an all-pervasive capacity—is also present, there is an effortless unfolding of rupakayas for the welfare of beings.

Accordingly, as the basic nature of things is all-pervasive, unless the signs on the path of self-existing wakefulness have reached their fullest degree, there is no understanding of when the time of the spontaneously present fruition has arrived and the practice becomes smug and lazy. This manual of signs and degrees of progress is therefore of utmost importance.

> Without it, your attachment to emptiness is no different from that of the
>   general vehicles.
> With it, the fruition will quickly be reached to fulfill the aims of
>   yourself and others.
> Through Vajrasattva's blessings, it arose in Garab Dorje's heart.
>
> He accepted Shri Singha, who then entrusted it to me, Padmasambhava.
> May it meet with a worthy person of karmic destiny.
> Hide it from the unworthy person with wrong views.
> When a suitable recipient appears, bestow the ultimate lineage.
> The scripture lineage has the seal of strictness.
>
> Ema, this amazing, sublime teaching,
> The quintessence of mind terma, concealed in Ludü's belly,

Is entrusted to the care of Gönpo Nagpo, Palchen, the dakinis,
And to the wrathful dharmapalas, teaching guardians, and treasure lords.
Safeguard it; be sure you protect these teachings!
Samaya. Seal, seal, seal.

SARVA MANGALAM

36

Song of Fruition

Lama Shabkar

Emaho!
Once more, fortunate and only heart-children,
Listen joyfully to this vajra song!

When you have gained realization in this way,
The whole phenomenal world is the book of oral instructions and the
    real mandala.
On the multicolored parchment of appearances,
Awareness, the bamboo pen of self-existing wisdom,
Inscribes the letters of nonfixation that are groundless and primordially
    free.
This is read as the nonduality of appearance and emptiness.

On this spontaneously perfect mandala of the three-thousandfold universe
Is sprinkled the water of naturalness.
The pathways are the natural lines of the design,
And your footsteps are the drawings in colored powder.
Your own appearing yet empty body is the form of the divine yidam.
Your speech, resounding and yet empty, is its vajra recitation,
While your naturally freed and unfixated thoughts are the mind of the deity.

The movements of your arms and legs are mudras,
And eating and drinking is the dharmata offering.
All appearance of form is the body of the deity.
All sounds and speech are musical offerings.
Beyond keeping and breaking, this is the naturally fulfilled samaya.

From Lama Shabkar Tsokdrug Rangdröl, *Flight of the Garuda* (Boudhanath:
Rangjung Yeshe Publications, 1988), "Song 23."

Whatever else such a practitioner does,
He does not need to depend on the teachings of effort, cause and effect,
Because in the state of the luminous dharmata,
The instructions, the stages of development, and the samayas are all
    complete.

The special quality of the Great Perfection, fortunate heart-children,
Is the swift and effortless attainment of the marvelous and wondrous siddhis.

If you truly practice in this way,
All the concepts of samsara and nirvana are liberated into the
    primordial ground,
Like clouds vanishing into the sky.

When you realize this luminous dharmakaya of self-existing awareness,
Radiant as the unobscured sun,
You will be able to revive the dead, to comprehend all secrets,
And to convert beings by displaying various miraculous powers.

Having perfected the virtues of all the paths and levels,
People of superior capacity are liberated in this very life.
Those of mediocre capacity are liberated at the moment of death.
The ones of inferior capacity will be liberated into the ground of
    primordial purity in the intermediate state.

Thereafter, continuously remaining in the inner space without
    separation from the wisdoms of the three kayas,
They will display emanation bodies to tame whoever needs taming in
    whatever ways are necessary,
Thus ceaselessly benefiting beings.

Keep the meaning of these words in your heart,
And the sun of happiness will surely arise from within.

The one who composed this realization in songs
Is the renunciant Tsokdrug Rangdröl.
By its virtue, may many fortunate disciples
Swiftly purify the stains of ignorance, emotions, and concepts
Into the original space of primordial purity
And attain fruition in this very life.

37

FRUITION

Tsele Natsok Rangdröl

The Nature of Fruition

Now, as a conclusion, I shall explain how to accomplish the final fruition of the kayas and wisdoms.

When you become completely adept in the practice, you will gradually exhaust all the gross, subtle, and extremely subtle defilements of momentary coemergent ignorance. The knowledge of self-cognizant wisdom will develop corresponding to the extent that the defilements are purified. That is the nature of things.

Take the example of a skilled doctor, who through medicine and treatment partially removes the obscuring factors from a person who has been blind since birth. When the blind person's eyes are opened, he will see only gross outlines, not fine details at first. Following this, by gradually having the remaining covers removed, he will finally see everything exactly as it is. The eyes are something he already possesses, not some new acquisition. Likewise, the nature of your sugata-essence, the original wisdom of primordial purity, is blinded by a temporary defilement. The doctor-like master with his medicine-like oral instructions and treatment opens up the kayas and wisdoms, which are like your eyes. Realizing this fact is called fruition. The three kayas, the wisdoms, and so forth, are not something new appearing from somewhere else. The *Sutra of Purified Karma* explains how to apply the methods for purifying the momentary defilements that have arisen, ensuring they do not reoccur.

Adapted from Tsele Natsok Rangdröl, *Circle of the Sun* (Boudhanath: Rangjung Yeshe Publications, 1990), "The Nature of Fruition."

The Time of Liberation

The basic manner of liberation common to both Mahamudra and Dzogchen is the dissolution of the aggregates into dharmadhatu without remainder within this lifetime. According to the *Tantra of the Jewel Mound*:

> Through understanding this in your own mind
> By means of unmanifest nonthought,
> All appearances naturally dissolve
> And everything, as complete openness,
> Becomes the nature of the great empty cognizance.
>
> The four elements—earth, water, fire, and wind—
> Do not manifest in their individual properties
> But vanish like mist into space.
>
> The manifold types of deluded clinging
> Are without arising, whatever one may think.
> Moreover, the aspects of perceiver and perceived naturally cease
> And are spontaneously exhausted without manifestation.
>
> Experiencing this in one's own cognition,
> All beings also become like this.

For the Tögal practitioner, the difference lies in the fact that all outer material objects that arise due to deluded perception cease and you gain mastery over the actual buddhafields of inner wisdom. Mastering both birth and entering through the illusory great transformation body, which is like the reflection of the moon in water, you act for the welfare of beings to the limits of the sky. People of middling capacity will inspire faith in disciples by means of relic bones, relic pills, seed syllables, sounds, earthquakes, rainbows, and rains of flowers. These are the signs that they will be liberated in one of the bardo states. Even those of lesser capacity will take rebirth from a lotus flower in a natural nirmanakaya realm. By receiving empowerment and prophecy, they will traverse the remainder of the path and attain enlightenment.

The Kayas

In any case, all the momentary obscurations of karma, disturbing emotions, habitual tendencies, and dualistic knowledge are naturally purified. This is because all conceptual thinking is exhausted; even the finest and most subtle concepts and tendencies are not present. To remain in the innate, empty, and cognizant state of great bliss—the circle of perpetual continuity of inseparable space and wisdom—is known as dharmakaya.

Different styles of teaching in the sutras and tantras, like stating that the dharmakaya remains in a form with face and arms, are meant to tame different types of people. But apparently there are people who proliferate many different treatises and create many points of controversy, clinging to particular segments of these quotations. According to my own understanding, one doesn't realize the natural state of dharmakaya by quarreling about whether or not a particular one-sided view can be established or whether or not it is real.

Dharmakaya is not an object of thought and description and does not lie within the confines of permanence and annihilation. Even if you exert yourself for one hundred eons in the intellectual refutations and affirmations of fixating thoughts, you will definitely not see the natural face of naked dharmakaya. Once you realize the ultimate nature of primordial purity as it is, I think it is sufficient to simply discover dharmakaya within yourself without any dialectic dispute.

From the natural radiance of unconstructed dharmakaya, the sambhogakayas of spontaneous presence automatically manifest as the fivefold wisdom mandalas of form endowed with the major and minor marks, acting effortlessly for the benefit of the bodhisattvas and vidyadharas on the ten bhumis.

By the unceasing power of the expression of the union of these two kayas and due to the ripened effect of the seeds of bodhichitta and aspiration made while on the path, the inconceivable number of compassionate nirmanakayas that tame whoever needs to be tamed manifest as countless and unfathomable creations in various places and as various species in conformity with those to be tamed. In essence, the nirmanakayas possess no deliberate notion or concepts such as subject and object. They do not fixate on self and others as being separate. But, by the power of aspiration and compassion they fulfill the hopes and desires of each being, just like the wish-fulfilling jewel or the wish-granting tree. This is the nature of the qualities and activities of all the victorious ones.

These three kayas, as well as other divisions like the four or five kayas or even the nine aspects of the three kayas, can actually be condensed into two: dharmakaya and rupakaya. In the ultimate sense, these two are of one taste in dharmakaya. As an example, they are like a mirror and its reflection or like the sky and a rainbow. In terms of the meaning, they are present as the kayas and wisdoms, the conditioned and the innate, cognizance and emptiness, essence and manifestation, space and wakefulness—the equal and perfect great sphere of spontaneous presence that is beyond change or alteration throughout the four times. This state is renowned as the inseparable kayas and wisdoms.

These details are found extensively in all the major authoritative scriptures. Here, I have only mentioned them in brief.

Epilogue

Throughout the entire billionfold universe
You will never find anything superior to the wondrous Great
    Perfection,
The ultimate extract of the extensive secret teachings of the victorious
    ones,
The quintessence of the innermost essence.

Though it was condemned with great effort by many people,
Such as Khugpa Lhatsey and Paldzin,
Who were blessed with the power of a demon,
Who can refute the numberless beings who attained the light body in
    India and Tibet?

These days when the sun of the teachings is about to set on the western
    mountains,
When the butter skins of rigid minds remain uncured by the butter,
Though they study a million dry words of sophistry and scholarship,
There is no way people haughty with learning will read this.

Even those who have entered the boat of the teachings of the Early
    Translations
Do not raise high the banner of renunciation
And do not vigorously apply the oars of detachment.
So who will uphold the bloodline of the vidyadhara lineage?

Hiding their enemy, ego-clinging, deep within their hearts,
Although they twirl rosaries for one hundred years

With the fierce mantras of Hung Hung! Phat Phat! Guard Guard! Foil Foil!,
There is no hope for them to subdue the vicious demon in their own minds.

Without knowing that spontaneously liberated freely resting
Is the nature of the realms of the three kayas, the magical display of
    awareness,
Won't the practitioner watching the enchanting spectacle of experiences
    and visions
Be like nothing but a cat hunting mice?

Through the primordial purity of Trekchö, strip rigpa to nakedness.
Without attachment, purify the realms through the luminous displays
    of Tögal.
Without hoping for or desiring the signs of the four visions,
Practice in this way and you will capture the kingdom of Samantabhadra.

Although an ignorant person like myself
Is unqualified to explain, teach, and compose,
I wrote this in response to the request
Of the yogi Tsültrim Zangpo.

All errors in language and meaning, and defects of incorrect points,
I confess openly before my teachers.
May all the virtue exemplified by my noble intention
Be dedicated to all beings, equal to space.

By the power and blessings of the wondrous compassion
Of all the buddhas and bodhisattvas of the Mind, Symbol, and Oral
    Lineages,
And by the power of the nature of the three kayas and the five wisdoms
That are spontaneously present in the nature of beings since the
    beginning,
May the lamp of the profound essence, the Dzogchen teachings,
Dispel the inherent obscurations of sentient beings.
In the expanse of dharmadhatu endowed with the threefold wisdoms,
May there be the auspiciousness of equal and perfect enlightenment.

AUSPICIOUS COMPLETION

.

Bardo Aspiration

The aspiration that is a pointing-out instruction for the bardos

Longchen Rabjam

OM AH HUNG

Please pay heed, victorious ones of all directions and all times.
By the goodness gathered in the threefold times, and what I now possess,
From the time without beginning up until this very day,
May enlightenment be reached by me and everyone without exception.

In every incarnation, while this is not attained,
May we see the basic essence, Great Perfection's deepest path,
Dharmata, directly, the increase of visions, and the culmination.
May the body made of matter then dissolve into a mass of light.

May we not be faced with anguish at the interrupted life.
May the gurus and the yidams, all the dakas and dakinis,
Appear in actuality, right before our very eyes,
Grant empowerment and predictions, and then guide us to the realms
   divine.

Since everything conditioned does not last, our death will surely come,
The breathing stops, the mind and body go their separate ways.
May we not become bewildered, start to cling, or be attached,
But remain in dharmakaya's natural and continuous state.

When the time has come to shed this body, this material illusion,
The perceptions and the skandhas, gross and subtle thoughts, all cease.
May we all be liberated, just when mind and body part,
Unbewildered, into all-pervasive vastness, timeless space.

From Longchen Rabjam's collected writings (Boudhanath: Rangjung Yeshe
Publications, 1993).

Then, one into another, untrue elements dissolve,
A lucid state, unmixed and pure, with lights of the five colors,
Without creating concepts, may the vajra chains in colors five,
Be undivided, unified, perfected in dharmata's realm.

When wrathful demons as enormous HUNGs and other forms,
When billion universes fill with roaring sounds of HUNG,
May we recognize the vital point: the HUNG sound is an empty knowing
And realize that every empty sound is like an echo.

When hordes of Yama's executioners surround us,
Attack, slay, kill, escape, give chase—may all this panic naturally
    dissolve.
Freed from illusory displays of being struck with fear and terror,
May we know them to be forms of yidams, both the peaceful and wrathful.

When the hordes of wrathful herukas come swarming forth
From the Blazing Blissful Palace in the mansion of the skull,
May we not behold them as the forms of dreadful demons,
But instead gain insight of the heart essence's pithy meaning.

When the multitude of peaceful ones dissolve in basic space
From the Palace of the Jewel Dome that is within the heart,
The moment the displays transpose and manifest as forms of light,
May awareness then dissolve into the brilliant expanse.

When the wheel of channels at the throat becomes unfastened
With a thousand roaring thunder claps of terrifying laughter,
May we recognize the peaceful-wrathful song of AH and HUNG
And free it as the nonarising sound of empty knowing.

When the white and red, the means and knowledge, are converging at
    the heart
From the Bliss Sustaining Palace in the secret center,
Untainted, may this natural state of blissful emptiness
Cause winds and mind to be absorbed within the central channel.

Then as we remain within dharmata's bardo state,
May consciousness not stray into oblivion,
But, having realized the vast and timeless purity, the natural liberation,
May we settle in the "other-empty" state where phenomena dissolve.

Upon seeing the reality of dharmata directly,
May the conceptual remedy, fixated mindfulness, be freed,
And realizing timeless purity, the nature of phenomena exhausted,
May we stay within the nonconceptual state devoid of constructs.

When the dome of fivefold wisdoms opens up its doors
From the palace of five-colored, interwoven rainbows,
And the realm is filled with deities and spheres,
May we meet the fivefold kayas and five wisdoms.

When we meet with the five kayas and five wisdoms
In the incandescent palace that is the empty bindu's lamp,
May we, freed from doubt, that vacillating dualistic feeling,
Fully merge into Samantabhadra's timeless state.

Having met the fourfold lamps, mind's essence, face to face,
In the incandescent palace that is the empty bindu's lamp,
May we reach spontaneous presence with a perfect steadiness
And transpose to space and rigpa's state of vastness.

May the luminous and empty lamp of dharmakaya shine.
May the dharmakaya emptiness of knowing be attained.
May sambhogakaya's ceaseless dual vision be attained.
May nirmanakaya's perfect natural knowing be attained.
Having reached the triple kayas, may we work for others' good.

This completes the aspiration for the bardo of dying and dharmata that liberates through hearing, written by Kunkhyen Longchen Rabjam.

Notes

1   From *The Mind Ornament of Samantabhadra* (Boudhanath: Rangjung Yeshe Publications, 2003).

2   Tulku Urgyen Rinpoche, *As It Is, Vol. I* (Boudhanath: Rangjung Yeshe Publications, 1999).

3   Longchen Rabjam, The Practice of Dzogchen, translated by Tulku Thondup (Ithaca, N.Y.: Snow Lion Publications, *1995*), pp. *131–32*.

4   Many so-called teachings appear in the world due to the influence of "demonic forces" to lead us astray. Demonic forces (or negative forces) are the manifestation of our own negative karma and emotions. They manifest as unhealthy images, sounds, teachings, or feelings, although some portray them as external spirits. If we stay on the right path, however, without letting ourselves be distracted by them, we transcend their influences, just as the Buddha transcended temptations before his enlightenment. [Tulku Thondup]

5   Tulku Urgyen Rinpoche, *The Light of Wisdom, Vol. IV*, pp. 17-18.

6   Tulku Urgyen Rinpoche, *As It Is, Vol. 1*, p. 50.

7   Here Tulku Urgyen Rinpoche plays on two words, *zagchey* and *zagmey*, which are sometimes translated as "material and insubstantial," sometimes as "conditioned and unconditioned." The usual translation, in the context of the sutras, is "tainted and untainted" or "defiling and nondefiling."

8   According to oral teachings from Tulku Urgyen Rinpoche, "self-arising and self-dissolving" (*rangshar rangdröl*)—rather than *by* themselves—means that thoughts arise from the dharmata nature itself and dissolve into this nature itself, like waves rising from and subsiding into a body of water.

9   Translator's colophon: *For the benefit of students at Chökyi Nyima Rinpoche's Dzogchen retreats at his Gomde centers, this was translated while following the oral instructions previously received from Tulku Urgyen Rinpoche, by Erik Pema Kunsang, during a single session at Nagi Gompa Hermitage in 2001 and then re-edited in 2003 with Michael Tweed. This text was included with special permission from Chökyi Nyima Rinpoche.*

10   The *Turquoise Scripture* in the *Vima Nyingtig* cycle mentions that Manjushrimitra's name at first was Manjushriprati.

11   The *Turquoise Scripture* in the *Vima Nyingtig* cycle mentions that Vimalamitra's other name was Jemalamudra, which in Tibetan is translated as Seal of Vastness (*phyag rgya rgya chen*).

12   A note within the original text says: Also known by the name Dharmapala.

13   The narration continues with the events that surrounded the Dzogchen teachings brought to Tibet by Jemalamudra (Vimalamitra).

14   One *drey* equals roughly two pounds or one kilo.

15   This is the *Treasury of the Supreme Vehicle (Tekchok Dzö)*, the first of the seven treasuries.

16   The *Treasury of the Natural State (Nelug Dzö)*.

17   The *Treasury of Oral Instructions (Man-ngag Dzö)*.

18   The *Treasury of Philosophical Views (Drubtha Dzö)*.

19   The *Wish-Fulfilling Treasury –(Yishin Dzö)*.

20   The *Treasury of the Meaning of Words (Tsigdon Dzö)*.

21   The *Treasury of Dharmadhatu (Chöying Dzö)*.

22   Cutting is the Chö practice of Machik Labdrön, and Pacification is the Shijey system of Padampa Sangye.

23   The *Three Portents* of the Dzogchen teachings refer to three primeval representations of enlightened body, speech, and mind: the statue of Vajrasattva, a self-resounding tantra, and the vajra of dharmata.

24   The fourth empowerment is often translated as "the empowerment of awareness display" or "the empowerment to the expression of awareness."

25   The four paths of training are those of accumulation, joining, seeing, and cultivation, while the "path without impediment" is their final point. In the sutras the vajralike samadhi is often mentioned in combination with two others: the samadhi of courageous movement and the samadhi of magical illusion. [Tulku Urgyen Rinpoche]

26   The most subtle defilements to be discarded that are difficult to destroy, vanquish, or defeat. The seven vajra qualities that destroy [defilements] such as being uncuttable and so forth are as mentioned in the *Vajra Vidarana*. It is also taught that the qualities such as being "solid, essential, and devoid of hollows," as mentioned in the *Peak Scripture* are most befitting in this context. [Jokyab Rinpoche]

27   Here, according to Kongtrül Rinpoche, *resolve (la bzla)* means "to transcend" (*la 'da' ba*). According to Khyentse Rinpoche it means "to resolve" (*thag chod pa*). [Jokyab]

28   1.   The ground of the natural state as the essential nature of things that is endowed with the three aspects of original wakefulness, before the split between confusion and liberation.

     2.   The way in which sentient beings were deluded from it.

     3.   The way the ground is present as kayas and wisdoms, even though beings are deluded from the spontaneously present capacity.

     4.   The abode of the self-knowing wakefulness which is the *Chitta Mandala* of the heart.

     5.   The pathways of this wisdom, which are the four channels, as well as the moving winds.

6. The gate for the wisdom to manifest, which is the eyes and so forth, and the essential characteristics of the lamps.

7. The key points of the fields, which are flawless space, the sun, moon, and butter lamp.

8. The way to put these into practice, which are Trekchö and Tögal.

9. The definitive signs to measure progress, which are the fourfold confidence and so forth.

10. The joining of the mother and child wisdom lamps in the intermediate bardo states, in case the practice has not been perfected.

11. The ultimate point of all this, the great state of liberation which is the original ground itself, and after being liberated how the capacity once more manifests.

Thus there is an outline of eleven points. [Jokyab]

Vimalamitra, in his *Great Commentary on the Hearing Lineage,* describes these eleven points—the eleven principal topics of the tantras of the Innermost Unexcelled Section—in the following way:

1. Stating the way in which the natural state of ground originally was, before buddhas appeared through realization and before sentient beings appeared through lack of realization.

2. Establishing how confusion occurred in this state.

3. Describing how the basis or seed of the truly perfected buddhahood is present in a sentient being during the time of confusion.

4. Stating where the location is situated in oneself.

5. The pathway through which this awareness-wisdom that is present in oneself manifests.

6. The gate through which this awareness-wisdom manifesting through that pathway appears.

7. The field in which this awareness-wisdom appearing through that gate is seen.

8. How the person seeing this field of revealed awareness-wisdom should practice.

9. Identifying the signs and marks of progress of practice.

10. The way in which it manifests in the bardo of dharmata for someone who, although possessing these pith instructions, got carried away by laziness and did not succeed in practicing.

11. Describing the ultimate state of the great liberation. [Erik Pema Kunsang]

29 "(of fruition)" is included based on Khenpo Rinchen Namgyal's commentary. [epk]

30 See *Dzogchen Essentials,* PART THREE.

31 As opposed to a wealthy, famous, or powerful man.

32 Here, awareness is rigpa.

33 This text is one of the last writings of Kyabje Dudjom Rinpoche.

34 "Permanent wishes" is a play on the name Samten, the person who requested these teachings.

35 In another source text, Shri Singha defined *Ati* as *nonarising self-existence.*

36 An alternative rendering could be: *All* refers to settling into a state within which no form is conceptualized.

37 In a similar conversation from another source ("The Cycle of Vital Points", *Lama Gongdü Shülen*), Padmasambhava says to Yeshe Tsogyal: "In *all-ground*, 'all' refers to conceptualizing thoughts and 'ground' is mingled with dharmakaya and is therefore a vessel for good and evil habitual tendencies. All-ground consciousness is mind that stirs from the all-ground and arises as thinking."

Moreover, since one or more of the segments in our manuscript of "Ten Profound Points of Essential Advice" seems to have been truncated over the centuries, I have used some of Padmasambhava's words from "The Cycle of Vital Points", a terma revealed by Sangye Lingpa in the 14th century. [epk]

38 To quote a similar passage from *Lama Gongdü Shülen* in which Padmasambhava tells Yeshe Tsogyal: *Vipashyana* is when you vividly and all at once see the nature of things. When applying this experientially to your own mind, after you have settled into the equal nature of dharmata, to experience vividly the nature of things in whatever you see and whatever you think—that is the vital point of the nonduality of shamatha and vipashyana.

39 This quote is taken from *Calling the Guru from Afar, A Supplication to Pierce Your Heart with Devotion,* written by the first Jamgön Kongtrül, Lodrö Thaye. Several English translations exist: one in *Journey Without Goal*, (Shambhala Publications), and one from Rangjung Yeshe Publications that includes extra verses for lineage masters.

40 *Three Words Striking the Vital Point (tshig gsum gnad brdeg)* is the famous pith instructions by Garab Dorje, the first human master in the Dzogchen lineage.

41 For instance, read the story of Ngaktrin Lama in Blazing Splendor, who when eight years old was pointed out the nature of mind by the old lama in charge of the chants for the protector shrine.

42 Please understand that we have omitted the detailed pointing-out instruction and left a skeletal semblance for reference. It is necessary to receive the teachings personally and in their entirety from a qualified master.

43 The vital point here in 'the differentiation of the practice' is for instance to distinguish between *sem* and *rigpa* through the experiential guidance of one's personal teacher.

44 The ritual of name-burning is performed for a recently deceased person to ensure a favorable rebirth either as a human being or in a pure land.

45 The *Tantra of the Great Vastness of Space (nam kha' klong yangs chen po'i rgyud)* is a Dzogchen tantra belonging to the Space Section.

Contributors

Adeu Rinpoche, Trulshik. A major living master of the Drukpa Kagyü and Nyingma lineages. He resides at the Tsechu Monastery in the Nangchen kingdom of Kham, Tibet.

Chökyi Nyima Rinpoche is the oldest son and a spiritual heir of the widely renowned late Dzogchen master Tulku Urgyen Rinpoche. He is the author of *Present Fresh Wakefulness, Indisputable Truth* and *The Union of Mahamudra and Dzogchen* (Rangjung Yeshe Publications). His Holiness the sixteenth Karmapa recognized Chökyi Nyima as a reincarnate bodhisattva and advised him to turn his efforts toward instructing Western practitioners, transmitting Tibetan Buddhism to the rest of the world. He is the abbot of one of the largest Buddhist monasteries in Nepal, located at the sacred Boudhanath Stupa in Kathmandu, Nepal. (www.shedrub.org)

Dudjom Rinpoche (1904–1987). The incarnation of the great treasure revealer Dudjom Lingpa. His Holiness was the supreme head of the Nyingma lineage after exile from Tibet. He is regarded as one of the most prominent scholars of our time.

Jamgön Kongtrül (1813–1899). Also known as Lodrö Thaye, Yönten Gyatso, and Padma Garwang and by his tertön name Padma Tennyi Yungdrung Lingpa. He was one of the most prominent Buddhist masters in the nineteenth century and placed special focus upon a nonsectarian attitude. Renowned as an accomplished master, scholar, and writer, he authored more than one hundred volumes of scriptures. The best-known are his *Five Treasuries*, among which are the sixty-three volumes of the *Rinchen Terdzö*, the terma literature of the one hundred great tertöns.

Jamgön Mipham Rinpoche—(1846-1912). A student of Jamgön Kongtrül, Jamyang Khyentse Wangpo and Paltrul Rinpoche. Blessed by Manjushri, he became one of the greatest scholars of his time. His collected works fill more than thirty volumes. Mipham was regarded as a direct emanation of Manjushri.

Khenpo Ngawang Palzang, alias *Khenpo Ngakchung* (1879-1941)—scholar-teacher at Katok monastic college and a very important reviver of the scholastic lineage of expounding the Dzogchen scriptures. Considered to be incarnation of both Vimalamitra and Longchenpa. Chatral Sangye Dorje is one of his last living disciples. Khenpo Ngakchung got his name because there was an older khenpo with the name Ngawang, so he became the "Younger Khenpo Ngawang." One of his works is available in English with a short biography in the introduction: Khenpo Ngawang Pelzang, *A Guide to the Words of My Perfect Teacher* (Shambhala Publications).

Lama Shabkar—(1781-1851). Literally, 'White Feet.' The name given to him because wherever he placed his feet the area became 'white' or virtuous. His autobiography, *The Life of Shabkar* (Snow Lion Publications), is a must-read.

Longchen Rabjam or Longchenpa (1308-1363) was a major lineage master and writer of the Nyingma tradition; an incarnation of Princess Pema Sal, the daughter of King Trisong Deutsen, to whom Guru Rinpoche had entrusted his own lineage of Dzogchen known as *Khandro Nyingtig*. He is single-handedly regarded as the most important writer on Dzogchen teachings. His works include the *Seven Great Treasuries*, the *Three Trilogies* and his commentaries in the *Nyingtig Yabzhi*. A more detailed account of his life and teachings is found in *Buddha Mind* by Tulku Thondup Rinpoche, (Snow Lion Publications).

Nyoshul Khen Rinpoche (1932 -1999)—one of the greatest recent khenpos of the Nyingma tradition; renowned for his spontaneous poetry and songs of realization; disciple of Shedrub Tenpey Nyima and one of the holders of the *Hearing Lineage of Nyingtig* which came through Jigmey Lingpa and Paltrul Rinpoche.

Padmasambhava is the miraculous great master who brought Vajrayana to Tibet in the eight century. He is also referred to as Guru Rinpoche, the precious teacher. For his biography, see *The Lotus-Born*, (Rangjung Yeshe Publications).

Paltrul Rinpoche was a great nonsectarian Tibetan master of the nineteenth century and one of the foremost scholars of his time. He was known not only for his scholarship and learning but also for his example of renunciation and compassion. His most famous works include *The Words of My Perfect Teacher* and his commentary on *Three Words Striking the Vital Point* (*Tsiksum Nedek*), the epitome of the Dzogchen teachings.

Samantabhadra is the primordial buddha who awakened to enlightenment many eons before this world was formed; forefather of the Dzogchen teachings.

Shakya Shri Jñana was a Tibetan mahasiddha of the nineteenth century; belonged chiefly to the Drukpa Kagyu lineage. Tulku Urgyen Rinpoche describes him in detail in his memoirs, *Blazing Splendor*, (Rangjung Yeshe Publications).

Shri Singha was the chief disciple and successor of Manjushrimitra in the lineage of the Dzogchen teachings. He was born in the city of Shokyam in Khotan and studied with the masters Hatibhala and Bhelakirti. Among Shri Singha's disciples were four outstanding masters: Jnanasutra, Vimalamitra, Padmasambhava and the Tibetan translator Vairotsana.

Thrangu Rinpoche, Khenchen, ranks as one of the foremost masters of the Kagyü lineage. He lives in Kathmandu, Nepal, and teaches in numerous countries around the world. He is also the author of *Songs of Naropa* and *King of Samadhi*, both Rangjung Yeshe Publications.

Tsele Natsok Rangdröl. (b. 1608) Important master of the Kagyü and Nyingma schools. His published works in English include *Mirror of Mindfulness, Lamp of Mahamudra, Circle of the Sun, Heart of the Matter*, and *Empowerment*, (Rangjung Yeshe Publications). About this master and his writings, Chökyi Nyima Rinpoche said: "People who harbor no ambition to become a great scholar, but who want to focus on truly realizing the ultimate point of Vajrayana training should study just a few of the writings of Tsele Natsok Rangdröl. In these, they will find the pith instructions that are the very heart of the Dharma."

Tsoknyi Rinpoche, Drubwang was recognized by His Holiness the sixteenth Gyalwang Karmapa as a reincarnation of Drubwang Tsoknyi, a renowned master of the Drukpa Kagyü and Nyingma traditions. Later he was brought up by the great master Khamtrül Rinpoche. Among his other teachers are Dilgo Khyentse Rinpoche, his late father Tulku Urgyen Rinpoche, Adeu Rinpoche of Nangchen, and Nyoshul Khen Rinpoche. Rinpoche is the head of the Drukpa Heritage Project to preserve the literature of the Drukpa Kagyü lineage. He is also the abbot of Ngedön Ösel Ling in the Kathmandu Valley of Nepal and author of *Carefree Dignity* and *Fearless Simplicity* (Rangjung Yeshe Publications). (www.pundarika.org)

Tulku Urgyen Rinpoche was born in eastern Tibet on the tenth day of the fourth Tibetan month in 1920 and passed away in Nepal on February 13, 1996. H. H. Khakyab Dorje, the fifteenth Gyalwang Karmapa, recognized him as an incarnate lama. He studied and practiced the teachings of both the Kagyü and Nyingma orders of Tibetan Buddhism.

In the Nyingma tradition, Tulku Urgyen held the complete teachings of the last century's three great masters: Terchen Chokgyur Lingpa, Jamyang Khyentse Wangpo, and Kongtrül Lodrö Thaye. He had an especially close transmission for the Chokling Tersar, a compilation of all the empowerments, textual authorizations, and oral instructions of Padmasambhava's teachings, which were rediscovered by Terchen Chokgyur Lingpa, his great-grandfather.

Tulku Urgyen established several monasteries and retreat centers in Nepal. The most important ones in the Kathmandu region are at Boudhanath, the site of the Great Stupa; at the Asura Cave, where Padmasambhava manifested the Mahamudra Vidyadhara level; and at the Swayambhu stupa. He primarily lived at the Nagi Gompa Hermitage above the Kathmandu Valley. He is the father of tulkus Chökyi Nyima Rinpoche, Tsikey Chokling Rinpoche, Drubwang Tsoknyi Rinpoche, and Yongey Mingyur Rinpoche.

Rinpoche instructed a growing number of Dharma students in essential meditation practice. He was famed for his profound meditative realization and for the concise, lucid, and humorous style with which he imparted the essence of the Buddhist teachings. His method of teaching was "instruction through one's own experience." Using few words, this way of teaching pointed out the nature of mind, revealing a natural simplicity of wakefulness that enabled the student to actually touch the heart of awakened mind.

Yeshe Tsogyal—The chief Tibetan female disciple of Guru Rinpoche who received almost all the transmissions he passed on in Tibet and later compiled his teachings.

Credits

Unless otherwise noted, all translations © by Erik Pema Kunsang, previously published or unpublished, are reprinted by arrangement with Rangjung Yeshe Publications, Boudhanath, www.rangjung.com.

"A Mirror to Reflect the Most Essential" is from a collection of Longchen Rabjam's writings, © 2005 Erik Pema Kunsang.

"Dzogchen Key Points" is from an unpublished oral teaching by Tulku Urgyen Rinpoche, © 2004 by Erik Pema Kunsang.

"The Vital Essence" by Shakya Shri Jñana, © 2004 by Erik Pema Kunsang.

"The Written Narration:—in India" is from Dzogchen Sangwa Nyingtig, by Vimalamitra © 2005 by Erik Pema Kunsang. (*ka. rdzogs pa chen po gsang ba snying tig yang zab bsdus pa'i snying po las ৪ lo rgyus kyi yi ge bzhugs so ৪.*)

"The Story of Vimalamitra and Vairotsana—from Sanglingma" by Yeshe Tsogyal, © 2001 by Erik Pema Kunsang.

"The History of the Heart Essence of the Dakinis" is from Khandro Nyingtig. Tibetan title: *mkha' 'gro snying thig gi lo rgyus bzhugs so ৪ mkha' 'gro snying thig* Vol. E, pp. 69-74, Taklung Tsetrül Pema Wangyal's edition. © 2005 by Erik Pema Kunsang.

"Historical Background" is from *Rainbow Painting* by Tulku Urgyen Rinpoche, © 1995 by Tulku Urgyen Rinpoche and Rangjung Yeshe Publications.

"Guidance Manuals" is from an introductory teaching by Tulku Urgyen Rinpoche in Circle of the Sun, © 1990 by Erik Pema Kunsang.

"Song of Encouragement to Read the Seven Treasuries" by Paltrul Rinpoche, © 1990 by Erik Pema Kunsang.

"The Aspiration for All the Writings of the Great Omniscient One" by Khenpo Ngakchung, Ngawang Palzang, © 1995 by Erik Pema Kunsang.

"The Dzogchen Scriptures" by Khenpo Ngakchung, Ngawang Palzang, © 1995 by Erik Pema Kunsang.

"The Prayer of Kuntuzangpo" translated by © 2005 Bhakha Tulku and Steven Goodman. Reprinted by arrangement with Steven Goodman. From: *kun tu bzang po'i dgongs pa zang thal du bstan pa'i rtsa rgyud.*

"Ati Yoga" is from *The Light of Wisdom, Vol. IV* by Padmasambhava and Jamgön Kongtrül, © 2001 by Rangjung Yeshe Publications.

"The Spontaneous Vajra Manifestation of Awareness and Emptiness" by Jamgön Mipham Rinpoche, © 1995 by Erik Pema Kunsang. (*jam dpal rdzogs pa chen po gzhi lam 'bras bu dbyer med pa'i don la smon pa rig stong rdo rje'i rang dgangs zhes bya ba*).

"The Fourth Dharma of Gampopa" is from *Repeating the Words of the Buddha* and *As It Is, Vol. 1* by Tulku Urgyen Rinpoche, © 1999 by Rangjung Yeshe Publications.

"Pointing the Staff at the Old Man" is from *Advice from the Lotus-Born* by Padmasambhava. Translated by Erik Pema Kunsang, © 1994.

"A Dear Treasure for Destined Disciples" by Dudjom Rinpoche is from *Crystal Cave.* Translated by Erik Pema Kunsang, © 1990. (*rdzogs chen ngo sprod skal ldan rnams kyi snying nor*).

"Ten Profound Points of Essential Advice" by Shri Singha. Rediscovered terma treasures by Rigdzin Gödem. © 1995 by Erik Pema Kunsang. (*gnad tig zhal gdams zab mo'i them bcu zhes bya ba bzhugs so ૹ*).

"The Inheritance" is from *As It Is, Vol. 2* by Tulku Urgyen Rinpoche, © 2000 by Tulku Urgyen Rinpoche and Rangjung Yeshe Publications.

"The Dzogchen Preliminaries" by Tulku Urgyen Rinpoche, © 1984 by Rangjung Yeshe Publications.

"Songs of Examining" is from *Flight of the Garuda* by Lama Shabkar. Translated by Erik Pema Kunsang, © 1990.

"Taking Direct Perception as the Path" is from *Crystal Clear* by Thrangu Rinpoche, © 2003 by Thrangu Rinpoche and Erik Pema Kunsang.

"Shamatha and Vipashyana" is from *As It Is, Vol. 2* by Tulku Urgyen Rinpoche, © 2000 by Tulku Urgyen Rinpoche and Rangjung Yeshe Publications.

"The Actual View of Trekchö" is from *Circle of the Sun* by Tsele Natsok Rangdröl, © 1990 by Erik Pema Kunsang.

"Buddha Nowhere Else" is from *As It Is, Vol. 1* by Tulku Urgyen Rinpoche, © 1999 by Tulku Urgyen Rinpoche.

"The Mirror of Essential Points" by Nyoshul Khen Rinpoche is from *Crystal Cave.* Translated by Erik Pema Kunsang, © 1990.

Contact Addresses
for Teachings and Retreats

For information regarding programs and recorded and published teachings in the lineage of Tulku Urgyen Rinpoche, please access one of the following websites:

SHEDRUB DEVELOPMENT MANDALA
www.shedrub.org

RANGJUNG YESHE GOMDÉ, USA
www.gomdeusa.org

RANGJUNG YESHE GOMDÉ, DENMARK
www.gomde.dk

RANGJUNG YESHE PUBLICATIONS
www.rangjung.com

PUNDARIKA
www.pundarika.org

MINGYUR FOUNDATION
www.yongey.org